VOLUME 6

FABLE—HERESY

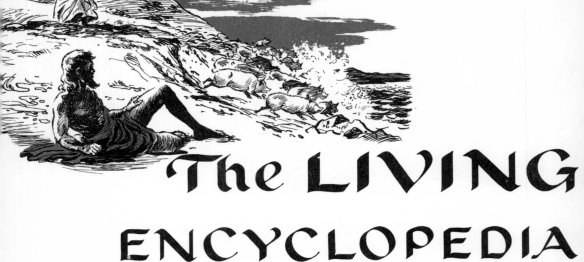

The LIVING
ENCYCLOPEDIA

This family library serves both adult and younger readers.
It combines THE ZONDERVAN PICTORIAL BIBLE DICTIONARY,
stories and narrative accounts from the KNOW YOUR BIBLE PROGRAM,
a gallery of 480 paintings based on Bible themes,
and the most fascinating photographs of contemporary
scenes and archaeological finds in the Holy Land.

BIBLE

in Story
and
Pictures

VOLUME 6

FABLE—HERESY

H. S. STUTTMAN CO., INC.
New York, New York 10016

"Then the band and the captain
and officers of the Jews
took Jesus and bound him.
And led him away...."
(JOHN 18:12, 13)

Cover illustration: This photograph shows the Church
and the Garden of Gethsemane, the site of Jesus' mid-
night arrest. The quiet of the olive trees with their deep
shadows, especially after dark, adds unusual vividness
to the record of events that took place here.

"And again, departing from the coasts of Tyre and Sidon, he came unto the sea of Galilee, through the midst of the coasts of Decapolis."

(MARK 7:31)

In New Testament times, a number of cities in eastern Jordan were united in a city union. There were ten in all, hence the name "Decapolis." Jesus was popular in the Decapolis. One of the ten cities was Gersa. Its ancient forum still stands and is shown in this photograph.

F

FABLE, usually defined as a narrative in which animals and inanimate objects of nature are made to act and speak as if they were human beings. The word "fable" is not found in the OT, but the OT has two fables: Judges 9:7-15 and II Kings 14:9. In the NT "fable" is found as the translation of *múthos* ("myth") in I Timothy 1:4; 4:7; II Timothy 4:4; Titus 1:14; II Peter 1:16. In II Peter 1:16 it has the general meaning of *fiction*, that is, a story having no connection with reality. The exact nature of the fables referred to in the pastoral epistles is beyond our knowledge, but they may have to do with some form of Jewish-Gnostic speculation.

FACE, in the OT, the translation of three Hebrew words: 1. *'ayin, eye;* 2. *'aph, nose;* 3. *pānîm, face;* and in the NT, of the Greek *prósopon, face.* The word is used literally, figuratively and idiomatically. Often "my face" is nothing more than an oriental idiomatic way of saying "I." Sometimes it means *presence,* and sometimes *favor.* The averted face was the equivalent of disapproval or rejection (Ps. 13:1; 27:9). To spit in the face was an expression of contempt and aversion (Num. 12:14). To harden the face means to harden one's self against any sort of appeal (Prov. 21:29). To have the face covered by another was a sign of doom (Esth. 7:8). Falling on the face symbolized prostration before man or God (Gen. 50:18). Setting the face signified determination (Luke 9:51). To cover the face expressed mourning (Exod. 3:6).

FAIR, a word translating more than a dozen Hebrew and Greek words, none of which have the modern sense of blond or fair-skinned. It has the meaning of beautiful, attractive (Acts 7:20); unspotted, free of defilement (Zech. 3:5); plausible, persuasive (Prov. 7:21); making a fine display (Gal. 6:12); good (of weather) (Job 37:22).

FAIR HAVENS (Gr. *Kaloí Liménes*), a small bay on the S coast of Crete, about 5 miles E of Cape Matala. Paul stayed there for a time on his way to Rome (Acts 27:8-12). The harbor was not suitable to spend the winter in, so it was decided to sail from there, with the hope of reaching Phoenix, a more secure harbor, also on the S coast of Crete.

FAIRS (Heb. *'izzāvôn*), a word found in KJV only in Ezekiel (27:12,14,16,19,27). The RV more accurately renders it "wares," the commodities bartered in Oriental markets. The KJV so translates the Hebrew word in Ezekiel 5:33.

FAITH (Heb. *'ēmûn,* Gr. *pístis*), has a twofold sense in the Bible, an active and a passive one; in the former, meaning "fidelity," "trustworthiness"; in the latter, "trust," "reliance." An example of the first is found in Romans 3:3, where "the faith of God" means His fidelity to promise. In the overwhelming majority of cases it has the meaning of reliance and trust.

In the OT (KJV) the word "faith" occurs only twice (Deut. 32:20; Hab. 2:4), and even the verb form, "to believe," is far from common, appearing less than 30 times. What we find in the OT is not so much a doctrine of faith, as examples of it. It sets forth the life of the servants of God as a life of faith. That which differentiates their lives from others is their self-commitment to God, implicitly involving unwavering trust in and obedience to Him. The foundation of Israel's faith was the revelation that God had made to the fathers and to Moses, the covenant He had made with them at Sinai, and the conviction that the covenant promises would some day be fulfilled. The observance of the Law and a life of faith were not for them incompatible. Faith lay behind the keeping of the Law as its presupposition. The Law was a mode of life incumbent upon those whose trust was in Jehovah. OT faith is never mere assent to a set of doctrines or outward acceptance of the Law, but utter confidence in the faithfulness of God and a consequent loving obedience to His will.

When used with a religious application, faith, in the OT, is sometimes in a specific word or work of God (Lam. 4:12; Hab. 1:5), or the fact of God's revelation (Exod. 4:5; Job 9:16), or the words or commandments of God in general (Ps. 119:66); or in God Himself (Gen. 15:6). Faith is put in the word of God's prophets because they speak for Him, and He is absolutely trustworthy (Exod. 19:9; II Chron. 20:20). NT writers, especially Paul and the author of Hebrews, show that the faith manifested by OT saints was not different in kind from that expected of Christians.

In contrast with the extreme rarity with which the terms "faith" and "believe" are used in the OT, they occur with great frequency in the NT — almost 500 times. A principal reason for this is that the NT makes the claim that the promised Messiah had finally come, and, to the bewilderment of many, the form of the fulfilment did not obviously correspond to the Messianic promise. It required a real act of faith to believe that Jesus of Nazareth was the promised Messiah. It was not long before "to believe" meant to become a Christian. In the NT, faith therefore becomes supreme of all human acts and experiences.

In His miracles and teaching Jesus aimed at creating in His disciples a complete trust in Himself as the Messiah and Saviour of men. Everywhere He offered Himself as the object of faith, and made it plain that faith in Him is necessary for eternal life, that it is the certain outcome of faith in the OT Scriptures that God requires it of men, and that refusal to accept His claims will bring eternal ruin. His primary concern with His own disciples was to build up their faith in Him.

The record in Acts shows that the first Christians called themselves "the believers" (Acts 2:44, etc.) and that they went everywhere persuading men and bringing them unto obedience to the faith that is in Jesus (Acts 6:7; 17:4; 28:24). Before long, as communities of believers arose in various parts of the Mediterranean world, the meaning and implications of the Christian faith had to be taught them in considerable fullness by the apostolic leaders, and so the NT books appeared.

It is in Paul's epistles that the meaning of faith is most clearly and fully set forth. Faith is trust in the person of Jesus, the truth of His teaching, and the redemptive work He accomplished at Calvary, and, as a result, a total submission to Him and His message, which are accepted as from God. Faith in His person is faith in Him as the eternal Son of God, the God-man, the second man Adam, who died in man's stead, making possible justification with God, adoption into His family, sanctification, and, ultimately, glorification. His death brings redemption from sin in all its aspects. The truth of His claims is attested by God's raising Him from the dead. Some day He will judge the quick and the dead. Faith is not to be confused with a mere intellectual assent to the doctrinal teachings of Christianity, though that is obviously necessary. It includes a radical and total commitment to Him as the Lord of one's life.

Unbelief, or lack of faith in the Christian Gospel, appears everywhere in the NT as the supreme evil. Not to make a decisive response to God's offer in Christ means that the individual remains in his sin and is eternally lost. Faith alone can save Him.   S.B.

FAITHFULNESS (Heb. ĕmûnâh), an attribute or quality applied in the Bible to both God and man. When used of God, it has in the OT a twofold emphasis, referring first to His absolute reliability, firm constancy, and complete freedom from arbitrariness or fickleness, and also to His steadfast, loyal love toward His people and His loyalty. God is constant and true in contrast to all that is not God. He is faithful in keeping His promises, and is therefore worthy of trust. He is unchangeable in His ethical nature. God's faithfulness is usually connected with His gracious promises of salvation. Faithful men are dependable in fulfilling their responsibilities and in carrying out their word. In the NT there are frequent exhortations to faithfulness. It is one of the fruits of the Spirit in Galatians 5:22.

FALCON (See Birds)

FALL, THE. The fall of man is narrated in Genesis 3 as a historical fact, not as a myth. It stands in a context of historical facts. Though not alluded to again in the OT, it is regarded as historical in the Apocrypha (i.e., not in the Palestinian canon) (Wis. 2:24) and in the NT (Rom. 5:12 f.; I Cor. 15:22). Some philosophers and theologians think the story is an allegory describing the awakening of men from a brute state of self-consciousness and personality—a fall upward, rather than downward, but such an explanation conflicts radically with Biblical teaching. There is no doubt that Paul takes the story literally and sees in the fall the origin of sin in the human race. The Scriptural view of sin and of redemption takes the fall for granted.

A denial of the fall requires that sin be made a necessity, with its origin in the Creation or in the Creator, and thus sin loses its character as sin; it becomes everlasting and indefeasible. If there has been no fall into sin, no redemption from sin is possible. Sin, moreover, becomes an inexterminable trait of man's nature. The Scriptures, however, teach us that man was created in God's own image, with a rational and moral nature like God's, with no inner impulse or drive to sin, and with a will perfectly free to do His will. There was nothing, moreover, in his environment to compel him to sin or to make sin excusable. God made him responsive to His call of love, and responsible for maintaining that responsivity. There was, indeed, outward solicitation to sin, on the part of the serpent, but there was no need to yield to the temptation.

The question Adam faced was whether ultimate happiness and fulfilment for him lay in theonomy or in autonomy, in the doing of God's will in love or in conducting his life in the way he chose, apart from the will of God.

The effect of the fall, as the rest of the Bible explicitly and implicitly brings out, was not merely immediate alienation from God for Adam and Eve, but guilt and depravity for all their posterity and the cursing of the earth.

Redemption from the effects of the fall is accomplished through the second man Adam, Jesus Christ (Rom. 5:12-21; I Cor. 15:21,22, 25-49).

FALLOW DEER. (See Animals)

FALLOW GROUND (Heb. nîr, untilled), twice found in the OT (Jer. 4:3; Hos. 10:12), is used in the sense of untilled ground.

FALSE CHRISTS (Gr. pseudó-christoi, false Christs). On Tuesday of Passion Week, Jesus warned His disciples that false Christs and false prophets would arise and that they would with great signs and wonders try to lead astray even the elect (Matt. 24:5,11, 23:25; Mark 13:6,21-23; Luke 21:8).

FALSE PROPHET, THE, is referred to only in the book of Revelation (16:13; 19:20; 20:10), but is usually identified with the two-horned beast of Revelation 13:11-18, who deceived the peoples of the earth with his lying wonders and killed those who refused to worship the image of the seven-headed beast (Rev. 13:1-10). The two beasts are clearly tools and instruments of Satan. In some way, the two-horned beast is a minister of the seven-headed one. In Revelation 16:13 we are told that three unclean spirits like frogs came out of the mouths of the dragon, beast, and false prophet. In Revelation 19:20 the beast (apparently the one with seven heads) and the false prophet, who is described as having performed deceiving miracles and killed those who refused to worship the image of the beast, are cast into a lake burning with brimstone. The devil is cast into that same lake of fire where the beast and the false prophet are (Rev. 20:10). Christian opinion is divided upon the interpretation of the two-horned beast.   S.B.

FAMILIAR SPIRIT (Heb. *'ôv*, etymology and exact meaning unknown). The term is generally used to refer to the spirit of a dead person which professed mediums claimed they could summon for consultation (Deut. 18:11). The word "familiar" has in this phrase the sense of the Latin *familiaris*, belonging to one's family, and hence ready to serve one as a servant. Such a spirit was thought to be able to reveal the future (Isa. 8:19; I Sam. 28:7). Since the voice seemed to come in a whisper from the ground, the medium was very likely a ventriloquist. Israelites were forbidden by Jehovah to consult familiar spirits (Lev. 19:31; Isa. 8:19). This was regarded as apostasy so serious that those who consulted them were put to death (Lev. 20:6). Saul put away mediums early in his reign, but consulted the witch of Endor, who "had a familiar spirit," when he became apostate just before his death (I Sam. 28:3-25; I Chron. 10:13). Manasseh dealt with familiar spirits (II Kings 21:6; II Chron. 33:6), but his grandson Josiah carried out the enactment of the Mosaic Law against them (II Kings 23:24). The practice of consulting them probably prevailed more or less to the time of the exile (Isa. 8:19; 19:3).
S.B.

FAMILY (Heb. *mishpahah, bayith, house, family;* Gr. *patriá, clan*). The OT has no term corresponding exactly to the English "family." The Hebrew family unit was larger than families today, and included some or all of the following: the father or master, the supreme head of the household; his mother, if she was living with him after the death of his father; his wives and concubines and their children; his children by other women; daughters-in-law and sons-in-law living on the paternal estate; other free Israelite friends and relatives; foreigners living under his protection; and male and female slaves. Since in primitive times the family assumed many of the responsibilities of modern government, like protection of life and property, large families were necessary.

Marriage was arranged not by the young people involved, but by the man (or his father) and the family of the bride, for whom a dowry, or purchase money, was paid to her father. In spite of this commercial aspect of the marriage contract, there is evidence that the love of the young people for each other often had an important part in the preliminaries of the marriage (Gen. 29; I Sam. 18:20). The wife was regarded as the property of the husband. He could divorce her, but she could not divorce him. Not only were polygamy and concubinage permitted, but no disgrace was attached to them. Wives, however, usually enjoyed more consideration than concubines.

Within his own domain, the authority of the head of the family was almost absolute. He could sell his children as slaves, and had power of life and death over them (Lev. 18:21; 20:2-5; II Kings 23:10). To dishonor a parent was a crime punishable with death (Exod. 21:15,17). He was also the chief religious functionary of the house, offering sacrifices to Jehovah on behalf of his family. Upon him rested the responsibility of training them in the ancient traditions.

While a wife was bought and paid for, her actual position was usually far from being a mere chattel. Her own family stood ready to avenge her in case she was mistreated by her husband. She had the chief place in the sub-family formed by her and her children in a polygamous household. The early training of the children was given mostly by her.

A large family was regarded as a great blessing. To be without children was a disgrace.

In the NT, Paul has much to say about family life. He stresses the need of bringing all family relationships under the principle of Christian love.
S.B.

FAMINE (Heb. *rā'āv*, hunger, famine, Gr. *limós, want of food*). In ancient times, in Palestine and Egypt, famines were not infrequent. They were produced by (1) want of rainfall in due season, (2) destructive hail storms and rain out of season, (3) destruction of crops by locusts and caterpillars, and (4) the cutting off of food supplies by a siege. Pestilence often followed, and the suffering was great. Famines which were the result of natural causes are recorded in the time of Abraham, who left Canaan and sojourned in Egypt (Gen. 12:10); in the time of Joseph, when the famine "was over all the face of the earth" (Gen. 41:56); in the time of the Judges (Ruth 1:1), of David, for three years (II Sam. 21:1), of Ahab and Elijah (I Kings 17:1; 18:2, and of Elisha (II Kings 4:38). Famines produced by sieges are mentioned in II Kings 6:25 — the siege of Jerusalem by Nebuchadnezzar. Nehemiah 5:3 tells of a "dearth" after the return from the Babylonian Captivity. The NT tells of a famine "throughout all the world" in the time of Claudius (Acts 11:28). In His Olivet discourse Jesus predicted famines in various places (Matt. 24:7), a prophecy believed to be partly fulfilled in the siege of Jerusalem by Titus, which is described with harrowing detail by Josephus, who says that "neither did any other city ever suffer such miseries" (*Wars*, V.x.5). Famines are sometimes said to be sent as punishments, and sometimes they are threatened as such (Lev. 26:19 f; Deut. 28: 49-51; II Kings 8:1; Isa. 14:30; 51:19; Jer. 14:12, 15; Ezek. 5:16). A special mark of God's favor and power is to be preserved in time of famine (Job 5:20; Ps. 33:19; 37:19). Sometimes the word "famine" is used in a figurative sense, as when Amos says that God will send a famine, not of bread and water, "but of hearing the words of the Lord" (Amos 8:11).   S.B.

FAN (Heb. *mizreh, winnowing fan*), a fork with two or more prongs used to throw grain into the air after it had been threshed, so that the chaff might be blown away. The work was done toward evening and at night when a wind came in from the sea and carried away the light chaff. Sometimes a shovel was used for the same purpose.

FARMING. The Israelites in the time of the patriarchs were a nomadic people. They first learned agriculture in Palestine, after the conquest of Ca-

"And when all the land of Egypt
was famished, the people cried to
Pharaoh for bread: and Pharaoh
said unto all the Egyptians,
Go unto Joseph; what he
saith to you, do."

(GENESIS 41:55)

Throughout Egypt during the years of plenty, Joseph stored up grain and other produce against the coming years of famine. Shown above is an Egyptian model of a granary; below, a bakery. These artifacts date from the 19th century B.C.

WINNOWING SCENE. Grain and chaff were tossed into the air, so that the wind would blow away the chaff.

REAPERS in barley fields north of Jerusalem. In Biblical times, the grain harvest lasted about seven weeks, from Passover to Pentecost.

naan. After that a large proportion of the people were engaged in agrarian pursuits. The pages of the Bible have much to say about agricultural occupations.

Agriculture was the background for all the legislation of Israel. At the time of the conquest every family probably received a piece of land, marked off by stones that could not be removed lawfully (Deut. 19:14; 27:17; Hos. 5:10). The soil of Palestine was generally fertile. Fertilizing was almost unknown. To maintain the fertility of the land, the law required that farms, vineyards, and olive orchards were to lie fallow in the seventh year (Exod. 23:10). On the year of jubilee those who had lost their ancestral estates recovered possession of them. Terracing was necessary to make use of soil on the hillsides. Irrigation was not required, since there was usually sufficient rainfall.

Plowing to prepare the land for sowing was done in autumn, when the early rains softened the ground that had become stone-hard in the summer sun. This was done with a crude wooden plough drawn by oxen; or, if the soil was thin, with a mattock. With such implements the surface of the ground was hardly more than scratched — perhaps three or four inches. Little harrowing was done, and was probably unknown in Palestine in early times.

The summer grain was sown between the end of January and the end of February. Usually the seed was scattered broadcast from a basket, but careful farmers put it in furrows in rows (Isa. 28:25). Between sowing and reaping the crops were exposed to several dangers: the failure of the latter rain, which came in March

PALESTINE PEASANT plowing with crude wooden plough drawn by oxen—a scene reminiscent of agriculture in Biblical times.

THRESHING GRAIN at the village of Sep-phoris, north of Nazareth. Open-air threshing was possible because the harvest season was rainless. Harvesters kept continual vigil upon the threshing floor, which was always in an exposed position, usually on a slope.

and April; the hot, drying easterly winds that often came in March and April (Gen. 41:6); hailstorms (Hag. 2:17); various kinds of pestiferous weeds like tares and thorns (Jer. 12: 13; Matt. 13:7, 25); injurious insects, especially the palmer-worm, the canker-worm, the caterpillar, and the locust (Amos 7:2); the thefts of crows and sparrows (Matt. 13:4); and fungus diseases, especially mildew (Deut. 28:22). As the harvest season approached, particularly valuable crops were protected by watchmen (Jer. 4:17); but the law permitted a hungry person to pick grain in passing by (Deut. 23:25; Matt. 12:1).

The time of harvest varied somewhat according to the climatic condition of each region, but usually began about the middle of April with the coming of the dry season. Barley was the first grain to be cut, and this was followed a few weeks later with wheat. The grain harvest generally lasted about seven weeks, from Passover to Pentecost. Whole families moved out of their village homes to live in the fields until the harvest was over. The grain was cut with a sickle and laid in swaths behind the reaper. It was then bound into sheaves and gathered into shocks (Exod. 22:6). In the interests of the poor, the law forbade a field to be harvested to its limits.

The grain was threshed in the open air, a custom made possible because the harvest season was free from rain (I Sam. 21:16 ff.). During the threshing-time the grain was guarded by harvesters who spent the nights upon the threshing floor (Ruth 3:6). The threshing floor was constructed in an

exposed position in the fields, preferably on a slight elevation, so as to get the full benefit of the winds. It consisted of a circular area 25 or 40 feet in diameter, sloping slightly upward at the edges, and was usually surrounded with a border of stones so as to keep in the grain. The floor was level and rolled hard. The sheaves of grain, brought in from the fields on the backs of men and animals, were heaped in the center. From this heap, sheaves were spread out on the floor, and then either several animals tied abreast were driven round and round the floor, or two oxen were yoked together to a threshing-machine, which they dragged in a circular path over the grain until the kernels of grain were separated from the stalks. The threshing machines were of two kinds, a board with the bottom studded with small stones or nails, or a kind of threshing wagon. While this was going on, the partly threshed grain was turned over with a fork. After that the grain was winnowed by tossing the grain and chaff into the air with a wooden fork or shovel so that the wind might blow away the chaff. This was usually done at night, to take advantage of the night breezes. The chaff was either burned or left to be scattered by the winds. The grain was then sifted with a sieve to remove stones and other impurities, and collected into pits or barns (Luke 12:18).

Of the large number of crops the Israelites cultivated, wheat and barley were the most important. Among other crops they raised were rye, millet, flax, and a variety of vegetables. See also AGRI-CULTURE.   S.B.

FASTING (Heb. *tsûm,* Gr. *nesteía, néstis*), meaning abstinence from food and drink for a longer or shorter period, is frequently mentioned in the Scriptures. Sometimes, instead of the single word "fast" the descriptive phrase "to afflict the soul" is used, the reference being to physical fasting rather than to spiritual humiliation. This term is used in various parts of the OT, but is the only one used to denote the religious observance of fasting in the Pentateuch (Lev. 16:29-31; 23:27; Num. 30:13; Ps. 35:13; Isa. 58:3,5,10).

The only fast required by Moses was that of the Day of Atonement. Before the Babylonian Captivity it was the one regular fast (Lev. 16:29,31; 23:27-32; Num. 29:7; Jer. 36:6). During this period there are many examples of fasts on special occasions, held because of transgression or to ward off present or impending calamity. Samuel called for such a fast (I Sam. 7:6); Jehoiakim and the princess proclaimed a fast after Baruch had read the condemnatory word of the Lord given through Jeremiah (Jer. 36:9); Jezebel hypocritically enjoined a fast when she sought to secure Naboth's vineyard (I Kings 21:9,12). We read of individuals who were moved to fast — for example, David, when his child became ill (II Sam. 12:16, 21-23), and Ahab on hearing his doom (I Kings 21:27).

After the Captivity four annual fasts were held in memory of the national calamities through which the nation had passed. They are mentioned only in Zechariah 7:1-7; 8:19. These fasts, established during the Captivity, were held on the fourth, fifth, seventh, and tenth months. The Mishna (*Taarith,* iv,6) and St. Jerome (in *Zachariam,* viii) give information on the historical events which these fasts were intended to commemorate. By the time of Christ they had fallen into disuse, and were not revived until after the destruction of Jerusalem by the Romans. In Rabbinic times the Feast of Purim, the origin of which is explained in Esther (9:31,32), was accompanied by a fast in commemoration of the fast of Esther, Mordecai and the Jews (Esther 4:1-3, 15-17). The OT gives a number of instances of other fasts in which the whole people joined (Ezra 8:21-23; Neh. 9:1). Examples of fasts by individuals are given in Nehemiah 1:4 and Daniel 9:3. A fast of great strictness was proclaimed by the heathen king of Nineveh to avert the destruction threatened by Jehovah through Jonah (Jonah 3:5).

Fasting among the Israelites was either partial or total, depending upon the length of the fast. When Daniel mourned three full weeks, he ate no "pleasant bread, neither came flesh nor wine in his mouth" (Dan. 10:2,3). The fast on the Day of Atonement was "from even till even" (Lev. 23:32); and no food or drink was taken. Other daylong fasts were from morning till evening. Longer fasts are mentioned in Nehemiah 1:4 and Daniel 10:2,3. The fasts of Moses and Elijah for forty days were exceptional (Exod. 34:28; I Kings 19:8).

Religious fasting was observed as a sign of mourning for sin, with the object of deprecating divine wrath or winning divine compassion. The prophets often condemn the abuse of the custom, for Israelites superstitiously thought that it had value even when dissevered from purity and righteousness of life (Isa. 58:3-7; Jer. 14:10-12; Zech. 7,8). Fasts were not necessarily religious in nature. They were commonplace when someone near

and dear died, as when the inhabitants of Jabesh fasted after they had buried Saul and Jonathan (I Sam. 31:13), and after the death of Abner (II Sam. 1:12).

There are few references to fasting in the Gospels, but what is said shows that frequent fasts were customary with those Jews who desired to lead a specially religious life. We are told that Anna "served God with fastings and prayers night and day" (Luke 2:37). Again, the Pharisee in the parable says, "I fast twice in the week" (Luke 18:12). Jesus fasted for forty days in the wilderness, but it is not clear whether this fast was voluntary or not. There is no reason to doubt that He observed the usual prescribed public fasts, but neither by practice nor by precept did He stress fasting. He was so unascetic in His ordinary mode of life that He was reproached with being "a gluttonous man and a wine-bibber" (Matt. 11:19; Luke 7:34). In all His teaching He spoke of fasting only twice. The passages are as follows:

Matthew 6:16-18. In this passage voluntary fasting is presupposed as a religious exercise, but Jesus warns against making it an occasion for a parade of piety. The important thing is purity and honesty of intention. Fasting should be to God, not to impress men. Jesus approves of fasting if it is an expression of inner contrition and devotion. The externalism of the Pharisees has its own reward.

Matthew 9:14-17; Mark 2:18-22; Luke 5:33-39. Here, the disciples of John and of the Pharisees ask Jesus, "Why do we and the Pharisees fast oft, but thy disciples fast not?" Jesus replies that fasting, which is a sign of mourning, would be inconsistent with the joy which should characterize those who know that the Messiah has finally come and is now with them. The time will come, however, when He will be taken away, and then His disciples will mourn. It is obvious that the reference to His being taken away is to His crucifixion, not His ascension, for the ascension, signifying the completion of His redemptive work, is no occasion for mourning. Jesus here sanctions fasting, as He does in the Sermon on the Mount; but He refuses to enjoin it on His disciples.

The references to fasting in Matthew 17:21 and Mark 9:29 are regarded by textual scholars as corruptions of the text.

The Acts of the Apostles has a few direct references to fasting. The church at Antioch fasted and prayed before sending out Paul and Barnabas as missionaries (Acts 13:2,3). On Paul's first missionary journey, elders were appointed in every church, with prayer and fasting (Acts 14:23). The reference to the fasting of Cornelius, in Acts 10:30, is an interpolation. The only other direct references to fasting in the NT are found in II Corinthians 6:5 and 11:27, where Paul describes his sufferings for Christ; and here, most likely, he has in mind involuntary fasting.

There are, therefore, in the NT only four indisputable references to voluntary fasting for religious purposes, two by our Lord in the Gospels, and two in the Acts of the Apostles. Jesus does not disapprove of the practice, but says nothing to commend it. The apostolic church practiced it, but perhaps only as a carry-over from Judaism, since most of the early disciples were Jews.

FAT (Heb. *hēlev, helev*). 1. The subcutaneous layer of fat around the kidneys and other viscera, which, like the blood, was forbidden by the Mosaic law to be used for food, but was burned as an offering to Jehovah, for a sweet savor unto Him (Lev. 4:31). This had to be done on the very day the animal was slain, apparently to remove temptation (Exod. 23:18). The purpose of the law was to teach the Israelite that his best belonged to God. Long before the Mosaic law was given, Abel brought the fat of the firstlings of his flock to Jehovah; and we read that the Lord had respect unto Abel and to his offering. (Gen. 4:4).

2. Sometimes used in the KJV to refer to a wine vat, a receptable into which the grape juice flowed from the "press" above (Joel 2:24; Isa. 63:2).

FATHER (Heb. *'āv*, Gr. *patér*), has various meanings in the Bible. 1. Immediate male progenitor (Gen. 42:13). In the Hebrew family the father had absolute rights over his children. He could sell them into slavery and have them put to death. Reverence and obedience by children is prescribed from the earliest times (Exod. 20:12; Lev. 19:3; Deut. 5:16, etc.). The Scriptures many times set forth the character and duties of an ideal father.

2. Ancestor, immediate or remote. Abraham is called Jacob's father (Gen. 28:13), and God tells him he will be the "father of many nations" (Gen. 17:4). The founders of the Hebrew race, the patriarchs, are referred to as its fathers (Rom. 9:5); so also heads of clans (Exod. 6:14; I Chron. 27:1).

3. The word has many figurative and derived uses. A spiritual ancestor, whether good or bad, as Abraham, "the father of all them that believe" (Rom. 4:11); and the devil, "Ye are of your father the devil" (John 8:44). The originator of a mode of life ("Jabal: he was the father of such as dwell in tents, and of such as have cattle" (Gen. 4:20). One who exhibits paternal kindness and wisdom to another: "be unto me a father and a priest" (Judg. 17:10). A revered superior, especially a prophet and an elderly and venerable man (I Sam. 10:12; I John 2:13). Royal advisors and prime ministers: "God hath made me a father to Pharaoh" (Gen. 45:8). Early Christians who have died: "since the fathers fell asleep" (II Peter 3:4). A source: "Hath the rain a father?" (Job 38:28).

4. God is Father: as Creator of the universe, "the Father of lights" (James 1:17); as Creator of the human race, "Have we not all one father? hath not one God created us?" (Mal. 2:10); as one who begets and takes care of his spiritual children, "Ye have received the Spirit of adoption, whereby we cry, Abba, Father" (Rom. 8:15). In a special and unique sense, God is the Father of Jesus Christ (Matt. 11:26; Mark 14:36; Luke 22:42).   S.B.

FATHOM (See Weights and Measures)

FATLING. One of the clean animals (calf, lamb, kid, etc.) fattened for offering to God. See Psalm 66:15, II Samuel 6:13, etc.

FEAR (Heb. *yir'âh*, Gr. *phóbos*). This word in English has two principal meanings: first, that apprehension of evil which normally leads one either to flee or to fight; and second, that awe and reverence which a man of sense feels in the presence of God, and to a less extent in the presence of a king or other dread authority. A child feels the first of these in the presence of a cruel parent, and the second before one who is good, but who must also be just. There are 15 different Hebrew nouns which are rendered "fear" in KJV, but in the NT the Greek *phóbos* is used in both senses; i.g., in Matthew 14:26 the disciples cried out for fear, thinking that they saw a ghost; whereas in Romans 3:18, "There is no fear of God before their eyes," the second meaning is implied. The word "reverend" which occurs only in Psalm 111:9 means literally "to be feared," and is used only for God. For the two senses in the OT, contrast Psalm 31:13, "fear was upon every side," with Proverbs 9:10, "the fear of the Lord is the beginning of wisdom."   A.B.F.

FEASTS (Heb. *mô'ēdh, an assembling; hagh, dance, or pilgrimage*). The feasts, or sacred festivals, held an important place in Jewish religion. They were religious services accompanied by demonstrations of joy and gladness. In Leviticus 23, where they are described most fully, they are called "holy convocations." Their times, except for the two instituted after the exile, were fixed by divine appointment. Their purpose was to promote spiritual interests of the community. The people met in holy fellowship for acts and purposes of sacred worship. They met before God in holy assemblies.

1. The Feast of the Weekly Sabbath. This stood at the head of the sacred seasons. The holy convocations by which the sabbaths were distinguished were quite local. Families and other small groups assembled under the guidance of Levites or elders among them and engaged in some common acts of devotion, the forms and manner of which were not prescribed. Little is known of where or how the people met before the Captivity, but after it they met in synagogues and were led in worship by teachers learned in the law.

2. The Passover, or the Feast of Unleavened Bread. The Passover was the first in point or time of all the annual feasts, and historically and religiously it was the most important of all. It was called both the Feast of the Passover and the Feast of Unleavened Bread, the two really forming a double festival. It was celebrated on the first month of the religious year, on the 14th of Nisan (our April), and commemorated the deliverance of the Jews from Egypt and the establishment of Israel as a nation by God's redemptive act. The Feast of Unleavened Bread began on the day after the Passover and lasted seven days (Lev. 25:5-8). This combined feast was one of the three feasts the Mosaic Law enjoined to be attended by all male Jews who were physically able and ceremonially clean (Exod. 23:17; Deut. 16:16), the other two being the Feast of Weeks, or Pentecost, and the Feast of Tabernacles. These were known as the pilgrimage festivals; and on all of them special sacrifices were offered, varying according to the character of the festival (Num. 28,29).

3. The Feast of Pentecost. Other names for this are the Feast of Weeks, the Day of the First-fruits, and the Feast of Harvests. It was celebrated on the sixth day of the month of Sivan (our June), seven weeks after the offering of the wave sheaf after the Passover. The name "Pentecost," meaning "50th," originated from the fact that there was an interval of 50 days between the two. The feast lasted a single day (Deut. 16:9-12), and marked the completion of the wheat harvest. The char-

THE JEWISH SACRED YEAR

MONTH		SPECIAL DAYS
Nisan	(April)	14 — Passover
		15 — Unleavened Bread
		21 — Close of Passover
Iyar	(May)	
Sivan	(June)	6 — Feast of Pentecost — seven weeks after the Passover (Anniversary of the giving of the law on Mt. Sinai)
Tammuz	(July)	
Ab	(August)	
Elul	(September)	
Tishri	(October)	1 & 2 — The Feast of Trumpets *Rosh Hashanah,* beginning of the civil year
		10 — Day of Atonement
		15-21 — Feast of Tabernacles
Marchesvan	(November)	
Kislev	(December)	25 — Feast of Lights, Dedication, *Hanukkah*
Tebeth	(January)	
Shebet	(February)	
Adar	(March)	14 — The Feast of Purim

acteristic ritual of this feast was the offering and waving of two loaves of leavened bread, made from the ripe grain which had just been harvested. This was done by the priest in the name of the congregation. In addition to these wave offerings, the people were enjoined to give the Lord an offering of the first fruits of their produce. The amount of the offering was not designated.

4. The Feast of Trumpets, or New Moon. This was held on the first day of the seventh month, Tishri (our October), which began the civil year of the Jews. It corresponded to our New Year's day, and on it, from morning to evening, horns and trumpets were blown. After the exile the day was observed by the public reading of the Law and by general rejoicing.

CELEBRATING PASSOVER FEAST. Shown here is a Jewish family in Jerusalem, observing *sedar,* the feast celebrated on the first two days of Passover. Passover commemorates the deliverance of the Jews from Egypt and the establishment of Israel as a nation.

DURING FEAST OF THE PASSOVER, a Samaritan priest exposes the Scroll of the Law before the congregation on Mount Gerizim. The Passover was the most important of all the annual feasts.

5. The Feast of the Day of Atonement. This was observed on the 10th day of Tishri. It was really less a feast than a fast, as the distinctive character and purpose of the day was to bring the collective sin of the whole year to remembrance, so that it might earnestly be dealt with and atoned for. On this day the high priest made confession of all the sins of the community, and entered on their behalf into the most holy place with the blood of reconciliation. It was a solemn occasion, when God's people through godly sorrow and atonement for sin entered into the rest of God's mercy and favor, so that as the partakers of His forgiveness they might rejoice before Him and carry out His commandments.

6. The Feast of Tabernacles, or Booths, or Ingathering. This was the last of the sacred festivals under the old covenant, in pre-exilic times. It began five days after the day of atonement (Lev. 23:34; Deut. 16:13), and lasted eight days. It marked the completion of the harvest, and historically commemorated the wanderings in the wilderness. During this festival people lived in booths and tents in Jerusalem to remind themselves of how their forefathers wandered in the wilderness and lived in booths. The sacrifices of this feast were more numerous than at any other. The last day of the feast marked the conclusion of the ecclesiastical year. The whole feast was popular and joyous in nature.

Besides the above feasts, which were all pre-exilic and instituted by Jehovah, the Jews after the Captivity added two others, the Feast of Lights, or Dedication, and the Feast of Purim.

The Feast of Lights was observed for eight days beginning on the 25th day of Kislev (our December). It was instituted by Judas Maccabeus in 164 B.C. when the Temple which had been defiled by Antiochus Epiphanes, king of Syria, was cleansed and rededicated to the service of Jehovah. During these days the Israelites met in their synagogues, carrying branches of trees in their hands, and held jubilant services. The children were told the brave and stirring deeds of the Maccabees to rouse them to noble emulation.

The Feast of Purim was kept on the 14th and 15th days of Adar (our March), the last month of the religious year. It is said to have been instituted by Mordecai to commemorate the failure of Haman's plots against the Jews. The word Purim means "lots." On the evening of the 13th the whole book of Esther was read publicly in the synagogue. It was a joyous occasion.   S.B.

FELIX fē'lĭks, Gr. *Phélix, happy*), born Antonius Claudius, a Greek subject, was made a freedman by Claudius, the emperor from A.D. 41 to 54, and given the surname Felix (i.e. *Happy*) probably in congratulation. He and his brother Pallas were favorites of Claudius and later of Nero (A.D. 54-68), and so Felix evidently thought that he could do as he pleased. Tacitus said of him that "he revelled in cruelty and lust, and wielded the power of a king with the mind of a slave." His very title of "procurator" hints at his fiscal duties of procuring funds for Rome, which he seems to have accomplished with all sorts of tyranny. He began his career as procurator of Judea by seducing Drusilla, the sister of Agrippa II, and wife of the king of Emesa (modern Homs), and marrying her. Because she was Jewish (at least on one side) he learned much of Jewish life and customs.

Felix appears in the Biblical account only in Acts 23:24 - 25:14. He was susceptible to flattery, as the speech of Tertullus shows, and also to conviction of sin, as is shown by his terror when Paul reasoned before him of "righteousness, temperance and judgment to come." His conviction faded; he procrastinated; and then held Paul for about two years (c. 58 - 60), hoping that Paul would buy his freedom. He was then replaced by Festus, a far better man.

FELLOES (fĕl'ōz), the exterior parts of the rim of a wheel which unite the outer ends of the spokes. The word occurs only in I Kings 7:33.

FELLOW (Heb. *rē'a*, Gr. *hetaíros*), a word which in English has two diverse meanings: 1. A person, but usually implying a certain amount of contempt as in Judges 18:25, "lest angry fellows run upon thee," and I Samuel 29:4, "Make this fellow return," where AVS has, "Make the man return," which is technically correct but lacks the feeling of KJV.

2. A friend, companion, associate or partner, as in Hebrews 1:9: "God hath anointed thee . . . above thy fellows." In denying the Christian doctrine of the Trinity, the Koran says of "Allah," "He does not beget, nor is he begotten, and he has no fellow." In Judges 11:37 (KJV) the word occurs once in the feminine, but ASV has "companion."

FELLOWSHIP (Gr. *koinonía, that which is in common*). 1. Partnership or union with others in the bonds of a business partnership, a social or fraternal organization, or just propinquity. Christians are told not to be unequally yoked together with unbelievers (II Cor. 6:14-18) because such a union, either in marriage, business or society, is incompatible with that fellowship with Christians and with God.

2. Membership in a local Christian church or in *the* Church. From the very beginning of the Church at Pentecost, "they continued stedfastly in the apostles' doctrine and fellowship, and in breaking of bread, and in prayers" (Acts 2:42).

3. Partnership in the support of the Gospel and in the charitable work of the Church (II Cor. 8:4).

4. That heavenly love which fills (or should fill) the hearts of believers one for another and for God. For this love and fellowship, the Scriptures employ a word *"agape"* which scarcely appears in classical Greek. This fellowship is deeper and more satisfying than any mere human love whether social, parental, conjugal or other.

FENCED CITY. All of the six Hebrew words which are used for fenced cities are from the one root, *bātsar*, which means *to restrain, withhold,* or *to make inaccessible.* Owing to the usual insecurity in the East, most of the towns and even many of the small villages are enclosed in walls. It seems strange to ride through two or three miles of fields without a single building, and then to enter the gate of a little village and find the houses packed together with hardly a place to breathe. In the description of the kingdom of Bashan in the days of Moses (Deut. 3:5) we read of cities "fenced with high walls, gates, and bars," but the Israelites utterly destroyed them. The Edomite city of Bozrah (Mic. 2:12) gets its name from the same root. Figuratively, the word is used to show God's protection of Jeremiah — "I will make thee unto this people a fenced brazen wall . . . for I am with thee to save thee and to deliver thee, saith the Lord" (Jer. 15:20).

FERTILE CRESCENT, does not occur in Scripture but is a modern description of the territory which may roughly be described as reaching NW from the Persian Gulf through Mesopotamia, then W to the N of Syria, then SW through Syria and Palestine. In this crescent the land is mostly rich and fertile, and is watered by the Tigris, the Euphrates, the Orontes and the Jordan, besides numerous rivers descending the west side of Lebanon, and in most of the region irrigation has long been employed. Various grains like wheat and barley, and fruits such as grapes, olives, figs, oranges, lemons, pomegranates abound. If one attempts to cross in a straight line from one end of the crescent to the other he will find himself most of the way in the great Syrian desert, with only an occasional oasis. This configuration of the land explains much of Bible history.

FESTIVALS (See Feasts)

FESTUS, PORCIUS (Gr. *Pórkios Phéstos, festal, joyful*), the Roman governor who succeeded Felix in the province of Judea (Acts 24:27). The date of his accession in uncertain. Of the life of Festus before his appointment by Nero as procurator of Judea almost nothing is known, and he appears in the Bible (Acts 24:27 - 26:32) principally in his relationship with his prisoner, the apostle Paul. Festus was apparently a far better and more efficient man than his predecessor. At the very beginning of his rule, he took up the case of Paul, and as king Agrippa said, Paul "might have been set at liberty if he had not appealed unto Caesar." Paul had made this appeal when Festus, at the instance of the Jews, was considering bringing Paul to Jerusalem for trial. Festus evidently knew that Paul was a good man (Acts 25:25), but he was unable to understand Paul's reasoning with king Agrippa, and thought that Paul had gone mad with much study. (Acts 26:24). Festus died at his post, and was followed, c. A.D. 62, by Albinus.

FETTERS, bonds, chains or shackles, generally for the feet of prisoners and made of brass or of iron (Judg. 16:21; Ps. 105:18; 149:8). The NT word (Mark 5:4, Luke 8:29) indicates that the fetters were for the feet.

FEVER (See Diseases)

FIELD. The Biblical "field" was generally not enclosed, but was marked off from its neighbors by stone markers at the corners, and sometimes one or two along the sides. Because they were unenclosed, and because of the usually unsettled conditions, a watchman was ordinarily employed, especially when the crop was nearing maturity. Besides the danger of human intruders, there was sometimes danger from straying cattle or even of cattle driven by thieving men (Exod. 22:5), and of fire if a Samson (Judg. 15:5) or an angry Absalom (II Sam. 14:30) were about. The word is used also in a larger sense for "territory," as in Genesis 36:35, where "the field of Moab" is any place in Moabite territory; and as in the parable of the tares (Matt. 13:38), where "the field is the world." Many of the ancient "fields" were the habitat of wild animals (Ps. 80:13).

FIG (See Plants)

FILLET. In the description of the tabernacle in Exodus 27:10,11 and 38:10-19 the "fillets" were the rods between the columns that supported the hangings of the court. In Jeremiah 52:21 the word means a cord for measuring. Cf. ASV *in loco.*

FINING-POT, found only in Proverbs 17:3 and 27:21 and means the crucible in which silver or gold is melted to be purified from dross.

FIR (See Plants)

BREASTED'S FERTILE CRESCENT (c. 2000 B.C.)

"Then the devil taketh him up into the holy city, and setteth him on a pinnacle of the temple."

(MATTHEW 4:5)

The highest point of the Temple is its south-east corner, which is regarded as the pinnacle where Christ was tempted. Below is the Kidron Valley, and in the background is the Mount of Olives with the Garden of Gethsemane and the Russian Orthodox Church.

"When Jesus had spoken these words,
he went forth with his disciples
over the brook Cedron,
where was a garden,
into the which he entered,
and his disciples."
(JOHN 18:1)

This is a view of the majestic Kidron (Cedron) Valley. At the
right is the Garden of Gethsemane, the traditional site of the
garden where Christ met with his disciples. The garden is also
the site of Christ's agony and arrest.

FIRE (Heb. *'ēsh*, Gr. *pýr*), probably one of the earliest discoveries of man; perhaps first seen as a result of lightning, but man soon invented ways to use it and found it a most useful servant as well as a cruel master. The first use of the word "fire" in Scripture is in Genesis 19:24, which says that "fire from the Lord out of heaven" destroyed the cities of the plain; but the use of fire was far more ancient. Before the Flood, Tubal-Cain (Gen. 4:22) was the father of smiths, in the account of the Abrahamic covenant (Gen. 15:17) one reads of a smoking furnace and a flaming torch. Many students believe that God showed His acceptance of Abel's offering (Gen. 4:4) by sending fire to consume it. In the institution of the Aaronic priestly ceremonies, God sent fire from heaven to consume the first offering (Lev. 9:24) to show His acceptance. This fire was to be kept burning continually (Lev. 6:9). When the two sons of Aaron, Nadab and Abihu, offered "strange fire," probably when intoxicated (Lev. 10:1,9,10), God's fiery judgment descended upon them and slew them. The final destiny of the enemies of God is the "lake of fire" (Rev. 19:20; 20:10,14). This world will some day be consumed by fire (II Pet. 3:7-12).

God uses "fire" not only for judgment but also for testing, and so we learn that the works of all believers will be tested as by fire (I Cor. 3:12-15). God's glory is accompanied by fire (Ezek. 1:27), the seraphim are fiery creatures (Isa. 6:2), as were

the "fiery serpents" of Numbers 21:6 (from the same Hebrew verb *saraph* "to burn"), and our Lord is pictured with eyes as a flame of fire, hinting at his work of judgment (Rev. 1:14). Fire is used to refine gold and to cleanse us (Mal. 3:2).

FIREBRAND, from three Hebrew words: (1) a stick for stirring fire (Isa. 7:4, Amos 4:11), (2) brands, sparks (Prov. 26:18), and (3) a torch, as in Judges 15:4 and Judges 7:16. Job 12:5 has the same word, meaning a lamp that is burnt out.

FIREPAN (Heb. *mahtâh*), a vessel used for carrying live coals, as in Exodus 27:3. The Hebrew word is rendered "censer" 15 times, as in Leviticus 10:1, and "snuff dish" three times, as in Exodus 25:38. The meaning is evident from the context.

FIRKIN (See Weights and Measures)

FIRMAMENT (fîr′mà-měnt, Heb. *raqîa'*), the expanse of sky surrounding the earth, made by God on the second day of creation to "divide the waters from the waters" (Gen. 1:6). The Hebrews thought of the "firmament" as the apparent void above in which the clouds float and the lights of heaven are set by God. The Hebrew word suggests something stretched or spread out like a curtain (Isa. 40:22). It corresponds to the "empty space" of Job 26:7. The translators of the LXX rendered the Hebrew word *raqîa'* as *steréoma*, which has the meaning of a firm and solid structure — something beaten out, like brass. This fitted in with the Alexandrian conception of the universe as being a succession of spheres, each carrying a planet; but it is not in accord with the real meaning of the Hebrew word. St. Jerome, in the Vulgate, made c. A.D. 400, translated the word *steréoma* as *firmamentum*, which also suggests something solid or firm. Our English word "firmament" does not correctly suggest the real meaning of the Hebrew word. S.B.

FIRST-BEGOTTEN (Gr. *prótótokos*), a term applied to the Lord Jesus Christ in Hebrews 1:6 and in Revelation 1:5, the former referring to "the eternal generation of the Son of God" and the latter to his resurrection. ASV has "firstborn" in both places.

FIRSTBORN (Heb. *bekhôr*, Gr. *prótótokos*). The Hebrew word is used chiefly of men, but is used also of animals (Exod. 11:5). It appears that man early felt that God has the first claim on animals (Gen. 4:4). Among the ancestors of the Hebrews there was a sacrifice to the deity of the firstborn offspring of men and animals. Because the firstborn of the Israelites were preserved at the time of the

T HE STRANGE SIGN — lamb's blood sprinkled on the doorposts — would save the firstborn of the Hebrew families. For the Lord was to pass through Egypt that night and cause the firstborn of all Egyptians to die, but when He came to a house with blood on the doorposts, He would *pass over* that house.

first Passover, every firstborn male of man and beast became consecrated to Jehovah (Exod. 13:2; 34:19). The beasts were sacrificed, while the men were redeemed (Exod. 13:13,15; 34:20; cf. Lev. 27:6). At Sinai the Levites were substituted for the Israelite firstborn (Num. 3:12,41,46; 8:13-19). On the 30th day after birth the father brought his firstborn to the priest and paid five shekels to redeem him from service in the temple (cf. Luke 2:27).

Among the Israelites the firstborn son possessed special privileges. He succeeded his father as the head of the house and received as his share of the inheritance a double portion. Israel was Jehovah's firstborn (Exod. 4:22) and was thus entitled to special privileges, as compared with other peoples. Jesus Christ is described as the firstborn (Rom. 8:29; Col. 1:15; Heb. 1:6), an application of the term that may be traced back to Psalm 89:27, where the Messiah is referred to as the firstborn of Jehovah.   S.B.

FIRST FRUITS (Heb. *rē'shîth, bikkûrîm*, Gr. *aparché*). In acknowledgement of the fact that all the products of the land came from God, and thankfulness for His goodness, Israelites brought as an offering to Him a portion of the fruits that ripened first, these being looked upon as an earnest of the coming harvest. Such an offering was made both on behalf of the nation (Lev. 23:10,17) and by individuals (Exod. 23:19; Deut. 26:1-11). These first fruits went for the support of the priesthood.

FISH (See Animals)

FISH GATE, an ancient gate on the E side of the wall of Jerusalem, just W of Gihon, where in the days of Nehemiah, men of Tyre congregated to sell fish and various wares on the sabbath (II Chron. 33:14; Neh. 13:16). It is probably identical with the "Middle Gate" of Jeremiah 39:3.

FISHING (See Occupations and Professions)

FISHHOOK, not only the means of catching fish as is done today, but also of keeping them, at least for a time (cf. Amos 4:2 with Job 41:1,2). Peter generally used a net, but see Matthew 17:27, where the Lord told him to cast a hook.

FISH POOL (Heb. *berēkhôth, pool*), in KJV occurs only in Song of Solomon 7:4, but the word should be rendered "pool," as it is in the RV.

FITCH (See Plants)

FLAG (See Plants)

FLAGON, a large container for wine. The word *nevel* is rendered "flagon" in Isaiah 22:24, elsewhere "bottle." The word *'āshîshâh* rendered "flagon" in II Samuel 6:19 and other places in KJV should be "cakes of raisins" as in ASV.

FLAX (See Plants)

FLEAS (See Insects)

FLEECE, the shorn wool of a sheep. The first of the shearing was to be given to the priesthood, as a part of their means of support (Deut. 18:4). Gideon's experience (Judg. 6:37-40) has given rise to the custom of "putting out a fleece" in seeking God's guidance.

FLESH (Heb. *bāsār, shē'er*, Gr. *sárx*). 1. Literally, the soft part of the bodies of men and animals.

2. By metonymy, all animals, as in Genesis 6:19.

3. Again by metonymy, mankind in general, as in Numbers 16:22, "the God of the spirits of all flesh."

4. Our ordinary human constitution as opposed to our mental and moral qualities as in Matthew 26:41, "the spirit indeed is willing but the flesh is weak."

5. Human nature deprived of the Spirit of God and dominated by sin (Rom. 7:14; I Cor. 3:1,3; Col. 2:18; I John 2:16).

FLESH-HOOK (Heb. *mazlēgh*), a metal implement with one or more teeth, used for handling large pieces of flesh, especially around the sacrificial altar. In the tabernacle it was made of brass (Exod. 27:3; 38:3), but in the temple it was made of gold (I Chron. 28:17). In Samuel's time it was used to remove the priests' share of the meat offering (I Sam. 2:13,14).

FLIES (See Insects)

FLINT (See Minerals)

FLOCK, a collection of sheep under the care of a shepherd, sometimes including goats as well (Gen. 27:9). The larger animals such as cattle, camels, asses, etc. were counted as herds, not flocks. Israel lived in OT times in a pastoral civilization and a man's flocks made up most of his wealth, providing clothing, food, milk and animals for sacrifice. Figuratively both Israel and the Church are counted as flocks, and God is the Good Shepherd (Isa. 40:11; Matt. 26:31; Luke 12:32; I Pet. 5:2,3).

FLOOD, DELUGE.

I. Historical Background of Flood Interpretations. The Noahic flood has been a subject for discussion among scientists and theologians for many centuries.

During the middle ages the Church was the authority in all areas of thought. Science as we know it today did not exist, for with its theological orientation the Church looked with disfavor upon observations which did not have theological explanations. It was only natural then that when the early geologists observed many thousands of feet of sedimentary rocks (those formed from particles of previously existing rock or chemically precipitated from solution) in the mountains of Europe and the British Isles, they should turn to the Church for an explanation. The easiest answer for the layers of sediments was that they were laid down by the Noahic Flood. As the sedimentary layers were studied further, problems arose when it was discovered that not all the layers were contemporaneous. It was also readily observed that some sediments had been deposited, hardened into rock, folded into mountain ranges, eroded off and then covered with new sediments. At some places the sedimentary rock layers were cut by formerly molten rock material which indicated volcanic activity after the sediments were deposited. Sixteenth and seventeenth century scientists attempted to harmonize the interpretation of field observations with church tradition.

As a result, many interpretations of the meaning and physical characteristics of the Flood have been suggested, modified, abandoned, and sometimes reproposed. These interpretations have produced some highly improbable explanations of the events of the deluge which have so confused the issue that it is difficult to separate intelligent exegesis of the Biblical accounts from fanciful eisegesis of the same passages. The reality of the Flood can hardly be questioned, however, because of the many references to it in both the Old and New Testament. Among these are chapters 6, 7, and 8 of Genesis, Genesis 9:11, 28; 10:1, 32; Matt. 24:38, 39; Luke 17:27; II Peter 2:5.

II. The Purpose of the Flood. An important aspect of the deluge is that God preserved some men, for Noah and his family were saved from destruction by going into an ark which Noah made according to God's specifications, and in which he gathered animals and birds preserved to replenish the earth.

It is apparent from Gen. 6:5-7 and other passages such as II Peter 2:5, 6 that the Flood was brought upon the earth as a judgment on the sins of the people. Man had become so sinful that "it repented the Lord that He had made man on the earth" (Gen. 6:6 KJV). In Scripture the reference to the Flood is linked with the judgment at the second coming of the Lord (Matt. 24:39). It is also mentioned in relation to the destruction of Sodom and Gomorrah (Luke 17:27-29; II Peter 2:5, 6).

The purpose of God as stated in Genesis 6:7 indicates that His judgment was not against the inanimate rocks or against plants, but against "man and beast, and the creeping things and the fowls of the air."

III. The Phenomena of the Flood. In the following passage, however (Gen. 6:11-13), the earth is included in the judgment. There is again difference of opinion as to the meaning of Gen. 6:13 in which God said, "The end of all flesh is come before me: for the earth is filled with violence through them; and, behold I will destroy them with the earth" (KJV). That the earth was not utterly destroyed as it will be in the last times (II Peter 2:10) is apparent. Some writers would interpret Gen. 6:13 to mean that great geologic catastrophes overwhelmed the earth's surface, while others point out that Gen. 6:6, 7, 12, and 13 all stress that it was the sin of living things ("flesh") that was to be punished and that the effect upon the inanimate rocks of the world is only incidental to punishing man.

Despite all attempts at scientific explanation of the minute details of the Flood, there seems to be no doubt that God worked a miracle in causing the Flood. In II Peter 3:5, 6 the Flood is compared with the creation of the world and is a miracle of the same order. In the same passage, II Peter 3:7ff, the final destruction of the world is given the same miraculous explanation as the Noahic Flood.

IV. The Source of the Flood. The Biblical account of the accumulation and dispersal of the waters of the Flood is very brief. In Gen. 7:11 the source of the water is explained ". . . all the fountains of the great deep were broken up and the windows of heaven were opened."

The Hebrew word *Tehom,* translated *great deep* in the KJV, is the same used in Gen. 1:2. That this does not necessarily include all the oceans is shown by its use in Isaiah 51:10 when it refers to the escape of the Israelites through "the depths of the sea" (the Red Sea). The word "fountain" (Hebrew *ma'yan*) means literally *place of a spring.* This could mean that water rose from the ocean or from fresh water springs on the earth or both.

V. Suggested Causes of the Flood. Some would prefer to believe that the expression "fountains of the great deep were broken up" indicates that the ocean (actually the Persian Gulf, an arm of the ocean) invaded the land. Others have assumed this implies volcanic activity and that some of the water of the Flood is "juvenile water" which is formed from the oxygen and hydrogen which may occur as separate elements in the molten rock deep in the earth's crust. This school of thought would also attribute a great deal of diastrophism (movements

GREAT TIDAL WAVES swept in from the oceans, and underground rivers gushed up through cracks in the ground, filling first the small depressions, next the hollows, then the wide valleys. The raging torrent swept away homes, tents, cattle, and all living things.

of the solid crust which result in a relative change of position of the rock formations concerned) to this verse. This could account for the subsidence of the mountains of the earth so that they could be covered more easily by the waters of the deluge.

To attribute volcanic activity to Gen. 7:11 is highly speculative, for at no place in the Genesis account of the Flood is any more specific description of conditions given. The fact that igneous rock (rock formed by the cooling of molten rock material) is found between or cutting sedimentary rock layers is not good evidence for volcanic activity at the time of the Flood. Sediments which have been laid down during historic time have been cut by lava coming up to present day volcanoes. It has also been observed that the oldest layers are also cut by igneous rocks. It seems apparent, therefore, that volcanic activity has gone on throughout the world's history. It is not possible to designate any particular rock body as being coincident with the Flood.

"The windows of heaven were opened" has been accepted as a description of rain. Some have seen this as a torrential downpour greater than normally experienced on the earth today. A hypothesis has been proposed that the earth from the time of Creation (or at least man's creation) was surrounded by a canopy of water in some form until the time of the Flood. The canopy was suggested as being water vapor, ice or liquid water. If such a canopy existed, it is proposed that its transfer from around the earth to the earth as water would cause a rain for many days.

The canopy idea, although firmly entrenched in literature, has doubtful Biblical authority. The language of Ezekiel, "the likeness of the firmament upon the heads of the living creature was as the colour of the terrible crystal stretched forth over their heads above" (Ezek. 1:22), has been cited as authority, with "the terrible crystal" referring to an ice canopy. This theory seems highly speculative. Again it should be noted that if a miraculous explanation for the Flood is accepted, physical explanations are not necessary.

VI. The Duration of the Flood. The length of the Flood is generally agreed upon within a few days. The Hebrews used a solar calendar in contrast to the Babylonian lunar month and the Egyptian arbitrary 365-day year. Most authorities would put the number of days from the time the rain started (Genesis 7:11) to the time Noah left the ark (Genesis 8:14) between 371 and 376 days.

VII. Traditions of the Flood. Traditions regarding a disastrous flood which occurred long ago are handed down by many peoples. Isolated tribes in all parts of the world have been found to have such traditions. This is not surprising when the destruction caused by present day floods as well as hurricanes and tornadoes accompanied by great rains is considered. A tribe occupying a limited area could be destroyed completely by one storm. If there were survivors they would date their civilization from such an event. Some traditional floods have been dated as having occurred within the last few hundred years by archaeological evidence.

The Hebrews, Assyrians and Babylonians, who lived within the area of the Tigris-Euphrates basin, all had traditions of a great flood. These narratives

Tabulated Chronology of the Flood

1. The making of the ark (Gen. 6:14)	
2. Collection of the animals (Gen. 7:9)	7 days before the rain started
3. Fountains of the great deep were broken up and the windows of heaven were opened	Second month, 17th day in Noah's 600th year
4. Rain (Gen. 7:12)	40 days and 40 nights
5. All the high hills covered (Gen. 7:19)	
6. Water prevailed upon the earth (Gen. 7:24)	150 days
7. Water returned from off the earth (Gen. 8:3)	150 days
8. Ark rested upon the mountains of Ararat (Gen. 8:4)	Seventh month, 17th day
9. Waters decreased (Gen. 8:4)	
10. Tops of mountains seen (Gen. 8:5)	Tenth month, 1st day
11. Noah waited (Gen. 8:6)	40 days
12. Noah sent forth raven and a dove; dove returned (Gen. 8:7-9)	
13. Noah waited (Gen. 8:10)	7 days
14. Noah sent forth dove again (Gen. 8:10); dove returned with olive branch (Gen. 8:11)	7 days
15. Noah waited (Gen. 8:12)	7 days
16. Noah sent forth dove which did not return (Gen. 8:12)	7 days
17. Noah removed covering; face of the ground was dry (Gen. 8:13)	1st month, 1st day, Noah's 601st year
18. Earth dried; Noah left ark (Gen. 8:14)	2nd month, 27th day

stated the purpose of the flood to be punishment because the world was full of violence, but the Hebrew story remained simple and credible, whereas the other accounts became complex and fanciful. Only the Biblical account retained a monotheistic viewpoint. Although it is not possible to affirm dogmatically that all of these three histories had a common origin, it seems probable that they did.

VIII.   The Universality of the Flood. One of the great differences of opinion in describing the Flood concerns its extent. Traditionally most Biblical interpreters considered the submergence to be universal; that is, that it covered the entire globe including the highest mountains. The reasons proposed to defend this viewpoint include the fact that in the Gen. account universal terms are used. *"All* the high hills that were under the whole heaven were covered" (Gen. 7:19) and *"all* flesh died" (Gen. 7:21). It has been pointed out that if the Flood were local there would be no need for an ark to preserve Noah, for God could have directed him to move with the animals to an area that was not to be submerged.

The fact that many civilizations have flood traditions has been cited as an evidence for a universal flood. The same evidence could be used to argue for a local flood because the accounts of floods in other parts of the world are less like the Hebrew tradition than those of the Assyrians and Babylonians who lived in the same areas as the Hebrews.

Today many conservative scholars defend a local flood. The crux of their argument seems to center in the covenant relation of God to man. He deals with certain groups, such as the children of Israel. The reasoning in regard to Noah is that Noah was not a preacher of righteousness to peoples of other areas but was concerned with the culture from which Abraham eventually came. Physical arguments have also been raised against a universal flood: origin and disposal of the amount of water necessary to make a layer six miles thick over the whole world, the effect upon plant life by being covered for a year, the effect upon fresh water life of a sea which contained salt from the ocean, and the fact that many topographic features of the earth such as cinder cones which show no evidence of erosion by a flood and which are much older than the flood could possibly be. It seems, therefore, that a person can advocate either a local or a universal concept of the Flood and find evidence to support his view.

IX.   Chronology of the Flood. Although Ussher in his chronology placed the flood at 2348 B.C., most scholars recognize a much earlier date.

Scholars who have advocated that the earth has developed to its present condition by a series of major calamities have been called catastrophists. These consider the Noahic Flood as the greatest of these catastrophes and believe that the Pleistocene ice age was related to the Flood. If, as the catastrophists believe, the Flood was associated in some way with the end of the Pleistocene ice age, a date of at least 10,000 B.C. would have to be accepted. Archaeological and anthropological evidence has caused some scholars to put the origin of man back more than 100,000 years so that there is not any general agreement among conservative scholars concerning the actual date of the deluge. The lack of consensus with regard to the details of the Flood should make all aware of the danger of placing so much importance on the interpretation of this important event that the other lessons of the Bible are missed.   D.B.

THE FOLLOWING BIBLE STORY, *Noah's Ark,* was written by Jean Bell Mosley. It is based upon the events related in the Book of Genesis, Chapters 5 through 11. The characters Shael, Mija and Reuel are fictional.

Noah's Ark

HEY WERE making fun of Noah again, down at the Gathering Place in the cypress grove.

"You know what that fellow Noah is aiming to do *now?*" demanded Shael (SHAY-el), an evil-looking man with brutal, leering features.

"No. Tell us, Shael," the others begged.

Noah had earned the ridicule of his roistering neighbors for his steadfast refusal to take part in their drinking brawls and their indecent talk. And Shael knew that Noah's "strange notions" were always good for a laugh.

Shael picked up a jug and emptied it, drinking noisily. "Well," he began, his black eyes darting around to make sure he had a sizable audience left. He had been carrying this choice bit of news for several days now, and he didn't want to waste it on unappreciative listeners.

"What's Noah doing?" his companions asked again.

"Well, he's building a boat," Shael announced. "Can you imagine—a boat, over in the meadow by the gopher woods!"

There was a moment of silence while the information filtered into foggy, drink-sodden brains, then a mixture of loud guffaws and derisive shouts: "A boat! Why there isn't even a brook down there! Where will he float it?"

Pleased with the reaction, Shael spoke again. "I was over that way the other day, and I heard a noise like a tree falling, so I went a little way into the woods to see what was happening. And there was old Noah and the boys—Shem, Ham and Japheth (JAY-feth)—hewing away as if they had to get something done before dark. 'What are you doing' I asked them. The boys kept on working, but Noah looked right at me and said, 'Son, the Lord is sorry that He made man and He's going to destroy him...'"

"Destroy us!" Shael's hearers shouted, glancing around the circle at one another and holding their sides with mirth.

Shael wiped his eyes and went on: "I asked Noah where he got the news, and what the boat had to do with it. He told me he'd been talking with God, and that the Lord told him to make this boat to save the ones He didn't want to perish."

After the laughter had died down, a short, stout man who had been sitting in the outskirts of the crowd spoke up, haltingly.

"I haven't seen the boat," he began, "but I did speak to Noah a long time back and, come to think of it, he warned me that something terrible might happen if people didn't change their ways. He said that men were disobeying God, that the world was so full of drunkenness, violence and pride and lying and treachery, that he wondered how long those things could go on." The man's voice trailed off into silence. There was a brooding pause in the live chatter of the crowd. It was almost as if a foreshadowing of doom hung over the cypress grove, stifling all thought and discouraging all conversation.

Then, with a sudden movement, Shael struggled slowly to his feet, walked over to where the short man was sitting, and clapped him noisily on the back. "Cheer up, friend!" he cried with forced gaiety. "Don't you go spoiling our fun with those gloomy thoughts. Leave them to Noah. Remember—you're only alive once—enjoy yourself while you can. Come on, now, let's have another drink!"

The Building of the Ark

L ONG BEFORE the morning sun penetrated the darkness of the cypress grove, revealing the results of the previous night's wild party, Noah and his three sturdy sons were making another patch of woods ring with their axes and hammers.

There was need for long hours, Noah felt, for many of his fine, hewn boards had already been stolen, obliging him to repeat much of his exacting work. He had never attempted such a big project before and had never felt such a necessity for having every piece of board and every wooden peg shaped to the exact dimensions given to him by God. For was not the continuation of life on earth hanging on his every act? Although he was a big man, well over six feet, with powerful shoulders and arms, sometimes the immensity of his commission made his mouth grow dry and caused his hands to tremble as he shaped the beams and sharpened the pegs.

"Shem, Ham, Japheth," Noah called to his sons. "Come, let us look over our work for this day." A morning breeze ruffled the gray hair that fell to his shoulders, billowing the folds of his loose-fitting garment as he walked between the piles of gopherwood logs.

Noah had the plans for the Ark quite fixed in his own mind, but there was constant need to instruct his sons. Taking a long, pointed stick, he drew a line in a nearby stretch of sand which he used and reused to make his sketches. "Now here we have the bottom," he said, "four hundred and fifty feet long. And here is the width, seventy-five feet." He added more lines to the sketch. "Then the sides, going up like this, are to be forty-five feet high." He studied his sons' expressions, making sure they understood these were no childish pictures in the sand nor whims of an old man, but divine blueprints for a vehicle to a new world. Turning to Ham, Noah continued, "Have you studied the trees that are left, son?"

"Yes, Father, there are plenty. And I thought we could set the pots for melting the pitch right over here." Ham indicated a suitable spot.

"Good, good," Noah said approvingly. "Now let us work with love and care this day."

The rising sun sent long shafts of light through the bordering woods as if pointing out to the world, with golden fingers, what was going on there. Crows gathered in the treetops to discuss the odd proceedings in their raucous language. Rabbits, which had thought the meadow theirs, scampered off to the thickets, wrinkling their noses and twitching their whiskers at the disturbance.

As they worked, Noah repeated to his sons God's plan, and his voice was full of quiet conviction. "He is going to destroy man and beast and the creeping things and the fowls of the air. There will be a great flood of waters upon the earth, but we will be safe in the Ark, you and your wives and your father and mother and one pair of every kind of animal, for we will make room for them in the Ark."

"But why, Father?" Shem asked, deep lines of puzzlement creasing his broad forehead.

Noah, although he had answered the question before, answered it again with fatherly love and patience, knowing that it was hard for human understanding. "Because God has seen the wickedness of man. You know what goes on in the cypress grove, do you not?"

The sons nodded reluctantly.

"That is what goes on everywhere," Noah continued, "and there is no darkness that God cannot penetrate. He has seen it and He wishes to end it all and start anew."

"And He is saving *us*?" Japheth marveled.

"He has so promised," Noah replied, looking from one to the other of his sons, pleased with their straight, sun-browned backs and strong, well-built bodies. They were dutiful and loyal, in the face of what to them still seemed shocking and incredible news.

Noah Is Mocked

THE WORK progressed slowly, for the tools were crude and unwieldy. It had been a long time since Tubal-cain (TEW-bul-kane) had fashioned the first implement, and not much improvement had been made since then. Moreover, there were many interruptions, for Noah would drop any piece of work at any time to talk to those who came to look on and poke fun, trying in every way he knew to lift them out of the mire of sin and depravity into which they had fallen. Though he spoke with all the eloquence that comes to one who has walked and talked with God, he never reached the ear or heart of even one person who would heed his pleas.

The morning after Shael had told his companions about Noah's project, he and his crowd came to the site where the Ark was being built to taunt and jeer.

"You say you're getting tired of walking with God, so you're going to take a little boat ride, Noah?" Shael asked. "Is this thing of yours supposed to float on *dew?*"

"Son, son," Noah implored, laying down his hammer, "when you speak of God, do so with all reverence. It may be that in His mercy He will yet . . ."

"Oh, you mean like this?" Shael interrupted. He assumed an exaggerated position of supplication and a mocking expression of veneration, winking slyly at his companions.

"Our God," Noah continued, "made man to have dominion over all things and in order that he can, he must . . ."

"Be quick with a knife, eh, Mija (MY-jah)?" Shael interrupted again, nudging a companion in the ribs.

"Yeah," Mija agreed, "quick with a knife and handy with his fists."

"I hear you're going to fill that thing with animals and live with them a while, Noah," Mija twitted. "How would you like that, Shael, living with a boatful of animals?"

"I don't know. I've never tried that yet. At least they don't put on righteous airs!"

Ham, his dark eyes smoldering, took a few menacing steps toward Shael with his ax upraised, but Noah held up a quick, forbidding hand. "No, son! Keep on with your work."

The laughter of Shael's crowd was loud and harsh, and Noah's heart ached with compassion for them as he turned back to his labors. Perhaps tomorrow they would listen to him. It was a lonely position he held among men, being the only one to whom God had revealed His plan.

The Building Progresses

THE YEARS WENT BY. The Ark went upward, but man descended into even deeper pits of killing, stealing, committing adultery, lying, swearing, blasphemy, and all things evil. Torn between his God-given duty to construct the Ark and his self-imposed duty of trying to reform man, Noah developed a nervous habit of shading his eyes and looking off to the left and then to the right, as a lone and abandoned actor on some vast stage might look off into the darkened wings for help from someone who has been on before, or for someone awaiting his cue to come on. The crow's-feet at the corners of his eyes deepened, and the eyes themselves, dark and gleaming, seemed to recede farther and farther into his head.

The daily sketches in the sand grew bigger and more intricate as Noah with his pointed stick outlined the lower, second, and third decks, showing where the partitions should be, what beasts would occupy the compartments, and how big to make each stall.

Shem, Ham, and Japheth constructed the interior compartments with great care, being mindful of the variety of animals which, if they could believe their father, were to live there during the flood. Food storage bins for both the family and the animals were built. A door was placed on one side and a window at the top, through which only the sky was visible.

The thick, black pitch, gathered from the shores of nearby lakes where it oozed up from underground sources, boiled and bubbled night and day in the big pots and hardened to a fine weatherproof coating on both the inside and outside of the Ark.

"Here will be our living quarters," Noah told his sons one day, standing in an oblong room near the center of the Ark. "Let us arrange the room for eating and sleeping."

When the long work was almost finished, the wives began drying fruit and preparing food that could be stored. They sorted their few possessions, choosing those they thought would be most needed, leaving the rest behind. As they worked with their hands, their minds were occupied with thoughts of what it would be like on the "other side" of the flood, as they began to call it. Would the Ark stay where it was, and come down in the same place? Would the hills and valleys be the same? Would they drift off into an entirely new world? It was difficult for them to imagine. Nevertheless they went ahead with their preparations—for so much depended upon their obedience to God's commands at this crucial time.

The Animals Arrive

P ECULIAR THINGS began happening now in the cypress grove and the surrounding woods. Strange and eerie noises were heard, and at night there were many eyes shining in the darkness.

After that, reports began coming in daily that some new and different animal had been sighted down by this meadow or that thicket—spotted animals and striped animals and animals with long necks, short stumpy tails, swinging noses. Noah smiled to himself, knowing that God had not forgotten him, and he ordered a ramp to be laid down from the ground to the door of the Ark for the animals to use in going aboard.

"The day is near," Noah told his family, for he could read the unmistakable signs. Time and again he went to the Gathering Place in the cypress grove, warning the people of the disaster to come and pleading with them to change their ways, for there might still be time. But they only spat at him, called him crazy, and hurled vile insults about "living with animals."

One day, as Noah was smoothing out the sand for the last time, for all the plans had been drawn and completed, the Lord appeared again to Noah and said, "You have been righteous and have done all that I commanded. Go into the Ark now, you and your household, and see that a pair of all animals, fowls, and creeping things are there, for in seven days I will bring the flood. It will rain for forty days and forty nights, and every living thing remaining on the face of the earth will be blotted out."

Noah stood with bowed head, tears coursing down his wrinkled old face. They were tears for his fellow men who had not listened to him and for whom time had run out.

"Yes, Lord," he answered obediently.

It was a time of frantic, last-minute packing and arranging. Noah directed the placing of various objects and animals so that the Ark would balance and stay upright. "Shem," he called to his son, "are there any more animals coming up the ramp?"

"They stopped this morning," Shem replied. "There have been more of some kind than just a pair, Father. I have counted as many as seven pairs."

"Yes, that is according to God's plan, son," Noah replied. Then he added in tones of finality, "Now let us draw up the ramp."

For a long time Noah stood at the doorway of the Ark, where he could look out over the hills and valleys to the faraway horizon. He shaded his eyes in the old familiar searching gesture.

"What is it, Father?" Shem whispered softly, for he had seen this look in his father's eyes many times. "You seem to be looking for something."

"Oh, nothing, son, nothing," Noah replied, a bit startled. "Anyway, it was something I didn't find. Now go, Shem, and make sure that all the others are settled."

Noah turned back to the doorway. A haze, soft as a blessing, lay over the countryside. For six hundred years, as time was reckoned then, Noah had taken pleasure in the sunrise and birdsong and growing things, walking the woodland paths, observing the continuity of life and the order that prevailed. It had been many years since God had created the earth and all things in it. Just how many, Noah was not sure, but he knew, from his father's telling, that the generations had been long, starting with Adam and Eve and coming down through Seth, Enosh (EE-nosh), Kenan (KEY-nan), Mahalalel (ma-HAL-uh-lel), Jared (JAY-red), Enoch (EE-nock), Methuselah (muh-THOO-zuh-luh), and Lamech (LAY-meck) to himself. He knew, too, that during that time all of creation had gone about its duty and pleasure in its own natural way. But, of all the things that had been placed on the earth, or in the waters, or in the heavens during that time of creation, man alone, the very one designated to have dominion, got bent and twisted and grew in the wrong direction, as a broken limb or twig might do.

Noah shivered involuntarily because he was aware that he, too, was pitifully human. Having God's promise, however, that there would be a new world, a new beginning, he straightened his aged shoulders, took a deep breath, and let his eyes travel back from the horizon to the things nearest at hand — the cypress grove, the buildings and tents, the chips and shavings left from making the Ark. Embers from the dying fires under the pitch pots glowed fitfully in the stray breezes. Noah watched them flare up and go out. The door to the Ark was slowly and silently closed, shutting out the old world forever.

"Yes, Lord," Noah whispered, staring in awe at the closed door he had not touched. He knew that it was time to turn and face a new life. With firm steps, this tall man with the lofty destiny went into the living quarters of the Ark to be with his family, to strengthen and fortify them for the ordeal that was coming.

Noah was old, but he still had much work to do.

The Deluge

THEY HAD BEEN laying bets for seven days down in the cypress grove as to just how long old Noah would stay shut up in the Ark.

"Maybe he isn't there any more," Mija suggested. "Maybe he's just gone like that one he tried to tell us about who lived just so long and then, poof, no more. No hide, no hair, no skin. Just gone."

"You mean Enoch," Shael said. "Yeah, I've heard him tell that crazy story, too."

And as they recalled the various sayings of Noah, each one trying to outdo the other for laughs, they gradually shifted over under the shelter of the biggest trees, for it was beginning to rain.

The rain began softly, hesitantly, making cozy sounds on the roof of the Ark. The fowls, roosting on the highest rafters, heard it and settled down cooing and clucking contentedly. Soon the rain was beating down in a more lively tempo against the sides of the vessel.

The members of Noah's family, gathered in the center room, looked at him questioningly.

"Noah," his wife said softly.

There was a moment of expectant silence.

"Yes," Noah nodded, "it is the beginning."

All day the rain beat a steady tattoo against the Ark. By nightfall it gained in fury and came down in great silver sheets, from all directions at once, buffeting and battering the Ark as if to test its buoyancy and durability.

Noah and his sons fed and bedded the animals as best they could, not being familiar with the habits of all of them. The women took from the storage bins and, with nervous hands, prepared the frugal evening meal. There was not much talk, each being occupied with his own thoughts. For the sons and the wives it was a time of having their doubts gradually removed. Each one was coming to the conclusion that Noah must indeed have been right. Was there ever such a rainstorm?

Flood waters rising

Not only did the rain continue with unabated fury, but great tidal waves swept in from the oceans. Underground rivers gushed up through cracks in the ground, filling first the smallest depressions, next the hollows, then the wide valleys. The raging torrent swept away homes, tents, cattle, and all living things.

Noah's family was sitting down to another evening meal during this terrible onrush when the Ark made a great lurch sideways, upsetting the water jar and sending things rolling across the floor. The women screamed and the animals sent up horrible sounds of fear.

Then slowly, slowly, the Ark righted itself. The rolling objects on the floor came to a full stop, and there remained only the gentlest swaying motion. All eyes turned to Noah.

The last mountain top about to be covered

"We are afloat," he said quietly, as a light of triumph brightened his tired old eyes.

The Ark listed a little to the right, so Noah and his sons immediately changed the stalls of the elephants with those of the giraffes. This promptly restored the balance.

Meanwhile, the cypress grove was a scene of the wildest confusion. Water was already waist high and rising rapidly. The carcasses of drowned animals were floating among the trees. Blood-curdling screams of fear were cut short, ending in choking, gasping sounds as someone's hold gave way. Logs, rooftops, and islands of debris sped swiftly by.

"Look!" someone shouted, pointing to the north.

All eyes turned in that direction. Faces whitened with fear as a great wall of water, mountain high, came sweeping in.

Noah's neighbors laugh at his work.

COLOR ILLUSTRATIONS BY RICHARD MUNSELL

Rising waters drive the survivors to the highest ground.

*God instructs Noah to build
the Ark.*

*God was displeased by the sinful
ways of men and women.*

The Tower of Babel was an immense construction project.

Noah offers a thanksgiving sacrifice to God.

Confusion results when the Tower of Babel workers speak in many tongues.

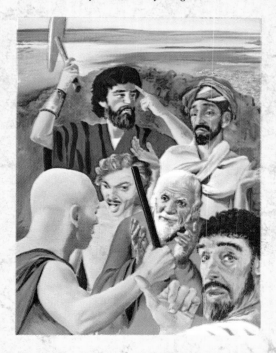

Building the great Ark.

Noah observes the rain starting.

Noah and Shem guide the birds and beasts into the Ark.

Shael and Mija and their companions had climbed to the first limbs of trees. Now they hurried on up. Crafty Shael had chosen the tallest tree of all, and seeing that there would not be enough room at the top for all the others who had chosen the same tree, he quickly climbed higher. Drawing his knife from his belt, he lashed out at the groping, grasping hands below, breaking their holds. The waters in the cypress grove turned red. Heads bobbed up and down, then sank out of sight.

Shael, his breath coming now in short painful gasps, climbed to the topmost branch and looked wildly around for something else to cling to. Over to the east he could see the Ark looming above the treetops, dancing lightly on the muddy waters, its door closed tightly. There was no human face visible anywhere for him to see, to call to. The curses were thick in Shael's throat until the mountain of water swept in, silencing him forever.

Only the Ark remained above water

The Voyage

THE DAYS passed slowly. There was not much to do inside the Ark except care for the animals and wait, wait, wait. The rain continued with such a deafening downpour that Noah sometimes thought he was losing his hearing. At such times he would climb to the third deck and sit underneath the now covered window, to be alone with his thoughts, to nourish his spirit, to weigh and test his understanding to make sure that all along the line he had done as God directed.

How tiny the Ark must look, he thought one day, riding the vast flood of waters. How slender the thread that held mankind! One crack of a seam, one twist of a joist, and it would all be over. The many years he had spent in building the Ark with such painstaking care seemed as nothing now, when his handiwork was being put to the test.

As Noah contemplated the sturdy construction that kept the Ark afloat, and as the rain drummed in his ears, his mind was caught up in a sort of fantasy wherein he seemed to see a larger meaning of his whole commission. The Ark became *man* and was able to withstand the floods of time and tide and adversity only because he had followed God's orders to the last detail, because the joists and beams and rafters of his inner self had been hewn and measured and cut to the proportions set down by God.

A swift, dizzy turning of the Ark as it was trapped in some swirling eddy brought Noah out of his dream and made him hasten below to comfort his family and allay their fears.

For forty days and forty nights the incessant rain lashed against the sides and pelted the roof of the Ark. The days inside the Ark were almost as dark as the nights. When tempers grew taut because of the close confinement and sharp words flared up, Noah would bid the members of his household sit down, and he would tell them stories that had been passed on to him by Lamech, his father, and Methuselah, his grandfather. He told them of the three brothers, Cain, Abel and Seth, and of the murder of Abel and the curse placed on Cain. He told them of old Jubal, who made and blew the first horn, of his brother Jabal, who fashioned the first tent, and of Tubal-cain, who made the first hammer.

One day, in the middle of a story, Shem suddenly broke in. "Father!" he interrupted, raising a quieting hand.

"What is it, son?"

"Listen," Shem whispered. "I think it has stopped raining."

The women ran to press their ears against the sides of the Ark.

"It is so!" Shem's wife cried, and there was gladness in her voice.

"Yes, it is the fortieth day," Noah replied. He was not surprised, for he had been making notches on a rafter for every period of what he could discern as light and darkness.

The warmth of the sun was soon felt against the roof, and when the animals were quiet enough the wind — no longer a menace — could be heard whistling around the decks.

"The wind will help to dry the land," Noah told them, adding to their rejoicing. However, when he noticed that the wives were making preparations to leave the Ark, he said, "Not yet, my daughters." There was kindness in his voice, for he knew it had been a trying time for them. "It will be a long time before the waters recede and the land gets dry."

The Long Waiting

THE TEDIOUS DAYS ticked by. Food supplies ran low, but the cow and goat supplied fresh milk daily and occasionally an egg was found unbroken. Noah continued making his notches on the rafter — fifty, sixty, seventy — and still the Ark floated — eighty, ninety, one hundred. Sometimes there would be periods of stillness when nothing dipped or swayed and Noah was tempted to announce that they had come to rest. But before long a gentle motion told him they were still afloat. Still the days crept by — one hundred ten, one hundred twenty, one hundred forty.

Some of the fowls dropped their feathers and grew new ones. The ravens flapped their great wings restlessly. There were days when the members of Noah's family paced silently back and forth in the Ark. Long ago each one had come to know, if he had held any doubts previously, that truly they were the only people who could possibly be alive. When their thoughts came to dwell on this fact, their hands grew moist and their throats tightened. It was a great responsibility they were entrusted with, peopling a new world.

One day, as each was meditating on the future, a loud, grating, splintery noise rose from somewhere down below.

"Shem, Ham, Japheth!" Noah called, hurrying down from the third deck. "The hull has given way!" His voice was sharp-edged with panic.

They met in the living quarters and there was naked fear in their eyes. A sudden lurch of the Ark knocked them all to the floor and loud cries, bellows, growls, and squawkings told them that terror was spreading among the animals, too.

Noah raised his head slowly, holding it to one side as if listening for the leak, and watching intently the rolling of the toppled furniture. "We are grounded," he said, and there was immense relief in his voice.

The Raven and Dove Are Sent Out

STILL MORE DAYS went by before Noah felt it would be entirely safe to remove the covering from the window. When there had been no motion of the Ark for many days he told his family of a plan.

"We will send the raven out the window and see what happens," he said, instructing his sons to remove the covering.

It was good to see the sky again, even though just a small part was visible, and they took turns standing beneath the window and looking up, breathing deeply of the fresh, clean air and exclaiming over the beautiful shade of blue they hadn't seen in so long or the piece of white fleecy cloud that happened to float within sight. For the first time since they had boarded the Ark they began to relax. The sight of the sky gave them a comfortable feeling of familiarity that soothed their tired bodies and spirits. When the raven flew up and outward, it was as if a part of them, too, had been released.

The raven did not come back and Noah, knowing that there was great strength in its wings, thought that it might fly back and forth across the waters until they were dried up.

"We will send forth a dove," he said, and once again they gathered at the window for the ceremony.

At dusk the dove returned to the Ark, for there was no other place for it to rest and it had not the strength of the raven in its wings.

At the end of another week, Noah sent the dove out again. And again at evening it returned. This time he caught it up in his hands.

"Shem, Ham, Japheth!" he cried, turning to show them what the dove had in its beak.

"An olive leaf!" Japheth exclaimed.

"A green olive leaf," Shem added.

711

Their hearts were too full of joy for any more speech then, but what excitement there was that night on the Ark! The women prepared a fine meal, for they were no longer so saving of the food that was left. They sang old familiar songs, made up new ones, and talked of the homes they would have when they left the Ark.

Noah waited another week and sent forth the dove again, and when it did not return he knew that it had found land on which to come to rest.

"Come, sons," he beckoned, "let us remove a larger portion of the covering and look out upon the earth."

Noah, as a boy, had watched the great and beautiful butterfly moths emerge from their dark, tight cocoons. The dramatic transition from one stage of life to another had always thrilled him. It was with such a feeling of release, and unfolding of wings, that he put his head and shoulders through the opening they had made and looked out upon the bright new world. There was the sun, still on duty, making such a bright light that Noah was forced to put his hands over his eyes and remove them slowly, as with blind eyes being restored to sight. The trees were faintly tinged with green, renewing life after seeming death. North, south, east, west, Noah gazed long and lovingly. All the slime and mud and corruption of death had disappeared. Everything was clean and bright and shiny. It was like looking upon another fresh creation. The beauty and wonder of it all made his voice ragged with emotion.

"We are at rest on the top of a mountain," he observed, and relinquished his place so that the others might look out upon the earth again.

"Let us go out at once," Ham proposed.

Noah shook his head, telling them for the first time how God had closed the door that first day. They must wait until God should tell them that it was time to leave. So they waited still longer, but this time the waiting was not so bad, for fresh air swept into the Ark from the opening and the sun sent in broad shafts of light.

At the end of eight more weeks, God came to Noah and said, "Go forth now, you and your household and all the animals. Be fruitful and multiply."

"Yes, Lord," Noah replied, and went immediately to tell his family what the Lord had bidden.

A wonderful sound of freedom went up from the Ark when the door was opened and the ramp let down. The fowls took to the air with a great rushing of wings, their molted feathers floating off on the breeze. The animals ran, leaped, and scampered about, stretching tired legs and switching cramped tails. Some stayed near the Ark because they sensed safety there. Others bounded off to places more to their liking.

As soon as Noah's feet touched the ground, he began looking for stones with which to build an altar and give thanks to God for the deliverance of his household.

He took from those animals and birds of which there were more than one pair and made a burnt offering to the Lord. This pleased God very much and He promised Noah that never again would He curse the ground or destroy every living creature, and that as long as the earth remained, there would be unchanging order in the universe — seed time, then harvest; summer, then winter; and day followed by night.

"Be fruitful now, and fill the earth with people," God said to Noah and his sons. "I give you dominion over all things. The green things that grow and every living thing that moves shall be food for you, except you shall not eat the blood with the flesh, nor shed the blood of your fellow man. And never again will I destroy all living things by flood. I give you now a sign of My promise."

"Oh, look!" exclaimed Japheth's wife, pointing to the sky. "There — to the east. See?"

All eyes turned eastward to behold a rainbow arching across the sky, faintly discernible at first, but growing in intensity, the colors deepening into their pure shades and each blending into the next. Noah and his family stood there, this little huddle of humanity, and watched until the last vestige of color disappeared, and then they ventured forth into the world, just a little lower than the angels and crowned with glory and honor.

Noah Plants a Vineyard

BECAUSE the winds were too strong and cold in the mountains where the Ark had landed, Noah and his wife descended to the lower slopes where the sun warmed the soil and caused things to grow in abundance. On a gently rolling hillside that sloped to the south and west, Noah chose to make his home, and there he planted a vineyard.

The strain of the voyage which had taken almost an entire year had left its mark on Noah. His commission was over, he knew that, but his taut nerves did not release as readily as the thoughts of his mind. Long afterwards he was haunted by nightmares that he was still on the Ark tossing to and fro on the raging waters, that the Ark had sprung a leak, or that the animals had broken loose in suicidal warfare. He would rise up in his sleep and shout for his sons to come and help. When he was awakened and made to realize that the journey was over and had been for some time, and that he had remained faithful in all things, the relief was so intense that it left him weak and shaken.

At such times Noah, so completely human, so pitifully mortal, would drink the wine that he had made from his grapes so that he might return to restful, dreamless sleep. And in the mornings, walking along the sloping hillsides of his vineyard, it was pleasant to remember that the hard times were behind him. He had kept stubbornly and faithfully to his work of building the Ark when Shael and his friends had stood around mocking him. He had managed the Ark and the animals and his household through the flood. The fate of the new world was no longer his responsibility. Shem, Ham, and Japheth were raising families and peopling the earth. It was up to *them* now. And, since no one was depending upon him any more, what was wrong with enjoying a good drink of wine?

As time went by, Noah did as so many men have done—he succumbed to the temptation of drinking too much.

On one such occasion he started undressing himself and then fell to the floor in a drunken stupor. Soon he was fast asleep, snoring loudly, and muttering incoherently from time to time.

Ham came home shortly thereafter to consult his father about a problem which had arisen. He was amazed to find his father naked. Then, stooping over the reclining form, he looked into Noah's face, listened to his heavy breathing and his strange babbling. Like a flash Ham rushed away to find his brothers, Shem and Japheth.

"That fine father of ours," he cried, "is lying on the floor drunk, without a stitch of clothes on. What a sight he is!"

Noah tending his vines

Shem and Japheth were pained and shocked... but Ham seemed to enjoy parading his father's disgrace.

"Let us go cover him," Shem said, turning to Japheth.

"I'm sure that father would not wish us to discover him in this state," Japheth protested.

"Then we will take a cloth and hold it up and walk backwards and cover him. That way we will not witness his shame."

When Noah later learned of the actions of his three sons, he was very angry with Ham and cursed his son Canaan, predicting that he should be slave to his brothers. And for their thoughtful actions, Noah poured out his blessings on Shem and Japheth.

Noah's Story Hours

SOMETIMES Noah's grandchildren and greatgrandchildren would come to visit him and sit on the pleasant hillside of the sloping vineyard and listen to him tell the old, old stories.

"Now, children," Noah would say, after they were all settled comfortably around him, "in the days before the flood, the people were very evil. And the Lord said to me that He was going to destroy the world."

"What did the Lord look like, Grandfather?" the children would ask from time to time.

Here Noah would pause, trying to remember in detail just how it was back then, almost four hundred and fifty years ago, when he walked and talked with God. But he was an old, old man now, almost nine hundred and fifty years of age as time was reckoned in those days, and his memory along some lines was dim. Still, it seemed very important that he tell these children exactly how it was. And as he tried so desperately to recall the face of God, it seemed that suddenly His features became a composite of all the people he had ever known. Then the answer came to him quite simply. "Why, God created man in His own image, children."

"And how big was the Ark, Grandfather?"

"It was four hundred and fifty feet long and seventy-five feet wide and forty-five feet high," Noah replied promptly, for these measurements had been burned into his memory. "It is still in the mountains to the north. You can see it if you journey that way. It looks like this." Here Noah would scratch out a place in the soil of his vineyard and with a sharpened stick once again draw a likeness of the Ark. "We coated it inside and outside with pitch."

"My father says there is a whole lake of pitch not far from here," one of the children said.

"Yes, it is plentiful in this country. Some day the people will use it to do more building," Noah replied.

"They already are," one of the boys reported. "Haven't you heard from the travelers of the great building that is going on to the southeast, Grandfather? They are baking bricks and using pitch to put them together. It is supposed to be built up to the heavens!" The little boy's eyes were wide with excitement at the telling.

"Has the Lord ordered someone to make the building?" Noah asked, his dim eyes sparkling with new interest.

"We have heard no one say, Grandfather."

Noah gazed thoughtfully at the distant horizon. Ah, if only he were younger, and could travel about and see what was going on ...

In the days to come, Noah would often sit on the sunny hillside mulling over in his mind the stupendous events he had been privileged to witness. His mind wandered back to the days before the flood ... to the taunts of his evil neighbors, the hard labor with axe, saw and hammer. He remembered the long days spent inside the Ark, the sending forth of the dove and its joyous return with a sign of fruitfulness in its beak. Years of blessing had followed. And now the heart of Noah rejoiced in the goodness of his Heavenly Father.

Then the old man suddenly remembered what the child had told him about a great new building which men were raising elsewhere in the land. Perhaps someone else had been called of God to carry out His will. Or maybe, on the contrary—and Noah passed a weary hand over his wrinkled forehead—maybe men were again doing something in defiance of God's will. For Noah knew only too well that men's hearts were prone to lapse into forgetfulness and disobedience. So often they did things for their own selfish pleasure, or to gratify their headstrong pride.

The Tower of Babel

THE PEOPLE of the first generation after the flood did not move far from the site of the landing of the Ark on the mountains of Ararat (AR-uh-rat), in what is now Turkey. But, as the generations increased in number, they began to migrate, and they came to the land called Shinar (SHINE-ar) and settled there in the rich plain between two rivers.

Living was easier than it had been before the flood, but of course these people did not know how it was back in those days, and the majority quickly forgot the stories that Noah and his sons had passed on, among them the one about the removal of the curse from the ground.

As the population grew, meeting places developed which were not unlike that evil Gathering Place in the cypress grove, except that perhaps the sins committed there were more those of stiff-necked pride and foolishness rather than sins of blasphemy and the flesh. Sometimes older men with good memories would attempt to hold the attention of the crowd at these gatherings and pass on the stories that had been told to them about Adam and Eve, Cain and Abel, and Noah and his Ark, but the younger generation was impatient with the happenings of the past and wanted to get on with new projects.

"You know what I think we can do?" a haughty man named Reuel (ROO-el) asked one day when he deemed a sizable enough crowd was present. He had been working out some plans in his mind for some time now and had not wanted to waste them on just a few. "I think we can build a tower, not a mere seventy-five feet wide and forty-five feet high, or whatever that Ark was supposed to have been — personally I have never seen it — but a tower that will reach to the heavens!" Reuel's dark eyes glowed feverishly with the immensity of his plans. He waited a few minutes for smaller minds to encompass the colossal idea.

"It will be a sort of central place to bind us together," he went on, "so that we will not become scattered. It will stand as a monument, showing to all what great things we can accomplish."

There were shouts of approval. "Yes, yes, let us do so. Let us build a tower so that it will disappear into the heavens. Let us show our might."

"And perhaps," continued Reuel, "if there ever should come another flood, as that story goes, we can be saved by climbing up to the top of this mighty tower."

"But we are never to have another such flood," a bearded old man interrupted. "The rainbow . . ."

"What about the rainbow?" Reuel demanded, irritated with the slightest suggestion of disagreement.

The old man disappeared into the crowd, cowed by the pompous manner of this important man.

"What about building material?" another man asked, not with any suggestion of disagreement, but with enthusiasm in his voice.

"We can make bricks and burn them and stick them together with the pitch, which is plentiful around here," Reuel said.

Attendance at the new Gathering Place increased as plans for such a building went forward.

"We will make it like this," Reuel said one day, placing wooden blocks on top of one another, each one smaller, so that it resembled a terraced pyramid. As Reuel kept adding block on top of block, more shouts of approval went up. "It will, indeed, touch the sky," they proclaimed.

The old bearded man who had earlier attempted to break into the discussion with his reminder of the promise of the rainbow spoke up again.

"The Ark was built according to specifications given by God. Has anyone received such instructions from God, or asked His guidance as to the building of this tower?"

"Who needs such instructions and guidance?" Reuel shouted angrily. "We can do it alone."

"Yah, old man," the others scoffed. "Why don't you go on off and milk your nanny goats?"

The Confusion of the Languages

THE SITE for the tower was chosen near the bank of the river. Once again fires were kindled under great pitch pots, and soon the acrid smoke of the bubbling asphalt ascended to the sky. Great stone ovens for baking the bricks were constructed nearby, and work progressed with reasonable speed, for everyone understood the orders and wishes of the others.

The keeper of the oven fires had a great many men working under him so that fuel was always on hand and temperatures evenly maintained.

The keeper of the pitch pots had another set of workers under him, as did the boss of the brickmakers, the boss of the bricklayers and the general boss of construction.

As the building went up and up, men began to swell with pride like fat, spring-singing toads, giving little if any consideration to the fact that the soil they used to make the bricks, the pitch which bubbled up from underground sources, the wood with which they kindled the fires, the very hands of men who shaped and handled these things, were all created by God.

When the tower reached such a height that the morning mists from the river shrouded its top, the workmen shouted with glee. "See, see what we have done. We are indeed at the heavens!"

"We are not through yet," Reuel told them, and ordered the work to proceed as usual.

The Lord was aware of all that was going on, of course. He observed the proud, haughty spirit of man. He heard Reuel say he did not need the help of God. He saw that if the building should be completed, man would go on to even more ambitious projects, until he would actually begin to believe that he could do anything without acknowledging the Source, or calling upon God for help. Perhaps a gentle reminder here at the beginning to forestall the creeping, belly-slithering sin of pride would be helpful in times to come.

So it was that one day, when the fires were burning too low in the brick ovens, the keeper of the fires shouted to the workers, "Build up the fires!"

The workers looked at him in astonishment. His words were a meaningless jumble of sounds to them. Then one of the workers broke out in a shout of laughter, and the others followed suit.

"He's either drunk or he's going crazy!" they said among themselves, going on with their work.

The same thing was going on over at the pitch pots.

"Fill up the pots again," the foreman shouted to his men.

His helpers stopped their activity, listening open-mouthed. The foreman's command was a blur of strange sounds to their ears.

"What are you trying to say?" they asked—but now *their* talk puzzled the foreman, and he upbraided them for their impudence.

And so they talked back and forth, accusing each other in alien tongues, not yet aware of what had happened.

Angry voices drifted down from the top of the tower. Men came in from the clay fields, mumbling what sounded like gibberish to the others. There was great flailing of arms, wild gestures and gesticulations. Fights broke out here and there. Dogs tucked their tails and ran off to hide under buildings. Even the birds ceased their singing, so loud was the uproar and confusion.

And then fear began to creep over the workers like a dark and dread disease — fear that blanched faces and silenced tongues. They left off with their work and crept home to their families, hoping that tomorrow it would all be over, hoping that someone had just got hold of some bad wine.

But the next day it was the same, and the next, and the next. The fires flared fitfully and went out. The pitch hardened in the pots. The pits in the clay fields filled with rainwater. No one appeared at the new Gathering Place. The last report about Reuel was that he was seen heading for the desert country in a whirlwind of dust.

Those who could understand each other came together and built their homes close together, so that they could protect themselves against those they could not understand and therefore feared. Other groups went off and built towns and villages in faraway places.

The unfinished tower stood as it had on that last day of work, except that pigeons and starlings came to roost on the open top and mud daubers built their intricate homes against the interior walls.

The years passed — seed time, then harvest; summer, then winter — as God had promised. Damp winds from the southeast blew up from the gulf. Sandy winds came in from the western desert, wearing away at the man-made bricks of the tower. In the summertime children came there to play. Their favorite game was one they called Babel (BAY-bul), in which they re-enacted the events of that long ago day, according to the tales passed down by their elders. Gay laughter could be heard echoing through the empty rooms as the children tried to outdo each other with their incomprehensible gabbling back and forth.

In the wintertime, bearded old men came to sit against the south walls, trying to soak up warmth from the bricks. Often they could not communicate in words, but their eyes would sometimes meet, travel to the top of the unfinished tower, and then look into each other's again and smile knowingly.

These were the old men who remembered and believed. These were the wise old men who cautioned their children that man was created only *in the image* of God, but that he is not God; the discerning old men whose thoughts were later to issue forth in such words of wisdom as: "Pride goes before destruction, and a haughty spirit before a fall...The Lord tears down the house of the proud...Commit your work to the Lord and your plans will be established...Many are the plans in the mind of a man, but it is the purpose of the Lord that will be established."

In years gone by, Noah learned the wisdom of submitting to God's purpose. How long before all his descendants will learn that wisdom, too?

FLOUR, fine-crushed and sifted grain, generally wheat or rye or barley (Judg. 7:13). Eastern flour was not quite as fine or as white as ours, and as a result, the bread was more wholesome. The "meat" offerings, were of flour. "Meat" here should be "meal." (Cf. Lev. 6:15 in KJV and ASV.)

FLOWER (See Plants)

FLUTE (See Music)

FLY (See Insects)

FOAL (See Animals)

FODDER, the mixed food of cattle, generally from several kinds of grain sown together (Job 6:5; Job 24:6 "corn" in ASV; Isa. 30:24).

FOOD, nutritive material taken into a living organism to sustain life, to promote growth and the repair of the tissues, and to give energy for the vital processes. The Bible says little about food for animals. Bible animals for the most part are herbivorous, though carnivorous ones are mentioned. Some omnivorous animals, like swine, are mentioned, but almost always in a contemptuous way (Matt. 7:6) and swine were forbidden as food (Isa. 65:4).

At the very beginning of human history, Adam's food for his first day was probably some ripe fruit near him as he awoke to consciousness, and when he began to hunger, his nose as well as his eyes directed him to his first meal. Food and water would of course be necessary from that first day. Before sin had entered into human history, God apparently prescribed a vegetarian diet, both for man and beast (Gen. 1:29,30), but one must not

COOKING IN A PEASANT HOME. Note the pottery cooking pot and the fire of thorns, reminiscent of Psalms 58:9.

build too much on silence here as regarding the content of diet. By the time that Noah built the ark, there was a distinction between clean and unclean beasts (Gen. 7:2,3) and when God made his covenant with Noah after the flood (Gen. 9:3,4) flesh was permitted as food. Blood was forbidden, and it seems that the reason for this prohibition was as much theological as sanitary for "the life (Hebrew *nephesh* or soul) is in the blood" (cf. Lev. 17:11). Coming down now to the time of Moses, fat was also prohibited as food (Lev. 3:16,17) and again, the reason given is religious but not hygienic. In the time of the Restoration (Neh. 8:10) Nehemiah encouraged the people to "eat the fat" while celebrating a national "Thanksgiving day." One might imagine here that Nehemiah had forgotten that "all the fat is the Lord's" (Lev. 3:16) until one notices that the Hebrew word for "fat" here is not the one used in Leviticus. The word in Nehemiah could just as well be rendered "dainties" and refers probably to the various rich confections of which Eastern people are so fond.

The animals most frequently mentioned in the Bible are the domestic herbivorous animals, and these are divided sharply into two classes; the clean and the unclean. (See Lev. 11) The clean animals were to be used for food and for sacrifice and the four-footed ones were distinguished by their hoofs and by their chewing the cud. The camel chews the cud but does not part the hoof and so was considered unclean, though its milk was and is greatly used by desert-dwellers. Swine part the hoof but do not chew the cud, and so were ceremonially unclean. They were perhaps prohibited as food because of the mischievous *trichina spiralis*, a worm which has long infested swine, and from half-roasted pork can enter the human body and create great harm. Of the seafood which was reckoned unclean the principal ones were oysters and shrimps. One can easily realize how dangerous they would be in a land where climate was hot and there was no refrigeration. In other words, most of the distinctions between "clean" and "unclean" foods were clearly based upon sanitary reasons.

In Palestine and Syria, fresh fruit can be obtained throughout the year. Oranges last in the spring till the very short season of apricots arrives. After the apricots come the plums, figs, pomegranates, etc., which last until the grapes appear, and they in turn remain until the oranges and lemons are again in season.

The preparation of food differs from Western custom. Generally meat is eaten not in steaks and roasts, but cut up and served with rice, and often imbedded in "coosa" (a kind of squash) or wrapped in cabbage or grape leaves. The bread is not as white and fine as is ours, but is far more healthful. A common laborer often takes as his lunch two hollow loaves of bread, one filled with cheese and the other with olives. There were several sorts of sweets, of which dried figs boiled in grape molasses (Gen. 43:11) was one of the best known. Near the sea, fish were very commonly eaten. Various kinds of vegetables were used: beans, lentils, millet, melons, onions, gourds; also spices: cummin, mint, mustard, and salt; and honey.

Food is a figure of spiritual sustenance. Peter tells his readers to "desire earnestly the sincere [unadulterated] milk of the Word, that ye may grow thereby." Peter was writing to young Christians (I Pet. 2:1-3) but Paul clearly distinguishes between Scripture which can be likened to "milk for babes" and that which can be compared with "strong meat," or solid food.   A.B.F.

FOOL, in modern usage, a dolt or a simpleton, but in Scripture generally impiety or lack of moral good sense is implied as well. "The fool hath said in his heart, There is no God" (Ps. 14:1; 53:1). Solomon in his writings, Proverbs and Ecclesiastes, makes about 80 statements about fools, showing their emptiness, their conceit and pride, their boasting and self-confidence, and in four cases in Ecclesiastes, their thick-headedness and their wordiness (Eccl. 2:19; 10:3,14). In Matthew 23:17 we read how the Lord called the scribes and Pharisees fools; not implying intellectual stupidity, but spiritual blindness. Men can be clever in mind, but at the same time fools in spiritual matters.

FOOT, the part of the body on which men and animals walk, or that part of furniture on which it stands. As regards furniture, the base of the laver just outside the tabernacle is several times called its foot (Exod. 30:18; 35:16, etc.). The foot of man, because in contact with the earth, is thought to be less honorable than the hand or the head, but in the Christian church "the foot" (i.e. the lowest member) should not suffer a feeling of inferiority or of envy, and say "Because I am not the hand, I am not of the body" (I Cor. 12:15) nor should the more prominent directing member ("the head") say to the foot, "I have no need of thee." In the East, shoes are ordinarily removed when entering a house. On entering a house, the lowest servant is detailed to wash the feet of the visitor. So the priests, before entering the tabernacle in divine service, must wash their feet as well as their hands at the laver, just outside, so that no trace of defilement would accompany their service. (For spiritual application, see John 13:10, Heb. 10:22). In lands where irrigation is practiced, men use shovels to move the earth for the larger channels, but a foot will suffice for a small channel to water a furrow (Deut. 11:10). To humiliate an enemy utterly, one sometimes put his foot upon the captives' necks as Joshua's captains did (Josh. 10:24).

FOOTMAN. 1. A member of the infantry as distinguished from the cavalry—horsemen and charioteers. The bulk of ancient armies consisted of footmen.

2. A runner, one of the king's bodyguard (I Sam. 22:17).

FOOTSTOOL (Heb. *keves,* Gr. *hypopódion*), a word is used in Scripture both literally (II Chron. 9:18; James 2:3) and figuratively: of the earth Isa. 66:1; Matt. 5:35), of the Temple (Lam. 2: 1), of the Ark (Ps. 99:5), and of subjection, especially of heathen enemies by the Messianic king (Ps. 110:1; Matt. 22:44; Acts 2:35).

FORD (Heb. *ma'var*), a shallow place in a stream where men and animals can cross on foot. In the small streams of Palestine and Syria, fording places are quite frequent and can easily be found simply by following the main roads which in many cases are mere bridle paths. Such probably were the fords of the Jabbok (Gen. 32:22) where Jacob halted, and of the Arnon (Isa. 16:2). The Jordan, however, is a strong and rapid stream, and its fording places are few and far between. When Israel crossed, God miraculously stopped the waters upstream by a landslide. John the Bap-

THE FORD of the Jabbok (Zerka) River. Near here Jacob wrestled with the angel, and received his new name, Israel, or "Prince of the Lords."

tist baptized at Bethabara (John 1:28 KJV), which name indicates that a ford was there. Joshua's spies (Josh. 2:7) evidently forded the Jordan, and Ehud (Judg. 3:28) took the same place to prevent Moabites from crossing there. Farther up the river and about two hundred years after Ehud, Jephthah (Judg. 12:5,6) made his famous "Shibboleth test" at a ford of the Jordan.

FOREHEAD, that part of the face which is above the eyes. Because it is so prominent, its appearance often determines our opinion of the person. In Ezekiel 16:12 KJV reads "I put a jewel on thy forehead," but ASV (more correctly) has, "I put a ring upon thy nose." The forehead is used as a very dishonorable word where we read of a "harlot's forehead" (Jer. 3:3) indicating utter shamelessness, and at the same time it stands for courage, as when God told Ezekiel (Ezek. 3:9) that he had made the prophet's forehead harder than flint against the foreheads of the people. The forehead is also the place for the front of a crown or mitre (Exod. 28:38), where the emblem of holiness on Aaron's forehead would make the gifts of the people acceptable before the Lord. A mark was put upon the foreheads of the men of Jerusalem who mourned for its wickedness, and they were spared in a time of terrible judgment (Ezek. 9:4). Similarly in Revelation 7 God's servants were sealed by an angel; and it seems that this seal not only saved the elect ones but it showed forth their godly character. In the ages of glory that are to come, the name of God will be marked on the foreheads of his own people (Rev. 22:4).   A.B.F.

FOREIGNER (Heb. *nokhrî, stranger*; Gr. *póroikos, sojourner*). The Jewish people divided all humanity into two groups, of which they belonged in the smaller and more select group; namely, Jews and Gentiles. "Lo, it is a people that dwelleth alone, and shall not be reckoned among the nations" (Num. 23:9b ASV). With the Greeks, the division was Greeks and Barbarians (Rom. 1:14). The common word for foreigner (Hebrew, *nokri*) is generally translated "stranger" and seems generally to be used with a slightly contemptuous meaning. "Are we not accounted of him strangers?" (Gen. 31:15). It generally implies also a heathen religion, as in I Kings 11:1 where "Solomon loved many strange women."

Foreigners were debarred from a number of privileges accorded only to Israelites: eating the passover (Exod. 12:43), entering the sanctuary (Ezek. 44:9), becoming king (Deut. 17:15). Israelites were forbidden to enter into covenant relations with them (Exod. 23:32), or to intermarry with them on equal terms (Exod. 34:12,16). They could be sold the flesh of animals that had died, which Israelites were forbidden to eat (Deut. 14:21); they could be loaned money with interest (Deut. 23:20); and debts could be collected from them even in the year of release (Deut. 15:3). In NT times the Jews even refrained from eating and drinking with Gentiles (Acts 11:3; Gal. 2:12). Foreigners, could, however, always become Israelites by fully accepting the Law and its requirements.   A.B.F.

FOREKNOWLEDGE (See Election)

FOREORDINATION (See Election)

FORERUNNER (Gr. *pródromos*). Rulers, intending a visit, often send advance agents to prepare the way for their reception; so John the Baptist was the forerunner of our Lord (Isa. 40:3; Luke 3:4-6). The word "forerunner" is used of Jesus, who has preceded us into the visible presence of God to insure our personal access to God (Heb. 6:20).

FORESKIN (Heb. *'orlâh*, Gr. *akrobustía*), the fold of skin which is cut off in the operation of circumcision. Just as the American Indians used scalps of enemies as signs of their prowess, so David presented two hundred foreskins of the Philistines (I Sam. 18:25-27). In Deuteronomy 10:16 the word is used figuratively meaning submission to God's law. In Habakkuk 2:16 it refers to the indecent exhibitionism of a drunken man.

FOREST (Heb. *ya'ar, sevakh, āvîm*), a piece of land covered with trees naturally planted, as distinguished from a park where man's hand is more evident. In ancient times, most of the highlands of Canaan and Syria except the tops of the high mountains were covered with forests. Several forests are mentioned by name, those of Lebanon the most often, for these were famous for the cedar and the fir trees. From the forest of Lebanon, Hiram of Tyre (I Kings 5:8-10) brought down cedar

and fir trees to the sea and floated them southward to the port which Solomon had constructed, from which his servants could transport the timbers to Jerusalem. Solomon's "house of the forest of Lebanon" (I Kings 7:2, etc.) was apparently his own house, and was so named because of the prevalence of cedar in its structure. KJV names the "forest of his Carmel" in II Kings 19:23 and Isaiah 37:24, but ASV renders it more truly the "forest of his fruitful field" without attempting to locate it. "The forest of Arabia" (Isa. 21:13) is also incapable of location upon a map. It was in a wood or forest in Ephraim that the crucial battle of Absalom's rebellion was fought (II Sam. 18) and "the wood devoured more people than the sword devoured" (v. 8).

FORGIVENESS (Heb. *kāphar, nāsā', sālah*; Gr. *apolúein, charízesthai, áphesis, páresis*). In the OT, *pardon*, and in the NT, *remission*, are often used as the equivalents of *forgiveness*. The idea of forgiveness is found in either religious or social relations, and means the giving up of resentment or claim to requital on account of an offense. The offense may be a deprivation of a person's property, rights, or honor; or it may be a violation of moral law.

The normal conditions of forgiveness are repentance and the willingness to make reparation, or atonement; and the effect of forgiveness is the restoration of both parties to the former state of relationship. Christ taught that forgiveness is a duty, and that no limit should be set to the extent of forgiveness (Luke 17:4). An unforgiving spirit is one of the most serious of sins (Matt. 18:34,35; Luke 15:28-30). The ground of forgiveness by God of man's sins is the atoning death of Christ. Jesus taught that the offended party is, when necessary, to go to the offender and try to bring him to repentance (Luke 17:3). God's forgiveness is conditional upon man's forgiveness of the wrongs done him (Matt. 5:23,24; 6:12; Col. 1:14; 3:13). Those forgiven by God before the Incarnation were forgiven because of Christ, whose death was foreordained from eternity. Christ's atonement was retroactive in its effect (Heb. 11:40). God's forgiveness seems, however, to be limited. Christ speaks of the unpardonable sin (Matt. 12:31,32), and John speaks of the sin unto death (I John 5:16). The deity of Christ is evidenced by His claim to the power to forgive sins (Mark 2:7; Luke 5:21; 7:49).   S.B.

FORK, mentioned only in I Samuel 13:21 as the translation of two words which could be rendered "a three-tined gatherer." It probably was the ancient type of our modern pitchfork.

FORNICATION (Heb. *zānâh*, Gr. *porneía*), unlawful sexual intercourse of an unwed person. It is to be distinguished from adultery which has to do with unfaithfulness on the part of a married person, and from rape which is a crime of violence and without the consent of the person sinned against. When these sins are mentioned in the Bible, they are often figurative of disloyalty. Idolatry is practically adultery from God. This ugly sin ought not even to be a subject of conversation among Christians (Eph. 5:3,4) and is commonly associated with the obscene worship of the heathen. For the spiritualizing of this sin, see Jeremiah 2:20-36, Ezekiel 16, and Hosea 1-3, where it applied to Israel; and Revelation 17, where it applies to Rome.

FORT, FORTRESS. Every city in ancient times was fortified by a wall and its citadel. The KJV often speaks of such cities as "fenced," and other terms are also used by the KJV and the RV. Even before the Israelites entered Canaan, they were terrified by the reports of cities "great and fortified up to heaven" (Num. 13:ff; Deut. 1:28). These cities were not necessarily large; they were usually, indeed, quite small. Jerusalem was so well fortified that it was not until the time of David that the city was captured from the Jebusites. Usually the city was built on a hill, and the fortifications followed the natural contour of the hill. Many times there was both an inner and an outer wall. The walls were built of brick and stone, and were many feet thick. After the Israelites entered the land, they too built fenced cities (Deut. 28:52; II Sam. 20:6).

FORTUNATUS (fôr-tū-nā'tŭs, Gr. *Phortounátos, blessed, fortunate*), a Christian who came with two others to bring gifts from the Corinthian church to Paul when he was about to leave Ephesus in A.D. 59 (I Cor. 16:17).

FORUM APPII, rendered Appii Forum in KJV (Acts 28:15), but more correctly in ASV as "The Market of Appius," a place 43 miles SE of Rome, where Paul was met by the brethren. It was a station on the famous Appian Way to Naples.

FOUNDATION (Heb. *yāsadh, to found;* Gr. *katabolé, themélios*), that upon which a building stands, or else the first layer of the actual structure; its walls. The word is often used figuratively. A temporal use of the word is found at least nine times in the NT, referring to the time of the foundation of the world. Some other figurative uses: as when the Church is built upon "the foundation of the apostles and prophets" (Eph. 2:20), or when simple Christian teaching is based upon "the foundation of repentance from dead works" (Heb. 6:1), or as when Jesus Christ is spoken of as the foundation of Christian theology (I Cor. 3:10,11).

FOUNTAIN, a spring of water issuing from the earth. In a country near the desert, springs, pools, pits, cisterns and fountains are of great importance and many towns and other locations are named from the springs at their sites: e.g., Enaim, "two springs" (Gen. 38:21 ASV); Enam, with the same meaning (Josh. 15:34); En-gedi, i.e., "the fountain of the kid" (Josh. 15:62); and a dozen others, like the English Springfield, or the French Fontainebleau. In the story of the Flood "the fountains of the great deep" were broken up, referring to great convulsions of the earth's surface (Gen. 7:11) which, with the rain, caused the Flood; and in the preparation of the earth for man, the Son of God (Wisdom personified) was with the Father before there were any "fountains abounding with water" (Prov. 8:24). The word is used both literally and figuratively, both pleasantly and unpleasantly. Figuratively, it refers to the source of hemorrhages (Lev. 20:18; Mark 5:29). In Proverbs, compare "a troubled fountain and a corrupt spring" (25:26) with "a fountain of life" (13:14; 14:27). In the Bridegroom's praise of his pure bride (S. of Sol. 4:12,15) she is first "a fountain sealed" then "a fountain of gardens." In the curse of Ephraim (Hos. 13:15), "his fountain shall be dried up" as a terrible punishment; but on the pleasant side, David speaks (Ps. 36:9) of "the fountain of life" as being with the Lord. In the Lord's conversation with the woman at the well (John 4:14), He told her of "a well of water

ANCIENT FORTIFICATIONS at Lachish. A wall and citadel guarded every city of ancient times. Walls were many feet thick.

springing up into everlasting life." Among the delights of heaven, will be "the fountain of the water of life" (Rev. 21:6). A.B.F.

FOUNTAIN GATE, the gate at the SE corner of the walls of ancient Jerusalem, mentioned only in Nehemiah (2:14; 3:15; 12:37).

FOWL (See Birds)

FOWLER (Heb. *yōkēsh*), a bird-catcher. Because fowlers used snares, gins, bird-lime, etc. and caught their prey by trickery, "fowler" is used to describe those who try to ensnare the unwary and bring them to ruin (Ps. 91:3; 124:7; Hos. 9:8).

FOX (See Animals)

FRANKINCENSE (Heb. *levōnâh,* from root meaning *whiteness*), a resinous substance obtained from certain trees of the *Boswellia* genus and the family of balsams. To obtain the frankincense, an incision is made through the bark of the tree deep into the trunk, and a strip of bark is peeled off. As the whitish juice exudes, it hardens in the atmosphere and is gathered after about three months' exposure in the summer. When sold, the frankincense is in the form of "tears" or of irregular lumps, and has been used as a perfume, as a medicine, and by Egyptians and Hebrews in their religious rites. It is spoken of as coming from Arabia (Isa. 60:6; Jer. 6:20) and perhaps from Palestine (S. of Sol. 4:6,14). It was an ingredient of the perfume for the most holy place (Exod. 30:34-38) which was exclusively reserved for this particular use. Frankincense was mingled with the flour in the meal-offering (Lev. 2:1,15,16) but was rigidly excluded from the sin-offering (Lev. 5:11) which was far from being an offering of a sweet savor. Soon after the birth of Jesus, the wise men presented to Him gifts of gold, of frankincense and myrrh; and these precious gifts, presented in worship may well have helped to finance His sojourn in Egypt (Matt. 2:11,15). See PLANTS.

The photograph at the top is of a reconstruction of a Persian king's harem. It belonged to Xerxes I, whose queen was the Hebrew Esther.

This tomb painting from Thebes shows an Egyptian harem. One of Solomon's 700 wives was an Egyptian princess. Solomon's harem included an additional 300 concubines.

"But king Solomon loved many strange women....
he had seven hundred wives, princesses,
and three hundred concubines:
and his wives turned away his heart."
(I KINGS 11:1-3)

FREEMAN, a rendering of two slightly different Gr. words, *apeleútheros,* found in I Corinthians 7:22, where it refers to a slave who has received his freedom, although in this verse the reference is to one who has received spiritual freedom from the Lord, and *eleútheros,* found in Galatians 4:22,23, 30, Revelation 6:15, where it means a free man as opposed to a slave.

FREEWILL OFFERING (See Offerings)

FRET (Heb. *hārâh, mā'ar*). 1. To fret is to be vexed, chafed, irritated, or to be angry; and the godly man is not to fret himself (Ps. 37:1,7,8). By contrast, one should have his mind stayed on the Lord (Isa. 26:3).

2. A fretting leprosy (Lev. 13:51,52) is a sharp, bitter, painful leprosy.

FRINGE (Heb. *tsîtsith, tassel, lock*), the tassel of twisted cords fastened to the outer garments of Israelites to remind them of their obligations as Israelites to be loyal to Jehovah (Num. 15:38, 39; Deut. 22:12). Later they became distinct badges of Judaism (cf. Zech. 8:23). They were common in NT times (Matt. 9:20; 14:36; 23:5).

FROG (See Plagues)

FRONTLET (Heb. *tôtāphôth,* from *tūph,* to bind), anything bound on the forehead, particularly phylacteries, which were worn on the forehead and on the arms. Phylacteries were prayer bands consisting of the following passages from the Law of Moses: Exodus 13:1-10; 11-16; Deuteronomy 6: 4-9; 11:13-21, which were put in small leather cases and fastened to the forehead and the left arm. They were worn by all male Jews during the time of morning prayer, except on the sabbath and festivals.

FROST, (Heb. *kephōr, hānāmāl*), usual in winter on the hills and high plains in Bible lands. Frosts in the late spring do great damage to fruit. The manna in the wilderness is compared to hoar-frost (Exod. 16:14). Frost is an evidence of God's power (Job 37:10; 38:29).

FRUIT (Heb. *perî,* Gr. *karpós*). The fruits most often mentioned in Scripture are the grape, pomegranate, fig, olive, apple; all of which are grown today; but the lemon, orange, plum and apricot were unknown or at least unmentioned. The word "fruit" is often used metaphorically: "the fruit of thy womb" (Deut. 7:13, cf. 28:11), "the fruit of their own way" (Prov. 1:31), "fruit unto life eternal" (John 4:36) etc. The fruit of the Holy Spirit consists of all the Christian virtues (Gal. 5:22,23).

FRYING PAN (Heb. *marhesheth*), properly a pot or saucepan in which things are boiled or baked. The word occurs only in Leviticus 2:7 and 7:9 and no frying is intended or implied.

FUEL (Heb. *'ōkhlâh,* or *ma'ăkhōleth, food*). In ancient times wood, charcoal, various kinds of thorn bushes, dried grass, and the dung of camels and cattle was used as fuel. There is no evidence that coal was used by the Hebrews as fuel; their houses had no chimneys (Isa. 9:5,19; Ezek. 4:12, 15; 15:4,6; 21:32).

FULLER (See Occupations and Professions)

FULLER'S FIELD (Heb. *sedhēh khôvēs*), a field, just outside of Jerusalem, where fullers washed the cloth material they were processing. A highway and a conduit for water passed through it (Isa. 7:3; 36:2). It was so near the city that the Assyrian Rabshakeh (*q.v.*), standing and speaking in the field, could be heard by those on the city wall (II Kings 18:17). Its exact site is in dispute.

FULLER'S SOAP, an alkali prepared from the ashes of certain plants and used for cleansing and fulling new cloth. The word is used figuratively in Malachi 3:2.

FUNERAL, the ceremonies used in disposing of a dead human body; whether by burying, cremation, or otherwise. The word does not occur in the Bible. The rites differed with the place, the religion, and the times; except for royal burials in Egypt, the elaborate ceremonies that are used with us today were not held.

In Palestine, as a general thing, there was no embalming and the body was buried a few hours after death; sometimes in a tomb, but more often in a cave. Coffins were unknown. The body was washed and often anointed with aromatic spices (John 12:7; 19:39). The procession of mourners, made up of relatives and friends of the deceased, were led by professional mourning women, whose shrieks and lamentations pierced the air. It was an insult to a man's reputation to be refused proper burial (Jer. 22:19). The "Tombs of the kings" on the E side of Jerusalem, and the "Garden tomb," where our Lord's body was laid, are evidences of the two types of burial. In Egypt, the bodies were embalmed so skillfully that many of them are recognizable today after the lapse of thousands of years.

FURLONG (See Weights and Measures)

FURNACE (Heb. *kivshān, kûr, attûn, 'ălîl, tannûr;* Gr. *káminos*). Furnaces for central heating are not mentioned in the Bible nor are they much used today in Bible lands. The burning fiery furnace of Daniel 3 was probably a smelting furnace and used only incidentally for the punishment of men. The most common word "tannur" could be and often is more properly rendered oven (cf. Gen. 15: 17 with Lev. 2:4; Hos. 7:4-7). Furnaces were used for melting gold (Prov. 17:3), silver (Ezek. 22: 22), brass or bronze (Ezek. 22:18) and including also tin, iron and lead and for baking bread (Neh. 3:11; Isa. 31:9). The word is often used figuratively, as in Deuteronomy 4:20 where it means Egypt and in Matthew 13:42, which refers to the punishment of the wicked at the end of the world. Quite recently, Solomon's ingenious smelting furnaces near Elath on the Gulf of Akaba have been found, arranged so that the constant north wind furnished a natural draft for melting the brass or copper. After being prepared there, the metal was taken to the plain of the Jordan for casting (I Kings 7:46).

FURNITURE (Heb. *kār, kēlîm;* Gr. *skevé*). In the Bible the principal reference to furniture is in the articles in and about the tabernacle and the temple. The main items were the large altar and the laver, outside; then the table of showbread (KJV "shewbread"), the lamp-stand, or "candlestick" and the altar of incense in the holy place, then in the holy of holies the ark of the covenant (Exod. 25-40). Generally beds were mats, spread upon the floor, and rolled up during the day, though Og of Bashan is said to have had a bedstead (Deut. 3:11). The tables in OT times were generally very low and people sat upon the floor to eat. Royal tables were often higher (Judg. 1:7), as were those in NT times (Mark 7:28).

FUTURE LIFE (See Immortality, Eschatology)

G

GAAL (gā'ăl, Heb. *ga'al, loathing*), a son of Ebed (Judg. 9:26-41), captain of a band of freebooters who incited the Shechemites to rebel against the rule of Abimelech. After the death of his father, Gideon, Abimelech murdered all but one of his 70 brothers so that he might become king of Shechem. After gaining the confidence of the men of Shechem, Gaal boasted under intoxication that he could overcome Abimelech if made leader of the Shechemites. Zebul, the prefect of Shechem, jealous of Gaal, secretly relayed this information to Abimelech who set up an ambush by night with four companies against Shechem. In the morning when Gaal went out and stood in the gate of the city, Abimelech and his army rose up out of hiding and chased Gaal and his company into the city, but Zebul thrust them out. Whereupon, Abimelech fought against the rebels and killed them and destroyed their city and sowed it with salt. Nothing more is known of Gaal, but clearly his weakness was foolhardy boasting which he failed to make good in action.

GAASH (gā'ăsh, Heb. *ga'ash, quaking*), a hill near Mount Ephraim. On its N side was Timnath-serah, the city given to Joshua (Josh. 19:49,50), where also he was buried (Judg. 2:9). The "brooks of Gaash" was the native place of Hiddai (II Sam. 23).

GABA (gā'-bà, Heb. *gāva'*), a Benjamite city (Josh. 18:24). Same as Geba (21:17; I Kings 15:22).

GABBAI (găb'-ā-ī, Heb. *gabbay, collector*), a chief of Benjamin after the captivity (Neh. 11:8).

GABBATHA (găb'à-thà, Aram. *gabbetha', height, ridge*), the place called the "Pavement" (John 19:13). Here Pilate sat on the Bema, or judgment seat, and sentenced Jesus before the people. Josephus (*Ant.* xv. 8, 5) states that the temple was near the castle of Antonia, and implies that Herod's palace was near the castle (xv. 11, 5). Therefore, if Pilate was residing in Herod's palace at Passover time in order to keep a watchful eye on the Jews, his residence was near the castle. An early pavement has been excavated near here consisting of slabs of stones three feet square and a foot or more thick. This may well have been the pavement where Jesus was brought forth from the judgment hall for sentencing.

GABRIEL (gā'brĭ-ĕl, Heb. *gavrî'ēl, man of God*, Gr. *Gabriél*), an angel mentioned four times in Scripture, each time bearing a momentous message. He interpreted to Daniel the vision of the ram and the he-goat (Dan. 8:16f). In Daniel 9:21f he explained the vision of the 70 Weeks. Gabriel announced to Zacharias the birth of John, forerunner of the Messiah (Luke 1:11-20), and he was sent to Mary with the unique message of Jesus' birth (Luke 1:26-38). His preparation is the ideal for every messenger of God: "I am Gabriel, that stand in the presence of God; and am sent to speak unto thee" (Luke 1:19). The Bible does not define his angel-status, but he appears in the Book of Enoch (chs. 9,20,40) as an archangel.

GAD (găd, Heb. *gādh, fortune*). 1. Jacob's seventh son; firstborn of Zilpah, Leah's handmaid (Gen. 30:9-11). Of his personal life nothing is known except that he had seven sons at the time of the descent into Egypt (46:16).

The Gadites numbered 45,650 adult males (Num. 1:24,25), but at the second census their number had fallen to 40,500 (26:18). Their position on march was S of the tabernacle next to Reuben. These two tribes and the half-tribe of Manasseh remained shepherds like their forefathers, and because of their "great multitude of cattle" they requested of Moses the rich pasture lands E of Jordan for their possession (Num. 32). This was granted (Josh. 18:7) on the condition that they accept their responsibility by accompanying the nine and a half tribes across Jordan in warfare against the Canaanites. The warriors of these two and a half tribes took the lead in the conquest of western Palestine (Josh. 1:12-18; 4:12) and returned to their families with Joshua's blessing (22:1-9). Fearing that the Jordan would alienate their children from the fellowship and faith of the western tribes, they erected a huge altar called Ed ("witness") as evidence of their unity in race and faith (Josh. 22:10-34). A satisfactory explanation removed the thought of war which seemed inevitable at first over a schismatic religion.

The territory of Gad, difficult to define, was formerly ruled by Sihon, king of the Amorites. It lay chiefly in the center of the land E of Jordan, with the half-tribe of Manasseh on the N and Reuben to the S. The northern border reached as far as the Sea of Chinnereth (Josh. 13:27); the southern border seems to have been just above Heshbon (13:26), although cities below this were built by Gad (Num. 32:34). One of these is Dibon, where the famous Moabite stone was found.

Genesis 49:19 seems to describe the military prowess of the Gadites: "Gad, a troop shall overcome him: but he shall overcome at the last" ("press upon their heel," ASV) meaning that they would put their enemies to retreat. Moses said of Gad: "Blessed is he that enlargeth Gad: he dwelleth as a lioness and teareth the arm, yea, the crown of the head," etc. (Deut. 33:20,21). Because they trusted in the Lord and cried to Him for help, they utterly defeated the Hagarites (I Chron. 5:18-22). It was natural for men of such faith and ability to extend their borders as far as Gilead (5:16). Of the Gadites who joined themselves to David it is said that they were "men of might, and men of war fit for the battle, that could handle shield and buckler," etc. (I Chron. 12:8,14,15). Other famous men of Gilead or Gad were Barzillai (II Sam. 17:27; 19:31-40) and Elijah. The land of Gad was long the battlefield between Syria and Israel (II Kings 10:33). Gad finally was carried captive by Assyria (II Kings 15:29; I Chron. 5:26) and Ammon seized their land and cities (Jer. 49:1).

2. The seer or prophet of King David. He advised David to get out of "the hold" and flee from Saul into Judah (I Sam. 22:5). Later, he gave David his choice of punishment from the Lord for his sin in numbering the children of Israel (II Sam. 24:11-17; I Chron. 21:9-17) and told him to build an altar to the Lord in the threshingfloor of Araunah (II Sam. 24:18). Gad assisted in arranging the musical services of the temple (II Chron. 29:25) and recorded the acts of David in a book (I Chron. 29:29).

3. A Canaanite god of fortune, seen in compound names such as Baal-gad (Josh. 11:17; 12:7; 13:5) and Migdal-gad (Josh. 15:37). In Isaiah 45:11f there is a curse against idolaters. "That troop" (Gad) is the Babylonian or Syrian deity *Fortune* and "that number" (Meni) is the deity *Destiny* (see ASV).   A.M.R.

GADARA, GADARENES (găd'a-rà, găd-à-rēnz', Gr. *Gádara, Gadarenón*). Gadara was a member of the Decapolis and is associated with "the country of the Gadarenes" in the Gospels (Mark 5:1; Luke 8:26,37; Matt. 8:28, Gr. text). Its ruins are identified with Um Keis today on a steep hill five miles SE of the Sea of Galilee and three miles S of the Hieromax or Yarmuk River. At the foot of the hill to the N were hot springs and baths. When Christ came across the lake from Capernaum, He landed at the SE corner where the steep bank descends from the eastern highlands into the Jordan valley. Two demoniacs met Him, and out of them Jesus cast many demons. There were swine feeding nearby, and when Jesus allowed the demons to enter them they ran headlong down the steep slope into the lake and were drowned. In the cliffs around Gadara, or Um Keis, tombs have been excavated out of the limestone, some measuring 20 feet square, with side recesses for bodies. Like the demoniacs, people still dwell in them today. Nearby there is a field of several acres strewn from stone coffins and their lids. This description would hardly fit Gerasa, a town some 50 miles S of the Sea of Galilee, although it might be appropriate to refer generally to it as the "country of the Gerasenes," which is the read-

GADARENE (GADARA) COUNTRY, viewed from the Lake of Galilee. It was in the "Country of the Gadarenes" that Christ cast the evil spirits out of the demoniacs. In nearby cliff rock-caves, people still dwell as they did in New Testament times.

ing of an important manuscript in Mark and Luke. Some texts of Matthew and Luke read "country of the Gergesenes," which is identified with the present Khersa farther N on the eastern shore of the lake. This might not be improper if the town were under the jurisdiction of the larger Gadara. Khersa's steep hill rising from the water's edge with rock-caves suitable for tombs does meet the narrative description of the Gospels. In Roman times Gadara was the best fortified city in Peraea, and its remains are impressive still. A Roman street can be seen with its colonnades prostrate on either side.　　　　　　　　　　　　　　　　A.M.R.

GADDI (găd'ī, Heb. *gaddî*), Manasseh's representative among the twelve spies (Num. 13:11).

GADDIEL (găd'ĭ-ĕl, Heb. *gaddî'al*), Zebulun's representative among the twelve spies (Num. 13:10).

GADI (gā'dī), father of Menahem who usurped the throne of Israel from Shallum (II Kings 15:14-20).

GAHAM (gā'-hăm), a son of Nahor, brother of Abraham, by his concubine Reumah (Gen. 22:24).

GAHAR (gā'hàr), a family of the Nethinim who returned with Zerubbabel to Jerusalem (Ezra 2:47).

GAIUS (gā'yŭs, Gr. *Gaíos*). 1. A Macedonian who traveled with Paul on his third missionary journey and was seized in the riot at Ephesus (Acts 19:29).

2. A man of Derbe who was one of those accompanying Paul from Macedonia to Asia (Acts 20:4).

3. A Corinthian whom Paul baptized (I Cor. 1:14). Since Paul wrote the Epistle to the Romans from Corinth, this may be the same Gaius in whose host and "of the whole church" (either in whose house the Christians assembled or were given lodging Rom. 16:23).

4. The addressee of III John. A convert of John, he is spoken of as "the wellbeloved" (III John 1) and is commended for his love and hospitality to traveling preachers of the Gospel (III John 5-8).

GALAL (gā'lăl), the name of two Levites: 1. I Chronicles 9:15.

2. I Chronicles 9:16; Nehemiah 11:17.

GALATIA (gà-lā'shĭ-à), the designation in NT times of a territory in north-central Asia Minor, also a Roman province in central Asia Minor The name was derived from the people called Galatians (*Galatai*), a Greek modification of their original name *Keltoi* or *Keltai,* Celtic tribes from ancient Gaul. After having invaded Macedonia and Greece about 280 B.C., they crossed into Asia Minor on the invitation of Nikomedes I, king of Bithynia, to aid him in a civil war. After ravaging far and wide, they were finally confined to the north-central part of Asia Minor, where they settled as conquerors, giving their name to the territory. Their chief city-centers were Ancyra, Pessinus, and Tavium. In 189 B.C. the Galatians were subjugated by Rome and continued as a subject kingdom under their own chiefs, and after 63 B.C. under kings. Upon the death of King Amyntas in 25 B.C., the Galatian kingdom was converted into a Roman province called Galatia. The province included not only the area inhabited by the Galatians but also parts of Phrygia, Pisidia, Lycaonia, and Isauria. The terms *Galatia* and *Galatians* henceforth carried a double connotation: geographically, to designate the territory inhabited by the Galatians, politically to denote the entire Roman province. That the cities of Antioch, Iconium, Lystra, and Derbe, evangelized by Paul on his first missionary jour-

ney, were in the province of Galatia is now recognized by all scholars.

The name *Galatia* occurs in I Corinthians 16:1; Galatians 1:2; II Timothy 4:10; and I Peter 1:1. In the last passage some scholars think the reference may be to the European Gaul. In Acts 16:6, 18:23 the name is an adjective (*Galatikē chōra*), the *Galatian country* or region. Luke apparently means the district, not the province, since in Acts, when speaking of Asia Minor, he employs the old ethnographic designations. The context in I Peter 1:1 seems clearly to indicate that the province is meant. Paul's general practice of employing political designations would point to that usage also in Galatians 1:1 and I Corinthians 16:1.

If *Galatia* in Galatians 1:1 means the Roman province, then the churches addressed were those founded on the first missionary journey (Acts 13-14); if it means the old ethnographic territory of Galatia, then the churches were established on the second missionary journey (Acts 16:6).

　　　　　　　　　　　　　　　　　　　D.E.H.

GALATIANS, EPISTLE TO THE, a short but very important letter of Paul, containing his passionate polemic against the perversion or contamination of the Gospel of God's grace. It has aptly been described as "the Magna Charta of spiritual emancipation" and it remains as the abiding monument of the liberation of Christianity from the trammels of legalism.

The contents of the epistle so unmistakably reveal the traces of Paul's mind and style that its genuineness has never been seriously questioned even by the most radical NT critics. The testimony of the early church to its integrity and Pauline origin is strong and unambiguous.

Written to "the churches of Galatia," it is the only Pauline epistle that is specifically addressed to a group of churches. They were all founded by Paul (1:8,11; 4:19-20), were all the fruit of a single mission (3:1-3; 4:13-14), and were all affected by the same disturbance (1:6-7; 5:7-9). Paul had preached among them the Gospel of the free grace of God through the death of Christ (1:6; 3:1-14). The reception of Paul and his message by the Galatians had been warm and affectionate (4:12-15). The converts willingly endured persecution for their faith (3:4) and "were running well" when Paul left them (5:7).

The startling information received by Paul that a sudden and drastic change in attitude toward him and his Gospel was taking place in the Galatian churches caused the writing of the epistle. The change was being induced by the propaganda of certain Jewish teachers who professed to be Christians, acknowledged Jesus as Messiah, but overlaid and obscured the simplicity of the Gospel of free grace by their insistence that to faith in Christ must be added circumcision and obedience to the Mosaic law (2:16; 3:2-3; 4:10,21; 5:2-4; 6:12). Paul realized clearly that this teaching neutralized the truth of Christ's all-sufficiency for salvation and destroyed the message of justification by faith. From this fatal mixing of law and grace Paul sought to save his converts by means of this epistle.

Due to the geographical and the political connotation of *Galatia* in NT times, two views concerning the location of the Galatian churches are advocated. The *North-Galatian* theory, which interprets the term in its old ethnographic sense to denote the territory inhabited by the Galatian tribes, locates the churches in north-central Asia Minor, holding that they were founded during Acts 16:6. The *South-Galatian* theory identifies these churches with those founded on the first missionary journey (Acts 13-14), located in the southern part of the province of Galatia. The former was the unanimous view of the Church Fathers. They naturally adopted that meaning since in the second century the province was again restricted to ethnic Galatia and the double meaning of the term disappeared. The majority of the modern commentators support the latter view. Supporting this view is the known practice of Paul of using provincial names in addressing his converts; it best explains the familiar reference to Barnabas in the epistle; Acts 16:6 gives no hint of such a protracted mission as the older view demands; the older view cannot explain why the Judaizers would bypass the important churches in South Galatia; known conditions in these churches fit the picture in the epistle.

Views concerning the place and date of composition are even more diverse. Advocates of the *North-Galatian* theory generally assign the epistle to Ephesus during the third missionary journey, near the time of Romans. *South-Galatian* advocates vary considerably; some place it before the Jerusalem Conference, while others place it as late as the third missionary journey. Advocates of the pre-Conference date place it at Syrian Antioch. Others place it on the second missionary journey, perhaps during the ministry at Corinth. The effort to date it before the Jerusalem Conference faces definite chronological difficulties. This early dating is not demanded by the silence of the epistle concerning the Conference decrees. The decrees were already known to the Galatians (Acts 16:4), while in writing the epistle Paul would desire to establish his position on grounds independent of the Jerusalem Church. Since apparently he had already twice visited the churches (4:13; 1:9), a date after Paul's second visit to the south-Galatian churches seems most probable (c. A.D. 52). During that second visit Paul had sought by warning and instructions to fortify his converts against the danger (1:9; 4:16; 5:3). The impact of the Judaizers upon the Galatians threatened to destroy his work. The result was this bristling letter.

The contents of Galatians make evident Paul's purpose in writing. The first two chapters show that he was compelled to vindicate his apostolic authority. The Judaizers, in order to establish their own position which contradicted Paul's teaching, had attempted to discredit his authority. Having vindicated his apostolic call and authority, Paul next sets forth the doctrine of justification in refutation of the teaching of the Judaizers. A reasoned, comprehensive exposition of the doctrine of justification by faith exposed the errors of legalism. Since the Judaizers asserted that to remove the believer from under the law opened the floodgates to immorality, Paul concluded his presentation with an elaboration of the true effect of liberty upon the Christian life, showing that the truth of justification by faith logically leads to a life of good works. The epistle may be outlined as follows:

THE INTRODUCTION. 1:1-10
1. The salutation. 1-5
2. The rebuke. 6-10
I. The Vindication of his Apostolic Authority. 1:11-2:21

1. The reception of his Gospel by revelation. 1:11-24
2. The confirmation of his Gospel by the apostles at Jerusalem. 2:1-10
3. The illustration of his independence. 2:11-21
II. The Exposition of Justification by Faith. 3:1-4:31
1. The elaboration of the doctrine. 3:1-4:7
   a. The nature of justification by faith. 3:1-14
   b. The limitations of the law and its relations to faith. 3:15-4:7
2. The appeal to drop all legalism. 4:8-31
III. The Nature of the Life of Christian Liberty. 5:1-6:10
1. The call to maintain their liberty. 5:1
2. The peril of Christian liberty. 5:2-12
3. The life of liberty. 5:13-6:10
THE CONCLUSION. 6:11-17
THE BENEDICTION. 6:18   D.E.H.

GALBANUM (gal'bà-nŭm), a gum resin from two Persian plants of the carrot family. It has a pungent, disagreeable odor and was mixed with other ingredients in the sacred incense to increase and retain its fragrance longer. (Exod. 30:34).

GALEED (găl'ē-ĕd, Heb. *gal'ēdh, a heap of witnesses*), the name given by Jacob to the heap of stones which he and Laban raised on Mount Gilead as a memorial of their brotherly covenant (Gen. 31:47,48). Sealing their compact of friendship with a common meal, Laban called the place *Jegarsahadutha*, the Aramaic or Chaldee equivalent, meaning "the heap of testimony."

GALILEAN (găl'ĭ-lē'ăn), a native or resident of Galilee (Matt. 26:69; John 4:45; Acts 1:11, 5:37) and detected as such by his dialect (Mark 14:70).

GALILEE (găl'ĭ-lē, Heb. *hā-gālîl, the ring or circuit,* Gr. *he Galilaía*), the most northerly of the three provinces of Palestine (Galilee, Samaria, Judea). Measuring approximately 50 miles N to S and 30 miles E to W, it was bounded on the W by the plain of Akka to the foot of Mt. Carmel. The Jordan, the Sea of Galilee, Lake Huleh, and the spring at Dan marked off the eastern border. Its northern boundary went eastward from Phoenicia to Dan. The southern border was in a southeasterly direction from the base of Mt. Carmel and the Samaritan hills along the Valley of Jezreel (Plain of Esdraelon) to Mt. Gilboa and Scythopolis (Bethshean) to the Jordan. The Valley of Jezreel was a vital communications link between the coastal plain and the center of Palestine. For this reason, decisive battles were often fought here for possession of this desirable pass. The city of Megiddo was important for the control of the valley and lends its name to *Har-Magedon,* the Hill of Megiddo, or Armageddon, where the conflict between Christ and the armies of the Antichrist is predicted to occur (Rev. 16:16).

An imaginary line from the plain of Akka to the N end of the Sea of Galilee divided the country into Upper and Lower Galilee. "Galilee of the Gentiles" refers chiefly to Upper Galilee, which is separated from Lebanon by the Leontes River. It was the territory of Asher and Naphtali. Here lie the ruins of Kedesh Naphtali, one of the cities of refuge (Josh. 20:7; 21:32). In this region lay the twenty towns given by Solomon to Hiram, King of Tyre, in payment for timber from Lebanon (I Kings 9:11). The land was luxurious and productive, a rugged mountainous country of oaks and terebinths interrupted by fertile plains. It was said of Asher, in the west, that he would eat fat for bread and yield royal dainties and dip his feet in oil (Gen. 49:20; Deut. 33:24,25). The olive oil of Galilee has long been esteemed as of the highest quality. Lower Galilee was largely the heritage of Zebulun and Issachar. Less hilly and of a milder climate than Upper Galilee, it included the rich plain of Esdraelon (or Jezreel) and was a "pleasant" land (Gen. 49:15) that would yield "treasures in the sand" (Deut. 33:19) The sand of these coasts was especially valuable for making glass. Important caravan trade routes carried their busy traffic through Galilee from Egypt and southern Palestine to Damascus in the NE as well as E and W from the Mediterranean to the Far East.

The northern part of Naphtali was inhabited by a mixed race of Jews and heathen (Judg. 1:33). Its Israelite population was carried away captive to Assyria to Tiglath-pileser and replaced by a colony of heathen immigrants (II Kings 15:29; 17:24), hence called "Galilee of the nations" or "Gentiles" (Isa. 9:1; Matt. 4:13,15,16). During and after the captivity, the predominant mixture of Gentile races impoverished the worship of Judaism. For the same reason the Galilean accent and dialect were noticeably peculiar (Matt. 26: 73). This caused the southern Jews of purer blood and orthodox tradition to despise them (John 7: 52). Nathanael asked, rather contemptuously, "Can there any good thing come out of Nazareth?" (John 1:46). Yet its very darkness was the Lord's reason for granting it more of the light of His presence and ministry than to self-satisfied and privileged Judea. He was sent "for a light of the Gentiles" (Isa. 42:6) as well as to the "lost sheep of the house of Israel" (Matt. 15:24). Wherever He found faith and repentance, He bestowed His blessing, whereas unbelief often hindered His activity (Matt. 13:58). He preached His first public sermon in the synagogue at Nazareth, in Lower Galilee, where He had been brought up (Luke 4:16-30). His disciples came from Galilee (Matt. 4:18; John 1:43,44; Acts 1:11, 2:7); in Cana of Galilee He performed His first miracle (John 2: 11). Capernaum in Galilee, the home of His manhood (Matt. 4:13; 9:1), is where the first three Gospels present His major ministry. Galilee's debasement made some of its people feel their need of the Saviour. This and its comparative freedom from priestly and pharisaical prejudice may have been additional reasons for receiving the larger share of the Lord's ministry.

After the death of Herod the Great in 4 B.C., Herod Antipas governed the tetrarchy of Galilee (Luke 3:1) until A.D. 39. Jesus referred to him as "that fox" (Luke 13:32). Sepphoris was his capital at first, three miles N of Nazareth, but about A.D. 20 he built a new capital on the shore of the Sea of Galilee and named it Tiberias, after the reigning emperor. Succeeding him was Herod Agrippa I with the title of "king." Upon his death in A.D. 44 (Acts 12:23), Galilee was joined for a while to the Roman province of Syria, after which it was given to Agrippa II. It became the land of Zealots and patriots who, in their hatred of foreign rule and in their longing for the Messiah, incited the populace to rebellion, which led Rome to destroy Jerusalem in A.D. 70. After the fall of Jeru-

salem, Galilee became famous for its rabbins and schools of Jewish learning. The Sanhedrin or Great Council was moved to Sepphoris and then to Tiberias on the western shore of the Sea of Galilee. This is most interesting in light of the fact that when Herod Antipas built his capital and residence on top of a cemetery, strict Jews utterly abhorred the place. Here the Mishna was compiled, to which the Gemara was added subsequently, forming the Palestinian Talmud. The remains of splendid synagogues in Galilee, such as those at Capernaum and Chorazin, still attest to the prosperity of the Jews there from the second to the seventh century.

In 1925 the famous "Galilee skull" was found in a cave near the Sea of Galilee; and in 1932, in a cave near Mt. Carmel, Dr. Theodore D. McCown discovered a Paleolithic skeleton resembling primitive Neanderthal man.   A.M.R.

GALILEE, SEA OF, so-called from its washing the E side of Galilee. It is also known by other names. It is called "the Sea of Gennesaret" (Luke 5:1), since the fertile Plain of Gennesaret lies on the NW (Matt. 14:34). The OT calls it "the Sea of Chinnereth (Heb. "harp-shaped," the shape of the sea, Num. 34:11; Deut. 3:17; Josh. 13:27) or "Chinneroth" (Josh. 12:3; I Kings 15:20), from the town so named on its shore (Josh. 19:35), of which Gennesaret is probably the corruption. "The Sea of Tiberias" is another designation (John 6: 1; 21:1), associated with the capital of Herod Antipas. All its names were derived from places on the western shore. Its present name is *Bahr Tabariyeh.*

Located some 60 miles N of Jerusalem, its bed is but a lower depression of the Jordan valley. The water's surface is 685 feet below the level of the Mediterranean and it varies in depth up to 150 feet. As the Jordan River plunges southward on its course from Mt. Hermon to the Dead Sea, it enters the Sea of Galilee at its northern end and flows out of its southern end, a distance of

SEA OF GALILEE, at the north end, showing inflow of the Jordan River and the mountains beyond, looking eastward.

SUNRISE ON THE SEA OF GALILEE. In Jesus' time, nine cities, with a population of more than 15,000, stood on these shores.

thirteen miles. Its greatest width is eight miles, at Magdala. The view from Nazareth road to Tiberias is beautiful. The bare hills on the W, except at Khan Minyeh (present Capernaum) where there is a small cliff, are recessed from the shore. From the eastern side, the western hills appear to rise out of the water to a height of 2000 feet, while far to the N can be seen snowy Mt. Hermon. The eastern hills rise from a coast of half a mile in width and are flat along the summit. The whole basin betrays its volcanic origin, which accounts for the cliffs of hard porous basalt and the hot springs at Tiberias, famous for their medicinal value. The warm climate produces tropical vegetation — the lotus thorn, palms, and indigo. The Plain of Gennesaret on the NW abounds with walnuts, figs, olives, grapes, and assorted wild flowers. Josephus called it "the ambition of nature which forces those plants that are natural enemies to one another to agree together" (Josephus iii. *Wars,* x.8). The fresh water is sweet, sparkling, and transparent, with fish in abundance. Smith paints an idyllic picture of the whole scene: "In that torrid basin, approached through such sterile surroundings, the lake feeds every sense of the body with life. Sweet water, full of fish, a surface of sparkling blue, tempting down breezes from above, bringing forth breezes of her own, the Lake of Galilee is at once food, drink and air, a rest to the eye, coolness in the heat, an escape from the crowd, and a facility of travel very welcome in so exhausting a climate. Even those who do not share her memories of Christ feel enthusiasm for her. The Rabbis said: 'Jehovah hath created seven seas, but the Sea of Gennesaret is His delight.' " (George Adam Smith, *The Historical Geography of the Holy Land,* New York: A. C. Armstrong and Son, 1908, p. 442). The Gospel accounts picture fishing as a prosperous industry here in Biblical times, but today, instead of fleets of fishing vessels, only a boat

or two is seen. On these shores Jesus called His first disciples, four of whom were fishermen, and made of them fishers of men (Matt. 4:18; Luke 5:1-11).

The Sea of Galilee is noted for its sudden and violent storms caused by cold air sweeping down from the vast naked plateaus of Gaulanitis, the Hauran and Mt. Hermon through the ravines and gorges and converging at the head of the lake where it meets warm air. It was just such a storm that Jesus rebuked with His "Peace, be still" (Mark 4:39). Another time, the disciples were trying to reach Bethsaida when "a great wind" turned the water into huge waves, preventing any headway. Then Jesus appeared, walking toward them on the tempestuous water. As soon as they took Him into the boat they reached their desired haven (Matt. 14:22-34; Mark 6:45-53; John 6:15-21). So impressed were the disciples that they worshiped Him saying, "Of a truth Thou art the Son of God."

The Sea of Galilee was the focus of Galilee's wealth. Nine cities of 15,000 or more stood on its shores. To the NW was Capernaum, the home of Peter and Andrew (Mark 1:29) and where Matthew sat at custom (Matt. 9:9). It was the scene of much of Jesus' Galilean ministry. Below this, on the western side, was Magdala (present Mejdal), the home of Mary Magdalene, and three miles S of here was Tiberias, the magnificent capital of Galilee. On the NE corner was Bethsaida Julias, the native place of Philip, Andrew and Peter (John 1:44), and one-time capital of Philip the tetrarch. Gergesa lay S of here. The sites of Capernaum, Chorazin (modern Kerazeh) to the N of it, and Bethsaida have long been in dispute. Whatever their locations may have been, their near obliteration accords with their condemnation by the Saviour for their unbelief (Matt. 11:20-24). Of these towns, once thriving with dyeing, tanning, boat building, fishing, and fish-curing, two are now inhabited, namely Magdala, consisting of a few mud huts, and Tiberias.   A.M.R.

SUDDEN STORM on the Sea of Galilee. Mark relates how Jesus calmed one of these storms, saying: "Peace, be still."

DRAWING IN THE NETS on the shores of the Sea of Galilee. On these shores Christ recruited his first disciples. He told Simon, Peter and his brother Andrew, "Follow me, and I will make you fishers of men." James and John were also fishermen.

GALL. 1. From a Heb. root meaning *bitter,* the human gall (Job 16:13; 20:25); the poison of serpents (20:14).

2. Heb. *rō'sh, head.* A bitter and poisonous herb, perhaps the poppy (Deut. 29:18; Jer. 8:14, 9:15; Hos. 10:4, "hemlock"). Criminals were given a potion before crucifixion to deaden pain. Thus, opium would suit well the drink given to the Lord: "vinegar (wine, ASV) mingled with gall" (Gr. *cholé,* Matt. 27:34, cf. Ps. 69:21). Mark says "with myrrh" (15:23). But Jesus chose to bear the full agony of death.

GALLERY, three terraced passageways or balconies running round the chambers in the temple of Ezekiel's vision (Ezek. 41:16; 42:3,5,6). The upper two stories were shorter due to the absence of supporting pillars.

GALLEY (See Ship)

GALLIM (găl'ĭm, Heb. *gallim, heaps*), a town of Benjamin enumerated with Laish and Anathoth (Isa. 10:30). By "daughter of Gallim" is meant the inhabitants. It was the home of Phalti the son of Laish (I Sam. 25:44). Site uncertain.

GALLIO (gal'ĭ-ō, Gr. *Gallíon*), Junius Annaeus Gallio, the Roman proconsul (AV, "deputy") of Achaia when Paul was in Corinth (A.D. 51). Luke accurately calls him "proconsul," for Achaia had been an imperial province administered by a legate, but in A.D. 44 Claudius gave it to the Senate whose provinces alone were under the rule of proconsuls.

Born in Cordova, Spain, as Marcus Annaeus Novatus, he was adopted into the family of Lucius Junius Gallio, the rhetorician, whose name he took. Of his amiable character Seneca said, "No mortal was ever so sweet to one as Gallio was to all," and, his brother adds, "to love him to the utmost was to love all too little." How exactly and undesignedly this independent testimony coincides with Acts 18:12-17! Alarmed over the inroads that the Gospel was making, the Jews in Corinth brought Paul before the judgment seat of Gallio. The charge: "persuading men to worship God contrary to the law." But which law? Meaning their own, they hoped to convince Gallio that Paul was guilty of an offense against a lawful religion and hence against the Roman Government itself; but he was not impressed. "If it were a matter of wrong or wicked lewdness, O ye Jews, reason would that I should bear with you," said he. "But since (Gr.) it is a question of words and names and your law, look ye to it; for I will be no judge of such matters. And he drave them from the judgment seat." The Greeks then beat the chief ruler of the synagogue, but Gallio remained indifferent to the incident. A governor more stern might have arrested the violence at once, but in the providence of God Gallio's action amounted to an authoritative decision that Paul's preaching was not subversive against Rome. This gave Paul the protection he needed to continue his preaching there. Had Gallio become a Christian, he might not have committed suicide later.

GALLOWS, a pole for executing and exhibiting a victim by impalement. Made 75 feet high by Haman for Mordecai (Esth. 5:14; 6:4).

GAMALIEL (gà-mā'lĭ-ĕl, Heb. *gamlí'ēl, reward of God,* Gr. *Gamaliél*). 1. Son of Pedahzur and chief of the tribe of Manasseh (Num. 1:10; 2:20; 7:54, 59; 10:23). He assisted Moses in numbering the people.

2. A Pharisee and eminent doctor of the law; grandson of Hillel and first of only seven rabbis to be given the title of Rabban. Paul was one of his pupils (Acts 22:3). When the enraged Sanhedrin sought to slay the Apostles for their bold testimony to Christ, Gamaliel stood up in the council and urged judicious caution on the ground that if the new doctrine were of God they could not over-

throw it, and if it were of man it would perish of itself (Acts 5:34-39). Held in esteem by all the people, his counsel was heeded, and God used it to give a needed respite to the infant Church. Inasmuch as Gamaliel believed in God's sovereign control, his advice was sound; but also underlying it was the premise of pragmatism that what succeeds is good and what fails is evil. Contrarily, the Scriptures point out that the wicked do prosper (Ps. 73:12) and the godly are often destitute (Ps. 109:22-26). Truth must be tested by the standard of God's word. The tradition that he afterward became a Christian is incongruous with the high esteem accorded him in the Talmud: "Since Rabban Gamaliel died, the glory of the Law has ceased."

GAMES. Not much is known concerning the amusements of the ancient Israelites, partly because the earnestness of the Hebrew character did not give them prominence. Instead of public games, the great religious feasts supplied them with their anniversary occasions of national gatherings. There are references to dancing (Ps. 30:11; Jer. 31:13; Luke 15:25). The dance led by Jephthah's daughter (Judg. 11:34) and the dances of the Israelitish women (I Sam. 18:6; 21:11; 29:5) were public dances of rejoicing to celebrate a warrior's victory. Religious dancing was engaged in by Miriam and the women of Israel at the Red Sea (Exod. 15:20); by the Israelites around the golden calf at Sinai (32:19); and by David before the ark (II Sam. 6:14,16). (See also Ps. 149:3; 150:4). Of course, children of every race have their games. Zechariah prophesied that "the city shall be full of boys and girls playing in the streets thereof" (8:5). "He will . . . toss thee like a ball into a large country," warned Isaiah (22:18). In the NT the only children's game mentioned is that of mimicking the wedding dance and funeral wail to the music of the flute (Matt. 11:16,17; Luke 7:32).

Jason's introduction of Greek games and a gymnasium, frequented by the priests, was among the corrupting influences which broke down the fence of Judaism against Hellenism and threw it open to the sacrilegious assaults of King Antiochus Epiphanes, c. 175 B.C. (I Macc. 1:14; II Macc. 4:12-14). Herod erected a theater and amphitheater at Jerusalem and Caesarea where contests in gymnastics, chariot races, music, and wild beasts were held every five years in honor of Caesar, much to the annoyance of the faithful Jews (Josephus, *Ant.*, XV, viii,1; ix,6).

The public games of Greece and Rome were common knowledge among Christians and non-Christians of the first century, providing the NT writers with rich source material from which to illustrate spiritual truths. Condemned criminals were thrown to lions in the arena as punishment and for sport. In I Corinthians 15:32 Paul alludes to fighting with beasts at Ephesus (though *his* frays were with beastlike men—Demetrius and his craftsmen—not with literal beasts, from which his Roman citizenship exempted him). When a Roman general returned home victorious, he led his army in a triumphal procession, at the end of which trailed the captives who were condemned to fight with beasts. Paul felt that in contrast to the proud Corinthians, God had *set forth* (exhibited prior to execution) the Apostles last as captives doomed to die, because they were made a spectacle to be gazed at and made sport of in the arena of the world (I Cor. 4:9). Nero used to

clothe the Christians in beast skins when he exposed them to wild beasts. Cf. II Timothy 4:17, "I was delivered out of the mouth of the lion" (viz. from Satan's snare, I Pet. 5:8).

In I Corinthians 9:24,25 the Isthmian games, celebrated every two years on the isthmus of Corinth, are vividly alluded to. Held in honor of the Greek gods, the festival consisted of foot races, horse races, chariot contests, jumping, wrestling, boxing, and throwing of the discus and javelin. To the Greeks they were a subject of patriotic pride, a passion rather than a pastime, and thus made a suitable image of earnestness in the Christian race: "Know ye not that they which run in a race run all, but one receiveth the prize? So run, that ye may obtain. And every man that striveth for the mastery is temperate in all things. Now they do it to obtain a corruptible crown; but we an incorruptible." The coveted crown was a garland made of laurel, olives leaves, or pine needles; our crown is incorruptible (I Pet. 1:4) and therefore demands greater fidelity. The competitor had to "strive lawfully" or else he was not crowned (II Tim. 2:5), i.e. he had to observe the conditions of the contest, keeping to the bounds of the course, having previously trained himself for ten months with chastity, abstemious diet, enduring cold, heat, and severe exercise. As in boxing, so in the Christian race, Paul beat his body and brought it under subjection, lest that by any means when he had preached ("heralded"; the herald announced the name and country of each contestant and displayed the prizes) to others, he should be rejected by the judge, not as to salvation but to the winner's crown of victory (James 1:12). In view of the reward, Paul denied himself, being servant of all in order to win more souls to Jesus Christ. The Christian does not beat the air, missing his opponent, but he fights certainly, with telling blows upon the enemy (I Cor. 9:18-27). As the runner looks intently at the goal and casts away every encumbrance, so the Christian runs, casting aside not only sinful lusts but even harmless and otherwise useful things which would retard him. He must run with *enduring perseverance* the race set before him, *looking off* unto Jesus who is the Captain and Finisher of our faith (Heb. 12:1,2). Paul used the same figure in addressing the Ephesian elders (Acts 20:24) and the Philippians (3:12-14). The Colossians were urged to let the peace of God *rule as umpire* in their hearts and thus restrain wrong passions that they might attain the prize to which they were called (3:15). Other allusions to the language of games are in Ephesians 6:12, "We wrestle not against flesh and blood" and II Timothy 4:7, "I have fought the good fight, I have finished the course" (Gr. *I have struggled the good contest,* not merely a fight). See also I Timothy 6:12 and Revelation 2:10.   A.M.R.

GAMMADIM (găm'à-dĭm, Heb. *gammādhîm*), occurs in Ezekiel 27:11 only as "gammadims" (KJV), but in ASV translated "valorous men." Foreigners would hardly be trusted to watch in the towers of Tyre. Variously interpreted, the ASV rendering seems most fitting as an epithet of the warriors of Tyre.

GAMUL (gā'-mŭl, Heb. *gāmûl*), the head of the twenty-second course of priests (I Chron. 24:17).

GARDEN (Heb. *gan, gannâh, a covered or hidden place,* Gr. *kéros*), a cultivated piece of ground, usually in the suburbs, planted with flowers, vegetables, shrubs, or trees, fenced with a mud or stone wall (Prov. 24:31) or thorny hedges (Isa. 5:5) and *guarded* (whence "garden") by a watchman in a lodge (Isa. 1:8) or tower (Mark 12:1) to drive away wild beasts and robbers.

The quince, citron, almond and other fruits, herbs, and various vegetables and spices are mentioned as growing in gardens. A reservoir cistern, or still better a fountain of water, was essential to a good garden. See Song of Solomon 4:15, "a fountain of gardens," i.e. a fountain sufficient to water many gardens.

The occurrence of no less than 250 botanical terms in the OT shows the Israelite fondness for flowers, fruits, and pleasant grounds. These are still a delight to the Oriental who lives in a hot, dry country. Every house court or area generally had its shade tree. The vine wound round the trellis or outside staircase, the emblem of the loving and fruitful wife and happy home (Ps. 128:3). The "orchards" (Heb. *paradises*) were larger gardens specially for fruit trees. Solomon's gardens and fruit orchards with pools of water for irrigation (Eccl. 2:4-6) very likely suggested the imagery of Song of Solomon 4:12-15. The "king's garden" (II Kings 25:4; Neh. 3:15; Jer. 39:4; 52:7) was near the pool of Siloam.

The Hebrews used gardens as burial places. The field of Machpelah, Abraham's burial ground, was a garden with trees in and around it (Gen. 23:17). Manasseh and Amon were buried in Uzza's garden (II Kings 21:18,26). The garden of Gethsemane was a favorite resort of Jesus for meditation and prayer (Matt. 26:36; John 18:1,2). In idolatrous periods, gardens were made the scene of superstition and image worship, the awful counterpart of the primitive Eden (Isa. 1:29; 65:3; 66: 17). The new Paradise regained by the people of God (Rev. 22:1-5) suggests in a fuller way the old paradise planted by God but lost through sin (Gen. 2:8).

Spiritually, the believer is a garden watered by the Holy Spirit (Jer. 2:13; 17:7,8; John 4:13,14; 7:37-39). The righteous "shall be like a tree planted by the rivers of water, that bringeth forth his fruit in his season" (Ps. 1:3). "A well watered garden" expresses abundant happiness and prosperity (Isa. 58:11; Jer. 31:12) just as "a garden that hath no water" (Isa. 1:30) expresses spiritual, national and individual barrenness and misery.
                                                          A.M.R.

GAREB (gā'rĕb, Heb. *gārēv, scabby*). 1. An Ithrite, a member of one of the families of Kirjathjearim (I Chron. 2:53) and one of David's mighty men (II Sam. 23:38; I Chron. 11:40).

2. A hill near Jerusalem to which the city would expand, as foreseen by the prophet Jeremiah (31: 39). The site is unknown.

GARLICK, GARLIC (See Plants)

GARMENTS (See Dress)

GARMITE (gàr'mĭt, Heb. *garmî*), a name applied to Keilah (I Chron. 4:19). Meaning is obscure.

GARNER (gàr'nêr, Heb. *māzû*), a *barn* or *storehouse* (Ps. 144:13); Heb. *'ōtsār*, a storehouse for precious items (II Chron. 32:27) and for food (Joel 1:17). Gr. *apothéke*, a barn used as a granary (Matt. 3:12; 6:26; Luke 3:17; 12:18,24).

GARRISON (Heb. *matstsāv* and *netsîv, placed*), a fortress manned by soldiers (II Chron. 17:2). Its primary reference is that of a military post for the occupation of a conquered country such as the

Philistines had when they held the land of Israel (I Sam. 10:5; 13:3; 14:1,6). David put garrisons in Syria and Edom when he subjugated those people (II Sam. 8:6,14). In Ezekiel 26:11, "thy strong garrisons" is a wrong rendering of *matstsévâh*. It refers to the pillars or obelisks in honor of the gods of Tyre which would totter before the conquering Nebuchadnezzar.

GASHMU (găsh'mū, Heb. *gashmû*, Neh. 6:6), a form of Geshem (2:19; 6:1,2), an Arabian who opposed Nehemiah's building of the wall of Jerusalem.

GATAM (gā'tăm, Heb. *ga'tām*), grandson of Esau; an Edomite chief (Gen. 36:11,16; I Chron. 1:36).

GATE (Heb. usually *sha'ar, opening*, Gr. *púle*), the entrance to enclosed buildings, grounds, or cities. The gates of a city were the place where the Oriental resorted for legal business, conversation, bargaining, and news. The usual gateway consisted of double doors plated with metal (Ps. 107: 16; Isa. 45:2). Wooden doors without iron plating were easily set on fire (Judg. 9:52; Neh. 2:3,17). Some gates were made out of brass, as was "the Beautiful Gate" of Herod's temple (Acts 3:2), more costly than nine others of the outer court that had been poured over with gold and silver (Joseph, *Wars of the Jews*, V,v,3). Still others were of solid stones (Isa. 54:12; Rev. 21:21). Massive stone doors are found in ancient towns of Syria, single slabs several inches thick and ten feet high, turning on pivots above and below. Gates ordinarily swung on projections that fitted into sockets on the post and were secured with bars of wood (Nah. 3:13) or of metal (I Kings 4:13; Ps. 107:16; Isa. 45:2).

Being the weakest points in a city's walls, the gates were frequently the object of a foe's attack (Judg. 5:8; I Sam. 23:7; Ezek. 21:15,22) and therefore flanked by towers (II Sam. 18:24,33; II Chron. 14:7; 26:9). To "possess the gates" was to possess the city (Gen. 22:17; 24:60). They were shut at nightfall and opened again in the morning (Deut. 3:5; Josh. 2:5,7).

Markets were held at the gate, and the main item sold there gave its name to the gate ("sheep gate," Neh. 3:1; "fish gate," Neh. 3:3; "horse gate," Neh. 3:28). The gate was the place where people met to hear an important announcement (II Chron. 32:6; Jer. 7:2; 17:19-27) or the reading of the law (Neh. 8:1,3) or where the elders transacted legal business (Deut. 16:18; 21:18-20; Josh. 20:4; Ruth 4:1,2,11). "Neither oppress the afflicted in the gate" meant to mete out impartial justice (Prov. 22:22). Psalm 69:12, "They that sit in the gate speak against me, and I was the song of the drunkards"; i.e., not only among the drunken revellers, but in the grave deliberations of the judges in the place of justice was he an object of abusive language. Amos 5:12, "they turn aside the poor in the gate"; i.e., they refuse them their right; vs. 10, "they hate him that rebuketh in the gate," viz. the judge who condemns them (Zech. 8:16). Isaiah 29:21, "They lay a snare for him that reproveth in the gate"; i.e., they try by bribes and misrepresentations to ensnare into a false decision the judge who in public court would reprove them for their iniquity, or to ensnare the prophet who publicly reproves them. "The Sublime Porte," the title for the Sultan of Turkey, was derived from the eastern usage of dispensing law in the gateway. It was also the king's or chief's place of audience

(II Sam. 19:8; I Kings 22:10). Daniel sat in the gate of King Nebuchadnezzar as "ruler over the whole province of Babylon" (Dan. 2:48,49). Regarded as specially sacred, the threshold in Assyrian palaces bore cuneiform inscriptions and was guarded by human-headed bulls with eagles' wings. In Israel, sentences from the Law were inscribed on and above the posts and gates of private houses (Deut. 6:9). Josiah destroyed the high places near the gates that were used for heathen sacrifices (II Kings 23:8).

Figuratively, gates refer to the glory of a city (Isa. 3:26; 14:31; Jer. 14:2) or to the city itself (Ps. 87:2; 122:2). In Matthew 16:18, the "gates of Hades" not prevailing against the Church may refer to infernal powers assaulting the Church or to the Church's greater power in retaining her members than the grave has for its victims.

A.M.R.

GATH (găth, Heb. *gath, winepress*), one of the five great Philistine cities (Ashdod, Gaza, Askelon, Gath, and Ekron, Josh. 13:3; I Sam. 6:17). Its people were the Gittites, of whom were Goliath (I Sam. 17:4) and other giants (II Sam. 21:19-22). In harmony with this fact is the record of the Anakims' presence in Gath after Joshua had destroyed the neighboring territory (Josh. 11:22). It was one of the five cities to which the Philistines carried the ark of God and thereby brought on the people God's heavy visitation with tumors (I Sam. 5:8,9). David fled from Saul to Gath where he feigned madness to save his life (I Sam. 21:10-15). The second time he visited Gath, King Achish assigned him Ziklag as a residence (I Sam. 27:2-6). During his sixteen months here, he won the

GAZA, the city as seen from the west. Here Samson pulled down the pillars and destroyed himself and his Philistine captors.

confidence of the king through subterfuge and intrigue (27:7-29:11). Some of David's six hundred followers were Gittites, one of whom was his loyal friend Ittai. They may have attached themselves to him at this time or when he smote and subdued the Philistines (II Sam. 8:1; 15:18-21). Though tributary to Israel after David conquered it (I Chron. 18:1), Gath retained its own king (I Kings 2:39). Rehoboam, Solomon's son, rebuilt and fortified the town (II Chron. 11:8). Later, Hazael, king of Syria, captured Gath from Jehoash, king of Judah (II Kings 12:17), but Uzziah won it back (II Chron. 26:6). From the fall of this walled city Amos sounds a warning lesson to those at ease in Zion (6:1,2). The omission of Gath from the list of the five cities (Amos 1:6,8; Zeph. 2:4,5; Zech. 9:5,6) indicates it had lost its place among them by that time. Its site today is uncertain. Gath lay on the border between Judah and Philistia, between Shocoh and Ekron (I Sam. 17:1,52). Tell es-Safiyeh favors this description, lying on a hill at the foot of Judah's mountains, ten miles E of Ashdod and ten SE of Ekron.

GATH-HEPHER (găth-hē'fêr, Heb. *gath ha-hēpher, winepress of the well*), a town on Zebulun's border (Josh. 19:12,13, ASV). Birthplace of Jonah the prophet (II Kings 14:25). Now el Meshhed, where his supposed tomb is still shown, on a hill two miles from Nazareth in Galilee.

GATH-RIMMON (găth-rĭm'ŭn, Heb. *gath rimmôn, winepress of Rimmon* or *pomegranates*). 1. A city of Dan on the Philistine plain, given to the Levites (Josh. 19:45; 21:24; I Chron. 6:69). 2. A town of Manasseh, W of Jordan, assigned to the Levites (Josh. 19:25). In I Chronicles 6:70 this is called Bileam, which is probably the true reading in Joshua 19:25, an error due to a copyist's eye catching "Gath-rimmon" in the previous verse.

GAULANITIS (gôl-ăn-ī'-tís), a province NE of the Sea of Galilee ruled by Herod Antipas. The name is derived from Golan, a city of Manasseh in Bashan and one of three cities of refuge E of the Jordan (Deut. 4:43; Josh. 20:8; 21:27).

GAZA (gā'-zà, Heb. *'azzâh, strong*, Gr. *Gáza*), one of the five chief Philistine cities and the most southwesterly toward Egypt. Originally a seaport, the town moved to a hill three miles inland on the great caravan route between Syria and Egypt. Here it became an important rest stop on the edge of the desert and a popular trading center. Its position and *strength* (as its name means) made it the key of this line of communications. It is called by its Hebrew name *Azzah* (Deut. 2:23; I Kings 4:24; Jer. 25:20).

Originally a Canaanite city (Gen. 10:19), Gaza was assigned by Joshua to Judah (Josh. 15:47) but was not occupied till after Judah had taken it (Judg. 1:18), as the Anakims were still present (Josh 11:22; 13:3). The Philistines soon recovered it (Judg. 13:1) and there Samson perished while destroying his captors (16:1,21). Solomon ruled over it (I Kings 4:24), but it was Hezekiah who gave the decisive blow to the Philistines (II Kings 18:8). God through Amos threatened Gaza with destruction by fire for her transgressions (Amos 1:6). This was fulfilled by one of the pharaohs of Egypt (Jer. 47:1). The predictions that Gaza would be forsaken (Zeph. 2:4) and that its king should perish (Zech. 9:5, i.e., its Persian satrap, or petty king subordinate to the great king of Persia) were fulfilled by Alexander the Great who

VILLAGE OF GEBA, in the territory of Benjamin, assigned to the Levites. Here Jonathan, attended only by his armor-bearer, surprised an outpost of Philistines, spreading panic to the main Philistine camp, and bringing victory to the Israelites.

took the city in 332 B.C., after it had resisted his siege for two months. He bound Betis the satrap to a chariot, dragging him round the city, and slew 10,000 of its inhabitants, selling the rest as slaves. It was desolated again by fire and sword by the Maccabees in 96 B.C. In turn, Gaza passed under the control of Syria and Rome.

Philip met the Ethiopian eunuch "S unto the way that goeth down from Jerusalem unto Gaza which is desert" (Acts 8:26). Once Gaza was the seat of a Christian church and bishop in the midst of Greek culture and temples, but it turned Moslem in A.D. 634. Now, of its 20,000 inhabitants, only a few hundred are Christians, the rest Moslems.

Modern Ghuzzeh is the metropolis of the Gaza Strip which is crowded with Arab refugees today. N of Ghuzzeh lies an extensive olive grove from the fruit of which soap is made. Its trade in corn is considerable, and there can still be heard the grinding of corn by millstones such as Samson was forced to work with in his prison house at Gaza (Judg. 16:21). The Tel el Muntar or "hill of the watchman" (II Kings 18:8), SE of Gaza, is the hill up which Samson carried the gates of the city (Judg. 16:3).   A.M.R.

GAZELLE (See Animals)

GAZER (See Gezer)

GAZEZ (gā'zĕz). 1. Son of Ephah.
2. Grandson of Ephah, Caleb's concubine (1 Chron. 2:46).

GAZZAM (găz'ăm), one of the Nethinim, whose posterity returned from exile (Ezra 2:48; Neh. 7: 51).

GEBA (gē'bà, gā'bà, Heb. *geva' hill*), a town in the territory of Benjamin (Josh. 18:24 ASV, RSV; Gaba in KJV), assigned to the Levites (Josh. 21: 17; I Chron. 6:60; 8:6). Jonathan defeated the Philistines at Geba (I Sam. 13:3). Saul and Jonathan then remained in Geba (I Sam. 13:16 ASV, RSV; KJV translates Gibeah, also in 14:5; see Judg. 20:10,33). Geba is SW of Wady Suweinīt, opposite Michmash (I Sam. 14:5), where Jonathan and his armor-bearer, by a bold stratagem won a signal victory. Geba should be Gibeon in II Samuel 5:25 (ASV margin has Gibeon), as in the parallel passage (I Chron. 14:16). Asa fortified Geba with stones and timber which Baasha had gathered to build Ramah (I Kings 15:22). In the time of Hezekiah Geba was the northernmost city of the kingdom of Judah, as Beersheba its southernmost (II Kings 23:8; II Chron. 16:6). The Assyrians, marching toward Jerusalem, stored their baggage at Michmash, crossed the pass to Geba and camped for a night (Isaiah 10:28,29). Men from Geba returned after the exile (Ezra 2:26; Neh. 7:30 ASV, RSV; Gaba in KJV). Levites from Geba helped in the rebuilding of Jerusalem (Neh. 11:31; 12:29). Zechariah 14:10 prophesied that the land will be made a plain from Geba to Rimmon, except for lofty Jerusalem.

GEBAL (gē'băl, Heb. *geval, border*, Gr. *Búblos, Bíblos*). 1. A seaport of Phoenicia, between Sidon and Tripolis; modern Jebeil, 25 miles N of Beirut. In the 15th century B.C. it was subject to Egypt. Its political history included periods of independence alternating with subjection to successive empires. In Greek and Roman times it was called Byblos, from the manufacture of papyrus there.

RUINS AT GEBAL, Phoenician seaport. In Greek and Roman times, it was known as Byblos, from the manufacture of papyrus there.

Joshua 13:5,6 refers to the land of the Giblites or Gebalites, the land of Lebanon at the foot of Mt. Hermon, as part of the land God gave to the children of Israel; God promised to drive out its inhabitants if Joshua would divide it by lot to the Israelites; but we have no record of Joshua accepting the offer, and the Israelites never controlled Gebal. In I Kings 5:17,18, ASV, RSV replaces "stonesquarers" of KJV with "Gebalites" or "men of Gebal." Expert stonemasonry was among the industries of Gebal. Shipbuilding was another, for Ezekiel 27:9 tells us that caulkers from Gebal worked on ships at Tyre. Skilled technologies, paper-making, fine stonework and seaworthy ship-building distinguished Gebal, rather than the extraction of raw materials or mass production alone.

2. A land between the Dead Sea and Petra; modern Jibâl, in northeastern Edom; allied with enemies of Israel, including Edom and Assyria (Ps. 83:6-8).

GEBER (gē'bêr). 1. One of Solomon's twelve purveyors for Southern Gilead (I Kings 4:13).

2. The son of Uri, who was over great pasture lands east of Jordan (I Kings 4:19). The two Gebers are sometimes identified as the same person.

GEBIM (gē'bĭm), a place near Anathoth and Nob, whose inhabitants fled at the approach of the Assyrian invaders (Isa. 10:31).

GECKO (See Animals)

GEDALIAH (gĕd'à-lī'à, Heb. *gedhalyâh*). 1. A son of Shaphan, king Josiah's secretary and Governor of Mizpah (II Kings 25:22-25; Jer. 39:14; 40:5-16; 41:1-18; 43:6). This Judean of high rank was the one who protected Jeremiah, whose views he shared, from the anti-Chaldeans. Nebuchadnezzar

made him governor over "the poor people left in the land." He ruled, however, for only two months. The anniversary of his treacherous murder is observed as one of the four Jewish feasts (Zech. 7:5; 8:19).

2. A priest, of the sons of Jeshua, who had taken a strange wife during the exile (Ezra 10:18).

3. Grandfather of the prophet Zephaniah (Zeph. 1:1).

4. One of the six sons of Jeduthun, a harper and head of the second of twenty-four companies, his consisting of twelve musicians (I Chron. 25:8,9).

g. A son of Pashur and the prince who caused Jeremiah to be imprisoned (Jer. 38:1-6).

GEDER (gē'dêr, Heb. *gedher*), Canaanite royal city near Debir, taken by Joshua (Josh. 12:13); perhaps Beth-gader (I Chron. 2:51) and the birthplace of Baal-hamon the Gederite (I Chron. 27:28).

GEDERAH (gĕ-dē'rà, Heb. *gedhērâh, wall*), a town on the heights between the valleys of Sorek and Aijalon in the Shephelah of Judah (Josh. 15:36,41) named with Gedorothaim (two walls) and Gederoth (walls). Modern Jedîreh. Jozabad (I Chron. 12:4) was a Gederathite. For KJV "those that dwelt among plants and hedges" ASV, RSV have "the inhabitants of Netaim and Gederah."

GEDOR (gē'dôr, Heb. *gedhôr, wall*). 1. A city in the hill country of Judah (Josh. 15:58); now Khirbet Jedûr, a few miles north of Hebron.

2. The town where Jeroham lived, whose sons were among the Benjamites who came to David at Ziklag (I Chron. 12:7); location unknown.

3. A descendant of Benjamin, who, with his father Jehiel and brothers, dwelt at Gibeon (I Chron. 8:31; 9:37).

4. Among the descendants of Judah, Penuel (I Chron. 4:4) and Jered (I Chron. 4:18) are both named as the "father" of Gedor: since the genealogical tables in which the names occur are different, two persons named Gedor must be meant.

5. In the time of Hezekiah, princes of Simeon went to Gedor to find pasture for their flocks, and finding it so good, they drove out the inhabitants and settled there.

GEHAZI (gē-hā'zī, Heb. *gêhăzî, valley of vision*), the servant of Elisha. He first appears when Elisha sought to reward the Shunamite woman for her hospitality (II Kings 4:8-37). When she declined to ask any reward, Gehazi answered, "Verily she hath no child, and her husband is old." Elisha promised her that she should bear a child, which came to pass. "When the child was grown," he died of sunstroke. The woman went with her sorrow to Elisha. He sent Gehazi with instructions to lay Elisha's staff upon the face of the child; but "the child is not awaked." Elisha then came himself and restored the child to life. Elisha had Gehazi call the woman to receive her son. Gehazi next appears when Naaman is healed (II Kings 5:1-27). Elisha refused any reward. After Naaman left, Gehazi determined to run after Naaman and ask something. Naaman gave him more than he asked. Gehazi hid his booty before he reached home, but Elisha knew what had happened, and rebuked Gehazi by invoking upon him the leprosy of which Naaman had been cured. Gehazi is last met with, talking with the king of "all the great things that Elisha hath done" (II Kings 8:4-6). As Gehazi was telling of the Shunamite woman's son

GEHAZI LOOKED IN HORROR at his right hand flaking with leprosy. It was of leprosy that Naaman had been cured, and when Gehazi sinned by taking money from Naaman, the same leprosy came upon him.

being restored to life, the woman herself appeared, to ask the king to restore to her the property which she abandoned upon the advice of Elisha during a seven years' famine. The king ordered her fully compensated. Because Gehazi appears in the court of the king, it has been inferred that he had repented and been healed of his leprosy, though II Kings 5:27 renders this doubtful. He shows no resentment against Elisha. Gehazi was an efficient servant, but weak enough to yield to avarice. He lacked his master's clear moral insight and stamina, and he bore no such relations to Elisha as Elisha bore to Elijah.

GEHENNA (gē-hĕn′à, Gr. *geénna*, a transliteration of the Aramaic form of Heb. *gê-ben-hinnôm, valley of the son of Hinnom*), a valley on the W and SW of Jerusalem, which formed part of the border between Judah and Benjamin (comparing Josh. 15:8 with 18:16); still recognized as the border after the exile (Neh. 11:30,31); modern Wadî er-rabâbi. Here Ahaz (II Chron. 28:3; see II Kings 16:3) and Manasseh (II Chron. 33:6; see II Kings 21:6) sacrificed their sons to Molech (Jer. 32:35). For this reason Josiah defiled the place (II Kings 23:10). After referring to the idolatrous barbarities (Jer. 7:31,32) Jeremiah prophesies a great slaughter of the people there, and in the siege of Jerusalem (Jer. 19:1-13). After the OT period, Jewish apocalyptic writers began to call the Valley of Hinnom the entrance to hell, later hell itself. In Jewish usage of the first century A.D., Gehenna referred to the intermediate state of the godless dead, but there is no trace of this sense in the NT. The NT distinguishes sharply between Hades, the intermediate, bodiless state, and Gehenna, the state of final punishment after the resurrection of the body. Gehenna existed before the judgment (Matt. 25;41). The word occurs 12 times in the NT, always translated "hell" ASV, RSV margin "Gehenna." Eleven times it is on the lips of Jesus; as the final punishment for calling one's brother a fool (Matt. 5:22); for adultery, when the severest measures have not been taken to prevent commission of this offense (Matt. 5:29,30); and others (Matt. 18:9; Mark 9:43,45,47); in a warning as to whom to fear (Matt. 10:28; Luke 12:5). A hypocrite is called a "son of hell" (Matt. 23:15) who cannot "escape the damnation of hell" (Matt. 23:33). James 3:6 speaks of the "tongue" as "a fire," being "set on fire of hell." A fire was kept burning in the Valley of Hinnom to consume the offal deposited there. Terms parallel to Gehenna include "furnace of fire" (Matt. 13:42,50); "lake of fire" (Rev. 19:20; 20:10 14,15); "eternal fire" (Jude 7); "cast down to hell" (II Pet. 2:4), where the Greek verb means "cast down to Tartaros," a Greek name for the place of punishment of the wicked dead. Its use by our Saviour Jesus Christ warns us of the destiny which even the love of God does not avert from those who finally refuse His forgiveness. See Hades, Hell   E.R.

GELILOTH (gē-lī′lŏth—lōth, Josh. 18:17), the name of a place on the border of Benjamin with Judah, E of Jerusalem; perhaps the same as the Gilgal of Joshua 15:7, whose name has a similar meaning (circuit). It cannot be the Gilgal near Jericho in the Jordan Valley.

GEMALLI (gē-măl′ī, *camel owner* or *rider*), the father of Ammiel, ruler of the tribe of Dan, and one of the twelve spies sent out to explore the land (Num. 13:12).

GEMARIAH (gĕm′à-rī′à, *Jehovah hath fulfilled* or *accomplishment of the Lord*). 1. A prince, son of Shaphan the scribe and brother of Ahikam (Jer. 36:10-25). This scribe with others sought in vain to keep king Jehoiakim from burning the roll which Baruch had written at the dictation of Jeremiah.
2. A son of Hilkiah, sent by King Zedekiah as ambassador to Nebuchadnezzar at Babylon. He also carried a letter from Jeremiah to the captive Jews (Jer. 29:3).

GENEALOGY (jĕn′ē-ăl′ō-jē, Heb. *yahas,* Gr. *genealogía*), a list of ancestors or descendants; or descent from an ancestor; or the study of lines of descent. Genealogies are compiled to show biological descent, the right of inheritance, succession to an office, or ethnological and geographical relationships. The word occurs several times in the English Bible (I Chron. 4:33; 5:1,7; 7:5,7,9,40; 9:22; II Chron. 12:15; 31:16-19; Ezra 2:62; 8:1; Neh. 7:5, 64; I Tim. 1:4; Tit. 3:9), but most Bible genealogies are introduced by other words, such as "the book of the generations of," or "these are the generations of," or are given without titles. Bible genealogies are not primarily concerned with mere biological descent. The earliest (Gen. 4:1,

2,17-22), by its emphasis on occupations (Abel, shepherd; Cain, farmer and city-builder; Jabal, cattleman; Jubal, musician; Tubal-cain, metal worker), in a family register of Cain's descendants, shows when new features of the culture were introduced. The genealogy of the line of Seth (Gen. 4:25,26; 5:1-32), a list of long-lived individuals, contrasts with the genealogy in Genesis 10:1-32, which is clearly a table of nations descended from the three families of Shem, Ham, and Japheth. Many of the names are Heb. plurals in "-im," signifying nations, tribes, cities or towns rather than individuals. The scope of Biblical genealogies narrows to the Chosen People and their close relatives (Gen. 11:10-22, Shem to Abraham; 22:20-24, Abraham's near kin). Next are the children of Abraham by Hagar (Gen. 16:15; 25:12-18); by Sarah (21:1-3; 25:19-28) and by Keturah (25:1-4); then the children of Jacob (Gen. 29:31-30:24; 35:16-26); and of his brother Esau (Gen. 36) for many generations in Edom. Jacob's posterity who came into Egypt are carefully enumerated (Gen. 46:8-27); part of them again (Exod. 6:14-27) to bring the genealogy down to Moses and Aaron; the inclusion of brief mention of the sons of Reuben and Simeon before the fuller genealogy of the Levites may be due to this list being taken from an earlier one. Numbers 26:1-56 is a census on genealogical principles, for the purpose of equitable division of the land. The military organization of the Israelites for the wilderness journey was by genealogy (Num. 1-3), and this included the priests and Levites (3:11-39), and provided for a tax and offerings (7:11-89) for the support of religion (3:40-51), as well as the order of march in peace or war (10). Many other references to persons must be taken into account in attempting a complete genealogy. Ruth 4:17-22 picks up the genealogy of Judah from his son Pharez, to carry it down to David, whose children are listed: those born in Hebron (II Sam. 3:2-5) and in Jerusalem (5:13-16). David's "mighty men" are named, with brief notices of their descent (II Sam. 23:8-39): Solomon's princes and providers of food are likewise treated (II Kings 4:1-19).

The major genealogical tables of the OT are in I Chronicles 1-9. They use most of the earlier genealogical material, but show differences which at a distance of time are puzzling. Satisfactory solutions are not available for many of these. Mistakes in copying would account for some; differences in the purpose of the recorders for others. The books of Kings and Chronicles contain information about the family relationships of the kings of Judah and of Israel. Ezra 2:1-63; 8:1-20 and Nehemiah 7:7-63 name by families those who returned with Zerubbabel from Babylonian captivity, including many whose descent could not be traced. Ezra 7:1-6 gives Ezra's own line of descent from Aaron. Ezra 10:18:44 names those who had married foreign women. Nehemiah 3 names those who helped rebuild the walls of Jerusalem. There follow lists of those who helped Ezra proclaim the law of God (Neh. 8:1-8); of those who sealed the covenant to keep the law (Neh. 10:1-27); of the leading inhabitants in Jerusalem (Neh. 11:1-10), in nearby Judah (11:20-24), and in more remote villages of Judah and Benjamin (11:25-36). Nehemiah 12 deals with the priests who accompanied Zerubbabel (1-9); the succession of high priests from Jeshua to Jaddua (10,11); the "priests, the chief of the fathers," in the days of Joiakim (12-21); Levites in this period (22-26); princes and priests who took part in the dedication of the wall of Jerusalem (31-42). The prophets usually begin their books with some indication of their genealogy (Isa. 1:1; Jer. 1:1; Ezek. 1:3; Hos. 1:1; Joel 1:1; Jonah 1:1; Zeph. 1:1; Zech. 1:1).

The genealogies of Jesus Christ will be dealt with in a separate article. Other NT persons generally appear without indication of their descent. Occasionally the father is named (e.g., James and John, the sons of Zebedee, Luke 5:10, etc.). Paul cherishes his pure Heb. descent (Phil. 3:4,5). I Timothy 1:4 and Titus 3:9 are sometimes thought to refer to pagan Gnostic series of beings intermediate between God and the created earth, but it is more likely that the rabbinic over-concern with human genealogies is meant, because the false teachers seem to be Jewish, and the term "genealogies" is not used by heathen authors of the pagan Gnostic series. Since the two genealogies of Jesus Christ in Matthew and Luke are known to have caused controversy a century or so later, it may not be improper to surmise that this difficulty was already troubling the churches.

It is certain that the NT shows far less concern for the genealogy of human beings than does the OT. In the OT, God was bringing forth a Chosen People who should be a nation peculiarly devoted to preserving the revelation of Him until in the fulness of time God sent forth His Son, Who should draw to Himself a new people, united not by descent from a common human ancestor, but by a genealogy of one generation only: a child of God by a new and spiritual birth.   E.R.

GENEALOGY OF JESUS CHRIST (jĕn′ē-ăl′ō-jē). Two genealogies are given in the NT: in Matthew 1:17, and in Luke 3:23-38. Matthew traces the descent of Jesus from Abraham and David, and divides it into three sets of fourteen generations each, probably to aid memorization. There are fourteen names from Abraham to and including David. From David to and including Josiah, and counting David a second time, there are fourteen names. (David is named twice in Matt. 1, v. 17). From Jechoniah to Jesus we have fourteen names. Matthew omits three generations after Joram, namely Ahaziah, Joash and Amaziah (I Chron. 3:11,12). Such an omission in Heb. genealogies is not peculiar to Matthew. He names Zerah as well as Perez, and mentions the brethren of Judah and of Jechoniah, which is unusual. Contrary to Heb. practice, he names five women: Tamar, Rahab, Ruth, Bathsheba (the wife of Uriah), and Mary, each name evoking associations, dark or bright, with the history of the chosen people. Matthew carefully excludes the physical paternity of Joseph by saying "Joseph the husband of Mary, of whom" (feminine singular in Greek) "was born Jesus" (1:16). The sense of "begat" in Heb. genealogies was not exact: it indicated immediate or remote descent, an adoptive relation, or legal heirship, as well as procreation.

Luke's genealogy moves from Jesus to Adam. Between Abraham and Adam it is the same as in I Chronicles 1:1-7,24-28, or the more detailed genealogies in Genesis; making allowance for the different spelling of names in transliteration from Heb. or Greek. From David to Abraham Luke agrees with OT genealogies and with Matthew. Between Jesus and David Luke's list differs from Matthew's, and there is no OT record to compare with Luke's, except for Nathan being one of David's sons, and for the names of Salathiel (Shealtil) and Zorobabel (Zerubbabel). At this point the two genealogies crossed, through adoption or otherwise.

As Matthew gave the line of the kings from David to Jechoniah, it is probable that from Salathiel to Joseph he named those who were heirs to the Davidic throne. Luke's record then would be that of physical descent, though crossing the royal line at one point. In Luke 3:23 there is a question as to how much should be considered parenthetical. Some would include "of Joseph" in the parenthesis: "(as was supposed of Joseph)," making Heli in some sense the father of Jesus, perhaps his maternal grandfather. This construction is awkward. Another supposition is that Joseph is really the son-in-law of Heli, through his marriage to Mary, thought to be Heli's daughter. If both genealogies are those of Joseph, his relationship to Heli must be different from his relationship to Jacob. Scholars have wrestled with the problems of the two genealogies from the second century, when pagan critics raised the difficulty. Many explanations have been more ingenious than convincing, involving complicated and uncertain inferences.

A relatively simple solution is given by A. T. Robertson in his *A Harmony of the Gospels for Students of the Life of Christ,* New York: George H. Doran and Co., 1922, pp. 259-262. In this view, widely accepted, Matthew gives the legal descent of heirship to the throne of David, through Joseph, while Luke gives the physical descent of Jesus through Mary. Matthew is concerned with the kingship of Jesus, Luke with His humanity. Both make plain His Virgin Birth, and therefore His Deity. In the light of these salient facts, on which the agreement of Matthew and Luke is obvious, their differences only accentuate their value as independent witnesses, in whose testimony the Holy Spirit did not see fit to cause them to collaborate. The question is fully discussed in J. G. Machen, *The Virgin Birth of Christ,* New York: Harper and Brothers, 1930, pp. 202-209, and in ISBE, vol. 2, pp. 1196-1199. Matthew's genealogy establishes the legal claim to the throne of David through his foster-father Joseph; Luke's establishes His actual descent from David through Mary. Luke 1:32 says that Mary's child "shall be called the Son of the Highest: and the Lord God shall give unto Him the throne of his father David." Romans 1:3,4 agrees with this: Jesus "was made of the seed of David according to the flesh," which could only be through Mary; "and declared to be the Son of God . . . by the resurrection from the dead." II Timothy 2:8 echoes this. Isaiah 11:1 indicates that Messiah is to be physically a descendant of David's father Jesse. The genealogies must be seen in the light of this fact. (Compare Matt. 22:41-46 and parallels with the answer in Rom. 1:4).   E.R.

GENERATION (jĕn′ĕr-ā′shŭn), in the OT, the translation of two Heb. words: (1) *tôledhôth,* from a root *yalad,* to beget, used always in the plural, refers to lines of descent from an ancestor, and occurs in the phrase "these are the generations of," introducing each of eleven sections of Genesis, from 2:4 to 37:2 (also elsewhere in Gen., Exod., Num., I Chron., and Ruth 4:18); (2 *dôr, a period of time* (e.g., Deut. 32:7, past; Exod. 3:15, future; Ps. 102:24, both); *all the men living in a given period* (e.g., Gen. 7:1; Judg. 3:2); *a class of men* *characterized by a certain quality* (e.g., Deut. 32: 5; Ps. 14:5); *a dwelling place or habitation* (Isa. 58:12; Ps. 49:19).

In the NT, *generation* translates four Greek words, all having reference to descent: (1) *geneá,* most frequent in the synoptic Gospels; for *lines of descent from an ancestor* (e.g., Matt. 1:17); or *all the men living in a given period* (e.g., Matt. 11: 16); or *a class of men characterized by a certain quality* (e.g., Matt. 12:39); also, *a period of time* (Acts 13:36; Col. 1:26). (2) *génesis,* in Matthew 1:1, in a heading to verses 2:17, used to mean "genealogy"; (3) *génnema,* in the phrase "generation of vipers" (Matt. 3:7; 12:34; 23:33; Luke 3: 7; ASV "offspring"; RSV "brood"); *génos,* race (I Pet. 2:9; ASV, RSV "race"); (4) Matthew 24:34 and parallels Mark 13:30 and Luke 21:32 present a special problem. If "this generation" (*geneá*) refers to the people then living, these verses, despite their position, must relate to the destruction of Jerusalem and not to the Second Coming of Christ. But the meaning may be that the generation which sees the beginning of the special signs of the Second Coming will see the end of them. Another interpretation is that "generation" here refers to the Jewish nation. *Geneá* may bear the sense of *nation* or *race.*   E.R.

GENESIS (jĕn′ĕ-sĭs), the first book of the Bible. The name is derived from a Greek word meaning "origin" or "beginning," which is the title given to the book in the Septuagint. The Hebrew name for the book is *berēshîth,* from Genesis 1:1 ("in the beginning"). The special phrase, "These are the generations of" divides the book into eleven sections (2:4, 5:1, 6:9, 10:1, 11:10, 11:27, 25:12, 25:19, 36:1, and 37:2), and serves as a superscription to the section that follows it. These sections do not describe the origin of the person mentioned in the superscription (or of "the heavens and earth" in the case of 2:4), but rather the further history of the one whose origin has already been described, plus that of his immediate offspring. A broader outline divides the book into two unequal sections. Genesis 1:1 through 11:26 describes the creation of the heavens, the earth, plants, animals, and man; the Fall and the Edenic curse; the antediluvian age and the great Flood; and the descendants of Noah down to Terah. Genesis 11:27 through 50:26 traces the history of Abraham and Lot; Ishmael and Isaac; Jacob and Esau; and Joseph and his brethren in Egypt.

GENESIS 1-11 AND UNIFORMITARIAN SCIENCE. Evangelical scholars have differed widely in their reaction to the claims of uniformitarian and evolutionary science that the earth has existed for billions of years, that animals preceded man by millions of years, that man has been on earth for hundreds of thousands of years, and that the Flood could have covered only a small part of the earth. Various attempts to harmonize Genesis with uniformitarian theories have gained wide acceptance among evangelicals, but such harmonizations reveal fatal inconsistencies and concessions which render them Biblically untenable. The Scriptural doctrine of a geographically universal and geologically significant Flood actually undermines the entire superstructure of uniformitarianism; for such a catastrophe, continuing for an entire year and covering all the high mountains of the antediluvian earth, must, of absolute necessity, have accomplished a vast amount of geologic work in a relatively short period (cf. H. C. Leupold, *Exposi-*

tion *of Genesis,* Columbus: The Wartburg Press, 1942, pp. 201, 296, 301; and J. C. Whitcomb and H. M. Morris, *The Genesis Flood,* Nutley, N. J.: The Presbyterian and Reformed Pub. Co., 1961, pp. 76, 123, 265-72). See FLOOD.

It is difficult to find room in Genesis 1-11 for the vast periods of time which are demanded by uniformitarians. The Scriptures reveal that the heavens, the earth, the sea, "and all that in them is" were created within six days, and therefore that man should labor for six days (Exod. 20:9-11). This is not the only indication that the days of creation were literal 24-hour days. (1) Although the word "day" sometimes refers to a period of undetermined length (cf. Joel 1:15), it always refers to a 24-hour period when a numerical adjective accompanies it, as it does six times in the first chapter of Genesis. (2) The phrase "evening and morning" is a technical Hebrew phrase meaning 24 hours (cf. Dan. 8:14 ASV). (3) Plants (created the third day) could hardly have survived a geologic age without sunlight (created the fourth day). If Moses had wanted to express the idea that the sun was simply made visible on the fourth day he could have used such a term as "appear" (verse 9). All attempts to make the days of creation correspond to the geologic ages have failed. For example, the Bible states that fruit trees were created two days before marine organisms; but paleontologists of the uniformitarian school insist that marine life existed millions of years before fruit trees. Other harmonization efforts, such as the revelatory view and the framework hypothesis, are contradicted by the plain reading of the text (cf. Paul A. Zimmerman, ed., *Darwin, Evolution, and Creation,* St. Louis: Concordia Pub. House, 1959, pp. 57-64).

The basic incompatibility of Genesis and uniformitarianism is seen further in the fact that Adam is said to have had dominion over the entire animal kingdom and that the diet of both man and beast was vegetarian (1:26-30; cf. Isa. 11:6-9). This could hardly have been the case if animals had been dying, devouring each other, and in many cases whole species becoming extinct millions of years before Adam's creation. Romans 8: 20-22 teaches that "the whole creation groaneth and travaileth in pain" under "the bondage of corruption" as a consequence of Adam's fall. To postulate a "reign of tooth and claw" during vast ages before Adam would be to undermine the force of this passage. In contradiction to uniformitarian hypotheses, Genesis reveals that God created the heavens and the earth as a dynamic, functioning entity. Thus, even as Adam was created instantly as a grown man, so also the earth and its living creatures were created fully "grown" within six days, with the oceans already containing the salts and chemicals necessary for sustaining marine life (1:2,10,20), the dry land equipped with a mantle of soil for plants and trees (1:11), the light rays from distant stars already performing their God-intended function of shining upon the earth (1:14-19), and the animals and plants created after their kinds (1:11,12,20-25). The "grown creation" doctrine is simply the Biblical doctrine of creation rightly understood, and is illustrated in the NT by the miracle of the changing of water to wine (John 2:1-11). The presuppositions which underlie the various age-determination methods of modern geology may be properly challenged, therefore, by those who accept the Biblical doctrine of creation (cf. John W. Klotz, *Genes, Genesis, and Evolution,* St. Louis: Concordia Pub. House, 1955, pp. 86-96).

GENESIS 12-50 AND ARCHAEOLOGICAL DISCOVERY. In spite of a century and a half of attacks by scholars of the critical school, the unity and Mosaic authorship of Genesis have been successfully defended by orthodox scholars, and the documentary hypothesis has been shown to rest upon false presuppositions (cf. O. T. Allis, *The Five Books of Moses,* Nutley, N. J.: The Presbyterian & Reformed Pub. Co., 1943). Furthermore, the entire field of OT studies has been revolutionized in recent decades by the discovery of vast numbers of clay tablets which shed important light upon ancient Near Eastern history and customs. Over 100,000 of these tablets date to the early second millennium B.C., and therefore fall within the patriarchal period (cf. D. J. Wiseman, *Illustrations From Biblical Archaeology,* Grand Rapids: Wm. B. Eerdmans Pub. Co., 1958, p. 25). Only a few of the discoveries which shed light on Genesis can be listed here.

Abraham's choice of Eliezer of Damascus to be his heir (15:2-4) corresponds to ancient Semitic and Hurrian custom, which provided that the adopted heir yield his rights in case a natural son should be born (Wiseman, *op. cit.,* p. 25). Sarah was only following the ways of her contemporaries when she gave Hagar to Abraham to bear a child for him (16:1-3), and Abraham was understandably grieved when Sarah later insisted on driving out both Hagar and Ishmael (21:11), for a Nuzi legal document (c. 1500 B.C.) states that "if Kelim-ninu (the bride) does not bear, Kelim-ninu shall acquire a woman of the land of Lullu (a slave) as wife for Shennima (the bridegroom), and Kelim-ninu may not send the offspring away" (James B. Pritchard, ed., *Ancient Near Eastern Texts,* Princeton University Press, 1950, p. 220). Furthermore, Nuzi sale-adoption documents have shed light on Jacob's relationship to Laban. We thus discover that possession of the household gods marked a person as the legitimate heir, and that the adopted son forfeited his inheritance if he took another wife outside of the family. This explains Rachel's theft of Laban's teraphim (31:19) and Laban's warning that Jacob should take no other wives besides his daughters (31:50) (Pritchard, *op. cit.,* pp. 219-220). We have also learned that personal names like Abraham, Isaac, and Jacob were current in those days; that Shechem, Ai, Bethel, and Dothan were thriving cities around 2000 B.C.; that the Negev region and the Jordan valley were also thickly populated; and that Sodom and Gomorrah were destroyed about that time and their ruins lie under the waters of the Dead Sea (Wiseman, *op. cit.,* pp. 29-30).

With regard to the patriarchs in Egypt, important archaeological discoveries have also been made (see EXODUS). For example, it is now recognized that Abraham could have had camels in Egypt (12:16) (cf. Joseph P. Free, "Abraham's Camels," JNES, July, 1944, pp. 187-93), and that groups of Semites migrated into Egypt as early as 2000 B.C. (tomb paintings at Beni Hassan). A recently published papyrus dating to about 1800 B.C. "lists seventy-nine servants in an Egyptian household, forty-five of whom are 'Asiatics', probably sold into Egypt as slaves . . . Some of them bear good Hebrew names like Shiphrah and Menahem" (Wiseman, *op. cit.,* p. 39). A great many examples

PLAIN OF GENNESARET and the Sea of Galilee, as viewed from Bethsaida. Today, as in Bible times, the plain is extraordinarily fertile. It has rich, loamy, well-watered soil.

of authentic Egyptian coloring in the patriarchal narrative of Genesis 39-50 have now been fully illustrated by archaeological discoveries (cf. M. F. Unger, *Archaeology and the Old Testament,* Grand Rapids: Zondervan Pub. House, 1954, pp. 132-34). In the words of the eminent archaeologist William Foxwell Albright, "So many corroborations of details have been discovered in recent years that most competent scholars have given up the old critical theory according to which stories of the Patriarchs are mostly retrojections from the time of the Dual Monarchy (9th-8th centuries B.C.)." (*From the Stone Age to Christianity,* 2nd ed., New York: Doubleday & Co., 1957, p. 241.) J.C.W.

GENNESARET (gĕ-nĕs'à-rĕt). 1. "The land of Gennesaret" (Matt. 14:34; Mark 6:53), a plain stretching about three miles along the northwest shore of the Sea of Galilee, extending about a mile inland: the modern el-Ghuweir. With a rich, loamy, well-watered soil, today as in Bible times it is extraordinarily fertile; the only easily tillable land bordering the Sea of Galilee. The fig, olive, palm and walnut trees, which ordinarily require diverse conditions, all grow well here.

2. "The Lake of Gennesaret" (Luke 5:1), elsewhere in Luke simply "the lake" (5:2; 8:22,23,33); the same as the Sea of Galilee (Matt. 4:18; 15:29; Mark 1:16; 7:31; John 6:1); or the OT "Sea of Chinnereth."

GENTILES (jĕn'tĭlz, Heb. *gôy,* plural *gôyîm, nation, people*), translated "Gentiles" in KJV of the OT 30 times, "people" 11 times, "heathen" 142 times, "nation" 373 times, "nation" being the usual translation in ASV, RSV. Sometimes *gôy* refers to Israel (Gen. 12:2; Deut. 32:28; Josh. 3:17; 4:1; 10:13; II Sam. 7:23; Isa. 1:4; Zeph. 2:9; translated "nation" or "people" in KJV as well as ASV, RSV). But *'âm* is the ordinary term for Israel.

Gôy usually means a non-Israelite people. In the NT, Greek *éthnos* renders *gôy*, while *laós, people,* corresponds to Heb. *'âm. Éthnos* is translated "Gentiles" in the NT in KJV, ASV and RSV. *Héllenes, Greeks,* is translated "Gentiles" in KJV, "Greeks" in ASV, RSV (John 7:35; Rom. 2:9,10; 3:9; I Cor. 10:32; 12:13).

Under conditions of peace, considerate treatment was accorded Gentiles under OT law (e.g., Deut. 10:19; 24:14,15; Num. 35:15; Ezek. 47:22). Men of Israel often married Gentile women, of whom Rahab, Ruth and Bathsheba are notable examples, but the practice was frowned upon after the return from exile (Ezra 9:12; 10:2-44; Neh. 10:30; 13:23-31). Separation between Jew and Gentile became more strict, until in the NT period the hostility is complete. Persecution embittered the Jew, and he retaliated by hatred of everything Gentile, and by avoidance, so far as was possible, of contact with Gentiles. The intensity of this feeling varied, and gave way before unusual kindness (Luke 7:4,5).

While the teachings of Jesus ultimately broke down "the middle wall of partition" between Jew and Gentile, as is seen in the writings of Paul (Rom. 1:16; I Cor. 1:24; Gal. 3:28; Eph. 2:14; Col. 3:11) and in Acts, yet Jesus limited His ministry to Jews, with rare exceptions (the half-Jewish Samaritans, John 4:1-42, the Syrophoenician woman, Matt. 15:21-28; Mark 7:24-30; the Greeks in John 12:20-36). He instructed His twelve disciples, "Go not into the way of the Gentiles, and into any city of the Samaritans enter ye not" (Matt. 10:5); but did not repeat this injunction when He sent out the Seventy (Luke 10:1-16). Jesus' mission was first to "his own" (John 1:11), the Chosen People of God; but ultimately to "as many as received him" (John 1:12). Limitations of time held His ministry on earth within the bounds of Israel; reaching the Gentiles was left to the activity of the Holy Spirit working through His disciples.

In Acts, from the appointment of Paul as the apostle to the Gentiles (9:15), the Gentiles become increasingly prominent. Even the letters addressed particularly to Jewish Christians (James; I Pet.; Heb.; Rom. 9-11) are relevant to Gentiles also. The division of all mankind into two classes, Jew and Gentile, emphasizes the importance of the Jews as the people through whom God made salvation available to all people.   E.R.

GENUBATH (gē-nū'băth, Heb. *genuvath, theft*), a son of Hadad the Edomite, the fugitive prince, by the sister of Queen Tahpenes, the wife of the pharaoh who governed Egypt toward the end of David's reign (I Kings 11:20).

GERA (gē'rà, Heb. *gērā', grain*), a name common in the tribe of Benjamin. 1. A son of Benjamin (Gen. 46:21).

2. A son of Bela and grandson of Benjamin (I Chron. 8:3,5).

3. Father of Ehud (Judg. 3:15).

4. A son of Ehud (I Chron. 8:7).

5. Father of Shimei (II Sam. 16:5; 19:16,18; I Kings 2:8). Some of these are thought to be the same person, taking "father" to mean a remote ancestor, and "son" a remote descendant.

GERAR (gē'ràr, Heb. *gerār, circle, region*), a town in the Negev, near but not on the Mediterranean coast south of Gaza, in a valley running northwest and southeast, and on a protected inland caravan route from Palestine to Egypt (Gen. 10:19). Here Abraham sojourned with its king, Abimelech (Gen. 20:1,2); and later Isaac (Gen. 26:1-33) had similar and more extended experiences with the king and people of the region. Here Asa and his army defeated the Ethiopians, and plundered Gerar and the cities round about (II Chron. 14: 13,14). Its site is thought to be the modern Tell ej-Jemmeh, which has been excavated, uncovering levels of occupation from the Late Bronze Age to the Byzantine period.

GERASA (gē-rà'sà), a city E of the Jordan midway between the Sea of Galilee and the Dead Sea, in the Decapolis at the eastern edge of the Peraea; partially excavated; the modern Jerash. The name does not occur in the Bible, but the adjective Gerasenes occurs in Mark 5:1 ASV, RSV, and the mar-

THE DEMONIAC, now miraculously cured, watched the herd of pigs run headlong into the Sea of Galilee. Jesus had commanded the unclean spirits to leave the demoniac and had permitted them to enter the swine.

ROMAN RUINS AT ANCIENT GERASA, showing the theater and the forum. Beyond the ruins lies the present village of Jerash. Gerasa was one of the leading cities of the Decapolis. The adjective "Gerasenes" occurs in the New Testament as one of the designations for the place where Christ healed the demoniacs. Another designation is "Gedarenes."

gin of Matthew 8:28 RSV and Luke 8:26,37 RSV. The MSS vary in all these passages between Gadarenes, Gerasenes and Gergesenes; and all the above occurrences relate to the region where Jesus healed a demoniac and permitted the demons which possessed the man to rush down a steep slope into the Sea of Galilee, hence this incident must have occurred on the shore. A possible location is at Kursi (Gergesa) on the eastern shore of the lake. Gadara (Muqeis) is SE of Lake Galilee. The place where the Gospel incident occurred may have been referred to sometimes as the country of the Gergesenes, a purely local name; or of the Gadarenes, from the nearest city; or of the Gerasenes, from the most important city of the district. See GADARA.

GERGESA (gûr-gē′sà), a place probably midway of the eastern shore of Lake Galilee, where the bank is steep. The adjective Gergesenes occurs in Matthew 8:28 KJV and RSV margin; Mark 5:1 RSV margin; and Luke 8:26,37 ASV, RSV margins. See GADARA.

GERIZIM (gĕ-rī′zĭm, gĕr′ĭ-zĭm), a mountain of Samaria, Jebel et-Tôr, 2,849 feet high, SW of Mt. Ebal. Through the valley between runs a main N-S road of Palestine, so that this pass is of strategic military importance. Moses commanded that when the Israelites came into the Promised Land, the blessing for keeping the law should be spoken from Mt. Gerizim, and the curse for not obeying it from Mt. Ebal (Deut. 11:29; 27:4-26), six tribes standing on the slopes of either peak (Deut. 27: 11-14). It is conjectured that Mt. Gerizim was selected for the blessing and Mt. Ebal for the curse, from the point of view of one looking eastward, to whom Mt. Gerizim would be on the right or "fortunate" side. From the top of Mt. Gerizim Jotham shouted his parable of the trees to the men of Shechem in the valley below, reminding them of all that his father Gideon had done for them (Judg. 9: 7-21). After the Israelites, returning from Babylonian exile, refused to let the mixed races of Samaria help rebuild Jerusalem (Ezra 4:1-4; Neh. 2:19,20; 13:28), the Samaritans built themselves a temple on Mt. Gerizim. "This mountain" referred to in John 4:20,21, is Gerizim, where the Samaritans worshiped in the open, after their temple was destroyed by the Maccabees. The small Samaritan community of Nablus still celebrates the Passover on Mt. Gerizim. Samaritan tradition maintains that Abraham attempted to sacrifice Isaac on this mountain (Gen. 22:1-19); that at a nearby Salem he met Melchizedek (Gen. 14:17-20); and that

745

MOUNT GERIZIM, towering above the ruins of the ancient ramparts of Shechem. The Samaritans built a temple on Mt. Gerizim, and worshipped in the open after their temple had been destroyed by the Maccabees.

Jacob's dream (Gen. 28:10-17) occurred at Khirbet Lanzah on Mt. Gerizim. The ruins of a fortress built by the Emperor Justinian in 533 A.D. remain. A rock with a cup-shaped hollow which could have been used for libations, is the traditional altar of the Samaritan temple. The Nablus community also possesses an important MS of the Pentateuch.

GERSHOM (gûr'shŏm, from Heb. *gārash, to cast out*, but in popular etymology explained as from *gēr, stranger*, Exod. 2:22; 18:3). 1. The first-born son of Moses and Zipporah. He was born in Midian (Exod. 2:22; 18:3; I Chron. 23:15,16; 26:24). The unusual circumstances of his circumcision are told in Exodus 4:21-28.

2. The eldest son of Levi, according to I Chronicles 6:16,17,20,43,62,71; 15:7). Elsewhere called Gershon. See Gershon.

3. One of the family of Phinehas, and one of the "heads of houses" who returned with Ezra from Babylon (Ezra 8:2).

4. Father of Jonathan, the Levite who became priest to the Danites who settled in Laish (Judg. 18:30). KJV calls him "son of Manasseh," but ASV, RSV have "sons of Moses," since the "n" in the Heb. text which converts the consonants of Moses into Manasseh is thought to have been inserted to disguise the fact that Moses had such a graceless descendant as this Jonathan.

GERSHON (gûr'shŏn, Heb. *gēreshôn*), firstborn of the three sons of Levi (Gen. 46:11; Exod. 6:16,

17; Num. 3:17,18,21,25; 4:22,28,38; 7:7; 10:17; 26:57; Josh. 21:6; I Chron. 6:1; 23:6). His descendants are also called Gershonites (Num. 3:21, 23,24; 4:24,27; Josh. 21:33; I Chron. 23:7; 26:21; 29:8; II Chron. 29:12). The functions of the Gershonites during the wilderness wanderings are described in Numbers 3:23-25; 4:21-28; for which functions two wagons and four oxen were deemed sufficient (Num. 7:7). They continued prominent in the service of the Temple of Solomon, and in that of Zerubbabel, especially as singers. See also GERSHOM 2.

GERZITES (gûr'zīts), **GIZRITES** (gĭz'rīts), or **GERIZZITES** (gĕ-rīz'īts, gĕr'ī-zīts), a tribe named between the Geshurites and the Amalekites (I Sam. 27:8), KJV Gezrites; ASV Girzites, margin Gizrites; RSV Girzites. They are called the ancient inhabitants of the land, on the way to Shur, toward Egypt; that is, in the S or Negev of Judah; not certainly connected with Gezer. If originally of Gezer, they may have been driven S by invading Israelites or Philistines.

GESHAM (gē'shăm), a son of Jahdai and descendant of Caleb (I Chron. 2:47). KJV Gesham; ASV, RSV Geshan, also the 1611 edition of KJV.

GESHEM (gē'shĕm), the Arabian who along with Sanballat and Tobiah, sought to oppose the building of the wall by Nehemiah (Neh. 2:19; 6:1,2). The same as Gashnu (Neh. 6:6).

GESHUR (gē'shûr, Heb. *geshûr, bridge*). 1. A country in Syria (II Sam. 15:8; ASV margin and RSV, Aram) on the western border of Og's kingdom of Bashan E of the Jordan (Josh. 12:5). Jair of Manasseh conquered Bashan up to Geshur (Deut. 3:14). Although in the territory of Israel, the Geshurites were not driven out (Josh. 13:11,13) but "dwelt in the midst of Israel." In fact, Geshur and Aram took from Jair sixty towns (I Chron. 2:23 ASV, RSV) though KJV makes it appear that Jair took the cities from Gilead. David made alliance with their king Talmai by marrying his daughter Maacah (II Sam. 3:3; I Chron. 3:2). Her son Absalom, after he murdered Amnon, sought refuge with her father (II Sam. 13:37,38), whence Joab brought Absalom back (II Sam. 14:23,32; 15:8).

2. A district between southern Palestine and Sinai, near Philistine territory (Josh. 13:2), unconquered at the close of Joshua's career; against which David made a raid when he was taking refuge from Saul among the Philistines (I Sam. 27:8). Whether these Geshurites were a branch of the same people as 1, is undetermined.

GETHER (gē'thêr), third of Aram's sons (Gen. 10:23; I Chron. 1:17). The latter reference reckons him among the sons of Shem.

GETHSEMANE (gĕth-sĕm'á-nē, probably from the Aramaic for "oil-press"), the place of Jesus' agony and arrest (Matt. 26:36-56; Mark 14:32-52; Luke 22:39-54; John 18:1-12—John tells of the arrest only). In Matthew 26:36; Mark 14:32 it is called "a place"; Luke does not give the name, says that the place was one to which Jesus customarily resorted, and that it was on the Mount of Olives; John 18:1, also without naming it, explains that it was a garden across the Cedron (Kidron) valley from Jerusalem. The traditional site, cared for by the Franciscans, is not far from the road, near the bridge over the Kidron, and is laid out in neat gardens. Within are eight large olive trees. If the Emperor Titus destroyed all the trees around Jeru-

GARDEN OF GETHSEMANE, beneath the east city wall of Jerusalem, traditional site of Jesus' agony and arrest. Within the garden is an olive grove, attended by Franciscans. Armenian, Greek and Russian churches claim other olive groves nearby as the true site.

salem during the siege of 70 A.D., as Josephus asserts, these trees cannot be so old as the time of Jesus, but they are certainly ancient, and they add to the atmosphere of a place where Christian devotion centers. Armenian, Greek and Russian churches claim other olive groves nearby as the correct site. It is certainly in the vicinity. The sufferings of Christ as His hour approached, portrayed by Matthew, Mark and Luke, and the humiliation of His arrest, told by all four evangelists, concentrate the reverent thought and feeling of believers, so that the very name Gethsemane evokes the love and adoration due to the Saviour who prayed here.   E.R.

GEUEL (gē-ū′ĕl), a son of Machi, a prince of Gad and the representative of the Gadite tribe sent out to explore Canaan (Num. 13:15).

GEZER (gē′zêr, Heb. *gezer, portion*), a fortified place, Tell-Jezer, 18 miles NW of Jerusalem, between the valley of Sorek and the valley of Aijalon. It lies S of the main road from Jerusalem to Jaffa (Haifa), and E of the railroad. The site was identified by M. Clermont-Ganneau in 1873, and excavated by R. A. S. Macalister in 1904-7. Prehistoric inhabitants occupied caves on the rocky heights. Its military importance, overlooking main routes through the country, has led to its occupation in many periods of history. The Egyptians captured Gezer about 1500 B.C., but their power decreased a century or so later. When Israel entered the land, Horam king of Gezer came to help Lachish, after their king had been killed following the battle of the day on which the sun stood still (Josh. 10:1-34). Horam and "his people," that is, his army, were destroyed completely, but Gezer was not taken. The king of Gezer is listed (Josh. 12:12) among those whom Joshua smote (defeated). Gezer is on the southern boundary of Ephraim, near the Bethhorons (Josh. 16:3-10; I Chron. 7:28). The inhabitants of Gezer were not driven out (Josh. 16:10; Judg. 1:29) but later became slave-labor. Gezer was one of the cities given to the Kohathite Levites (Josh. 21: 21; I Chron. 6:67). David smote the Philistines as far as Gezer (I Chron. 20:4; also Gazer, KJV, Gezer in ASV, RSV, in II Sam. 5:25; I Chron. 14:16), but it remained for Solomon to reduce the people of Gezer to forced labor, and to rebuild the city, which the pharaoh of Egypt had taken and burnt and given to Solomon as a dowry with his daughter (I Kings 9:15-17). Gezer was occupied in the Greek period. Though not mentioned in the NT, it was known in NT times as Gazara. The Crusaders fortified Gezer, and it has undergone several changes of owners since then. Archaeological remains illustrate the life of the people fully.   E.R.

GHOR, THE (gôr), the upper level of the Jordan valley, about 150 feet above the Zor or jungle through which the river channel winds.

GHOST (gōst), the human spirit as distinguished from the body. Ghost translates Heb. *nephesh, breath* (of life) in KJV, ASV of Job 11:20 (RSV, *breathe their last*), and Jeremiah 15:9 (RSV, *swooned away*). Heb. *gāwa', gasp out, expire,* is used of Abraham (Gen. 25:8), Ishmael (Gen. 25:17), Isaac (Gen. 35:29) and Jacob (Gen. 49:33); in all which cases RSV has "breathed his last." For *gāwa'* in Job 3:11; 10:18; 13:19; 14:10, RSV uses varied expressions. In the NT, "ghost" renders Greek *pneúma, breath, spirit,* in Matthew 27:50; John 19:30 KJV: ASV, RSV have "spirit." Gr. *ekpnéo, breathe out,* appears in Mark 15:37,39; Luke 23:46 KJV, ASV: RSV has "breathed his last." These four Gospel references all relate to Jesus. In Acts 5:5 (Ananias); 5:10 (Sapphira); 12:23 (Herod), RSV has "died" for Greek *ekpsýcho, lose consciousness, expire.* "Holy Ghost" in KJV is translated "Holy Spirit" in ASV, RSV.

GIAH (gī'á), an unknown place near Gibeon, where Joab overtook Abner (II Sam. 2:24).

GIANTS. The first mention of giants in the Bible is in Genesis 6:4, where ASV, RSV have *Nephilim,* a Heb. word of uncertain etymology. Nephilim were found in Canaan when the spies went through the land (Num. 13:33; KJV giants). Beside their huge stature the spies felt like grasshoppers. Once (Job 16:14) "giant" translates Heb. *gibbôr,* which RSV text renders "warrior," ASV margin "mighty man," its usual meaning. The other Heb. words translated "giant" are *rāphā', rāphâh,* and the plural *rephāîm,* of uncertain etymology. The giants whom the Israelites met when they attempted to enter Canaan through Moab (Deut. 2:11,20), are called Rephaim in ASV, RSV. They resembled the Anakim, and the Moabites called them Emims, while the Ammonites called them Zamzummims. They were tall, large-framed and powerful. The last of this race was Og, king of Bashan, whose iron bedstead, nine cubits long, was famous (Deut. 2:11; Josh. 12:4; 3:12). The giant Rephaim were a vanishing race when the Israelites came out of Egypt. The land of the giants (Rephaim) is referred to in Joshua 17:15; the valley of the giants or Rephaim, located southwest of Jerusalem, in Joshua 15:8; 18:16. The Rephaim are named in Genesis 14:5; 15:20; the valley of Rephaim in II Samuel 5:18,22; 23:13; I Chronicles 11:15; 14:9; Isaiah 17:5. So the memory of this fearsome race persisted in their ancient haunts. II Samuel 21:15-22 records encounters of some of David's mighty men with descendants of the giant (Raphah). But the best known giant of all, Goliath of Gath, champion of the Philistines, whom David as a youth slew (I Sam. 17), though described as of a huge stature and great strength, is not called a giant on that account. It was not necessary to name the obvious. Thus giants terrorized the Israelites from their entry into Canaan until the time of David. Tall men like Saul were admired (I Sam. 10:23); the Lord had to remind Samuel not to consider height when choosing the next king (I Sam. 16:7). Isaiah 45:14 notes that the Sabeans were tall. The question, How tall is a giant? can be answered only in terms of the average height of the race which is using the term. Giants were abnormally strong, yet they had their weak points, as David's victory over Goliath proved.

GIBBAR (gĭb'ár), a man whose children returned from captivity with Zerubbabel (Ezra 2:20). Perhaps the Gibeon of Nehemiah 7:25.

GIBBETHON (gĭb'ē-thŏn), Tell el-Melât, W of Gezer in the territory of Dan (Josh. 19:44), allotted to the Kohathite Levites (Josh. 21:23). Baasha killed King Nadab at Gibbethon while Israel was besieging the city, which was now in the hands of the Philistines (I Kings 15:27). A quarter century later Israel again besieged Gibbethon, and Omri was made king there by the army, upon receiving news that Zimri had killed Baasha (I Kings 16:15-17), whereupon the army abandoned the siege of Gibbethon.

GIBEA (gĭb'ē-à), a son of Sheva, and grandson of Caleb (I Chron. 2:49).

GIBEAH (gĭb'ē-à). 1. A city in the hill country of Judah, site unknown (Josh. 15:57).

2. A city of Benjamin (Josh. 18:28), modern Tell el-Fûl, in NT times Gabath Saul; on the E side of the N-S road a few miles north of Jerusalem and on a height commanding a view of the latter; Gibeah of Saul, where excavation has uncovered the rustic but strong fortress-palace from which Saul ruled Israel. Here in the time of the Judges took place the abuse of a Levite's concubine, which brought on war between Benjamin and the rest of Israel (Judg. 19,20). The transactions at Gibeah during the reign of Saul are recorded in I Samuel 10:26; 11:4; 13:2,15,16; 14:2, (ASV, RSV have Geba); 14:16; 15:34; 22:6; 23:19; 26:1. Also ASV margin has Gibeah instead of "the hill," referring to the place where stood the house of Abinadab to which the ark of God was brought when it was returned by the Philistines (I Sam. 7:1), and whence David brought it to Jerusalem (II Sam. 6:3). Here seven of Saul's descendants were hanged to satisfy the vengeance of the Gibeonites (II Sam. 21:6; RSV has Gibeon). One of David's mighty men was from Gibeah of Benjamin (II Sam. 23:29; I Chron. 11:31). The people of Gibeah fled when the Assyrians marched toward them (Isa. 10:29). Hosea calls for a warning (Hos. 5:8) at Gibeah because of the sins Israel has committed "from the days of Gibeah" (Hos. 9:9; 10:9); the sins of Saul's reign had been remembered for centuries.

GIBEATH (gĭb'ē-äth, Josh. 18:28), probably the same as Gibeah of Saul, which see. RSV text has Gibeah; margin Heb. Gibeath.

GIBEON (gĭb'ē-ŏn, Heb. *giv'ôn, pertaining to a hill*), a city of Benjamin (Josh. 18:25) NW of Jerusalem; in NT times Gabao; modern ej-Jib. It was given to the priests (Josh. 21:17). At the time of the Conquest, Joshua, without consulting the Lord, was deceived by the ambassadors of Gibeon into making a treaty with them (Josh. 9) whereby he promised not to destroy them. Upon discovering the deception, though their lives were spared, they were made woodcutters and water-carriers. A coalition of Canaanite kings attacked Gibeon because they had made peace with Joshua (Josh. 10), whereupon Joshua came to the aid of Gibeon, and the battle was fought in which Joshua called upon the sun to stand still to give him time for more fighting (alluded to in Isa. 28:21). No other city made peace with Israel (Josh. 11:19). Gibeon was the chief of four Hivite cities (Josh. 9:17). Abner representing Israel, and Joab representing David, met at a pool, the remains of which may still be seen, at Gibeon; and here, after an indecisive contest between two groups of twelve men each, a disastrous battle was fought (II Sam. 2:1-28; 3:30), following which Abner and Joab agreed to a cessation of the fighting. At a great stone in Gibeon Joab slew Amasa (II Sam. 20:8). David smote the Philistines from Gibeon on the north to Gezer on the south (I Chron. 14:16). Zadok the priest was assigned to minister at the high place in Gibeon (I Chron. 16:39,40; 21:29). Solomon, at the outset of his reign, came to Gibeon to sacrifice, and to dream — to good purpose (I Kings 3:3-15; II Chron. 1:2-13). Again Solomon received a message from the Lord here (I Kings 9:1-9). In I Chronicles 8:29; 9:35 we read of the father of Gibeon, husband of Maachah, dwelling there. People from Gibeon returned to Jerusalem from the captivity and helped build the walls (Neh. 3:7; 7:25). Jeremiah confronted a false prophet from Gibeon in the temple (Jer. 28:1). Gibeon is the scene of a rescue of Israelites during the Assyrian occupation (Jer. 41:11-16).   E.R.

GIBEONITES (gĭb′ē-ŏn-īts), the inhabitants of Gibeon; Hivites (Josh. 9:3,7), Hurrians or Horites (Gen. 36:20; Deut. 2:12) who had formerly lived in Edom. Because of the deceitful manner in which they gained the favor of Joshua, they were made slave-laborers for menial tasks such as chopping wood and drawing water (Josh. 9). They were the peasants of the Mittannian empire which in 1500 B.C. reached from Media to the Mediterranean. Its rulers were Indo-Aryans, its peasants of another but non-Semitic race. The Gibeonites and their allies, at the time of the Conquest by Joshua, controlled a tetrapolis of four cities — Beeroth, Chephirah, Kirjath-baal and Gibeon. Because of a prolonged famine, David inquired of the Lord and learned that the cause was blood-guilt because

VILLAGE OF GIBEON, northwest of Jerusalem. The battle in which Joshua called upon the sun to stand still was waged to aid Gibeon against the Canaanites.

THE GIBEONITES were a pitiful sight as they hobbled into Joshua's camp. They were ragged, hungry, wore torn sandals, and carried old, patched water bags. Joshua felt sorry for the Gibeonites and gladly made a treaty with them. When he discovered their treachery, he reprimanded them severely and decreed that henceforth some of their people would always be slaves for the Israelites.

Saul had massacred the Gibeonites; wherefore David delivered up seven descendants of Saul to their vengeance (II Sam. 21:1-9). A Gibeonite was leader of David's thirty mighty men (I Chron. 12:4). Gibeonites helped repair the walls of Jerusalem (Neh. 3:7).

GIBLITES (gĭb'lĭts), the inhabitants of Gebal or Byblos (Josh. 13:5; ASV, RSV Gebalites). The Gebalites (ASV) or men of Gebal (RSV) are called stonesquarers in KJV of I Kings 5:18. See GEBAL.

GIDDALTI (gĭ-dăl'tī), a son of Heman, and one of the heads of music (I Chron. 25:4,29).

GIDDEL (gĭd'ĕl). 1. A member of the family of Nethinims who returned from exile with Zerubbabel (Ezra 2:47; Neh. 7:49).

2. Sons of Giddel; descendants of Solomon's servants who also came up to Jerusalem from exile (Ezra 5:26; Neh. 7:58).

GIDEON (gĭd'ē-ŏn, Heb. *gidh'ôn, feller* or *hewer*), the son of Joash, an Abiezrite (Judg. 6:11), who lived in Ophrah, not far from Mt. Gerizim, not the Ophrah of Benjamin (Josh. 18:23). The record about Gideon is found in Judges 6:1-9:6. When he is first mentioned he was a mature man. His first-born, Jether, was a youth (8:20). Gideon had already become a noted warrior (6:12), perhaps by waging "underground" warfare against the marauding Midianites. The extent to which the people had been enslaved is shown by the fact that Gideon had to hide in a winepress to do the threshing (6:11). That the messenger who called Gideon to lead Israel was from God was attested to by supernatural fire which consumed a sacrifice which he had placed upon a rock (6:17-23).

Gideon responded to the call and, with the help of some friends, overthrew the altar of Baal and

GIDEON'S FOUNTAIN, at the foot of the Mountains of Gilboa. Gideon delivered Israel from the Midianites.

cut down the sacred grove around it. He erected instead a new altar, naming it Jahveh-Shalom, *Jehovah gives peace* (6:24). For his daring feat the followers of Baal wanted to slay him, but his father intervened. Instead of death he was given a new name, Jerubbaal, or "Contender with Baal" (6:28-32). Later the name was changed to Jerubbesheth, "Contender with the Idol," evidently to eliminate any recognition of Baal (II Sam. 11:21). Gideon then issued a call to adjoining tribesmen to war against the Midianites. Having gathered a formidable host, he sought to know the surety of his faith and so put forth the famous test of the fleece (6:36-40). As further assurance, he was instructed to slip into the enemy's camp, and there he overhead one soldier tell another of a dream and interpret it as meaning that Gideon's smaller army would win the battle (7:9-14). To prevent human boasting over victory, God instructed Gideon to reduce his force to 300 picked men by (1) letting the faint-hearted go home; and (2) by choosing only such men as were cautious enough to dip their drinking water while passing over a stream (7:1-8). Thus came the famous army of 300.

By a piece of strategy, involving psychological warfare, Gideon's small band surprised the enemy by a night attack. Three groups of 100 each attacked from three directions. At the proper time a signal was given, shields for the lights were removed, and trumpets blared forth. The sleeping Midianites were terrified. So complete was their rout that they slew one another in the mad flight (7:15-22). Gideon then called upon his allies to join in the chase. Ephraim captured two of the kings (8:1-3). Gideon pursued the other two northward and captured them near the confluence of the Sea of Galilee and the Jordan (8:4-21). Thus the country was delivered all the way to the Jordan (7:22,23; 8:1-21). When his people would have made him king, Gideon refused and instead called for an offering of the golden trinkets which had been captured from the Midianites. With these he made an ephod, either an image of Jehovah, or a sacred vestment worn by a priest in the sanctuary. Because of its worth and beauty, it later became an object of worship (8:24-27). Gideon's ability and statesmanship are shown in his long and fruitful ministry of forty years as judge (8:28). During his life he begat 71 sons, one, Abimelech, by a concubine of Shechem. After Gideon's death idolatry returned (8:32-35), Abimelech seized an opportune time, engaged mercenaries, invaded the land of Gideon, and destroyed all the seventy sons except Jotham who escaped by a bit of strategy (9:1-6).   J.D.F.

GIDEONI (gĭd'ē-ō'nī, *cutter down*), a prince of Benjamin's tribe (Num. 7:60) whose son ruled them (10:24).

GIDOM (gĭ'dŏm, Heb. *gidh'ōm, desolation*), mentioned only in Judges 20:45. An isolated place east of Bethel, to which the routed Benjamites fled from angry brethren.

GIER EAGLE (See Birds)

GIFT, GIVING. Giving played a great part in the social life of Bible times. At least fifteen words in the Bible are used for it: *eshkār,* a reward (Ps. 72:10); *minhâh,* an offering to a superior (Judg. 3:15); *mattān,* that given to gain a favor (Gen. 34:12), or as an act of submission (Ps. 68:29); *mattenā'* and *mattānâh,* an offering (Gen. 25:6;

Dan. 2:6); *shōhadh,* a bribe (Deut. 16:19). In the NT, *dósis* and *dóron,* anything given (Luke 21:1; James 1:17); *dóma,* a present (Matt. 7:11); *cháris,* and *chárisma,* special enduement (Rom. 1:11; I Tim. 4:14); to be cherished (I Cor. 12:31).

GIFTS, SPIRITUAL (Gr. *charísmata*), a theological term meaning any endowment that comes through the grace of God (Rom. 1:11). They make possible good works (Eph. 2:10). Paul discussed at length in I Corinthians 12 the enduements for special tasks in and through the churches (Rom. 6:23; II Cor. 1:11; I Pet. 4:10). They are found in ability to speak an unlearned tongue (I Cor. 14:1-33); power to drive out evil spirits (Matt. 8:16; Acts 13:7-12); special ability in healing the sick (I Cor. 12:9); prophecy (Rom. 12:6); keenness of discernment (wisdom) and knowledge (I Cor. 12:4-8). These gifts are to be sought diligently (I Cor. 12:31), but never at the risk of neglecting the "more excellent way" of pursuing faith, hope and love, of which love is the greatest gift (I Cor. 13:13). Fruits of the Spirit are given in Galatians 5:22-23.

Everyone is accountable for any gift bestowed upon him (I Pet. 4:10; I Cor. 4:7). Claims of having such gifts are to be tested by doctrine (I Cor. 12:2,3) and on moral grounds (Matt. 7:15; Rom. 8:9). Ability in preaching is a spiritual gift (I Cor. 2:4; II Tim. 1:6). To know the deep things of God requires spiritual insight (I Cor. 2:11-16). The gifts are distributed by the Holy Ghost (Heb. 2:4).   J.D.F.

GIHON (gī'hŏn, Heb. *gîhôn, burst forth*). 1. One of the four rivers in Eden (Gen. 2:8-14). The name indicates that it arose either from some large spring or a cataract. Since it "encompasseth the whole land of Ethiopia" it is supposed to be the Nile whose origin from lakes Albert and Victoria would account for the name. However, Ethiopia was the name given to the land occupied by the descendants of Cush, and covered a vast area. Isaiah called it the land of Cush (11:11). Cushan appears in Habakkuk 3:7. Since Eden was probably in the Tigris-Euphrates Valley, it is possible that Gihon was a small stream in that region. Reliable evidence confirms the claim of some scholars that Cush refers to an area in northwest India. *Kassi* (Cush) appears in some ancient records of the region.

2. Gihon is also the name of a noted spring near Jerusalem. Solomon was anointed there to succeed David (I Kings 1:32-40). That the spring provided a goodly supply of water is shown by the fact that Hezekiah, during his prosperous reign, had its water diverted by a tunnel to serve the growing population of Jerusalem (II Chron. 32:27-30). Recent discoveries show that this tunnel was that connected with the Pool of Siloam, so-called because it fed that watering place in the city. Remains of an ancient canal have been found through which the water once entered and it may be of this that Isaiah wrote (8:6). This spring was originally controlled by the Jebusites (II Sam. 5:6) who cut a tunnel to bring it near enough to the wall for it to be drawn without exposure of their women to raiders.   J.D.F.

GILALAI (gĭl'à-lī), a member of a band of musicians who under Ezra's direction had part in the dedication of the wall of Jerusalem (Neh. 12:36).

GILBOA (gĭl-bō'à, Heb. *gĭlbō'a, bubbling*). It has been identified as Jabel Fuku'a, a range of barren hills on the eastern side of the Plain of Esdraelon,

DAVID ordered the priest Zadok and the prophet Nathan to take the young prince Solomon to the sacred spring at Gihon, near Jerusalem, and there to anoint him. All the people now knew that the king had decided upon Solomon as his successor.

named from a noted spring. The mean elevation of the hills is about 1,600 feet. Ain Jalud on the northern slope of the range has been identified as the location of the spring. Saul gathered his forces here to await an attack by the Philistines. Fear drove him to consult the Witch of Endor (I Sam. 28:4-7). During the battle he was wounded; his forces were routed; and he committed suicide (I Chron. 10:1-8).

GILEAD (gĭl'ē-ăd, Heb. *gil'ādh, rugged*). The name is used to indicate Israel's possession E of the Jordan River. Josephus so understood it (*Ant.* XII; 8:3). It extended from the lower end of the Sea of Galilee to the northern end of the Dead Sea, and from the Jordan eastward to the desert, a plateau of some 2,000 feet elevation. At the time of Moses it was a lush region with goodly forests, rich grazing lands, and abundant moisture. A scenic gorge of the noted brook, Jabbok, running into the Jordan, divided it. Jacob camped at Gilead when fleeing from Laban (Gen. 31:7-43). Overtaken at that place, he made a covenant with Laban which was confirmed by a pile of stones which Jacob named *Galeed,* "Heap of Witness" (Gen. 31:47 marg.). During succeeding years it came to be applied to the entire region which included Mount Gilead (Gen. 31:25), the land of Gilead (Num. 32:1), and Gilead (Gen. 37:25).

When Canaan was allocated to the Israelites, Gilead fell to the Reubenites, Gadites and to half the tribe of Manasseh (Deut. 3:13). An account of the conquest of the region is found in Deuteronomy 2 and 3. Moses was permitted to see the goodly plain before his death (Deut. 34:1). After the land was conquered a great altar was erected beside the Jordan that true worship might not be forgotten (Josh. 22:10).

IN THE LAND OF GILEAD, showing the Yarmuk River and the road to Damascus. Gilead was famous for its medicinal balm.

Gilead became famous because of some of its products. Balm was exported to Tyre (Ezek. 27:17); Jeremiah knew of its curative power (8:22; 46:11; 51:8). The Ishmaelites who bought Joseph carried balm to Egypt (Gen. 37:25). Beside the Jabbok Jacob had his reconciliation with Esau (Gen. 32:22-33:15). Jair, a Gileadite, served for twenty years as judge over Israel (Judg. 10:3). Jephthah, a great grandson of Manasseh, was also a judge. Being the son of a concubine, he was banished by his brothers, but when Gilead was in dire distress, he was recalled by the elders (Judg. 11:1-3). He defeated the Ephraimites and prevented fugitives from crossing the Jordan by resorting to the noted password, Shibboleth (Judg. 12:1-7). Absalom gathered his forces in Gilead when he rebelled against David (II Sam. 15:13-23). The Gileadites finally fell into gross idolatry (Hos. 6:8; 12:11), were overcome by Hazael (II Kings 10:32-34), and led into captivity by Tiglath-pileser (II Kings 15:27-29).   J.D.F.

GILGAL (gĭl'găl, Heb. *Gilgāl, circle of stones*), the first camp of Israel after crossing the Jordan (Josh. 4:19,20). While encamped there Joshua restored the Hebrew rite of circumcision in response to God's promise to "roll away the reproach of Egypt" (Josh. 5:2-9). The town which grew up was near the northern border of Judah (Josh. 15:7). Most authorities agree that this is the town included in the judicial circuit of Samuel (I Sam. 7:16). And it is certain that the altar-memorial of stones erected there became a pagan shrine of later years against which Hosea (4:15) and Amos (4:4) warned the people. According to Josephus, Gilgal was about ten miles from the Jordan and two miles or more from Jericho.

It was to Gilgal that Saul was sent by Samuel to be confirmed as king over Israel (I Sam. 11:15). There Saul later grew restless because of the delay in the coming of Samuel and offended Jehovah by presuming to act as priest and make his own sacrifice (I Sam. 13:1-10). Judah gathered at Gilgal to meet David when he returned from defeating the rebels under Absalom (II Sam. 19).

Gilgal is not mentioned in the NT and its location is not known. The town from which Elijah ascended was not this Gilgal (II Kings 2:1). Gilgal furnished singers who had part in the dedication of the wall of Jerusalem (Neh. 12:27-43). A large pool has been located at modern Jiljuliyeh, which may mark the site. Some authorities disagree with the idea that Gilgal near Jericho was the city in Samuel's circuit, and others claim that the Gilgal mentioned by Hosea and Amos was another city near Shechem.   J.D.F.

GILOH (gī'lō), home of Ahithophel, one of David's counsellors who rebelled with Absalom (II Sam. 15:12), also a town of Judah (Josh. 15:51).

GIMZO (gĭm'zō, *place of lush sycamores*), a town some three miles southwest of Lydda, off the Jerusalem highway, captured by Philistines during the reign of Ahaz (II Chron. 28:18). Jimza is no doubt its present location.

GIN, a trap to ensnare game (Amos 3:5) or to deceive and destroy (Ps. 140:5; 141:9); a pitfall (Job 18:9) or an offense (Isa. 8:14).

GINATH (gī'năth, *protector*), the father of Tibni, a contender for the throne of Israel (I Kings 16:21).

GINNETHO (See Ginnethon)

GINNETHON (gĭn'ē-thon), a priest who returned to Jerusalem with Zerubbabel (Neh. 12:4) and signed the Levitical covenant (Neh. 10:6. Gennetho in KJV).

GIRDLE (See Dress)

GIRGASHITES (gûr'gà-shītes), one of seven Canaanite tribes conquered by Joshua (Deut. 7:1). They were descendants of Ham (Gen. 10:15,16). Their land was promised to Abram (Gen. 15:21) and to Israel (Josh. 3:10). Tradition says they fled to Africa.

GISPA (gĭs'pà, *listener*), an overseer of the Nethinims, in Nehemiah's time (Neh. 11:21).

GITTAH-HEPHER (See Gath-hepher)

GITTAIM (gĭt'ā-ĭm, Heb. *gittayim*, perhaps *two wine presses*), a town of Benjamin to which the Beerothites fled (Neh. 11:31,33), probably at the time of Saul's cruelty (II Sam. 4:3), and lived as protected strangers. Exact site unknown.

GITTITES (gĭt'īt, *of Gath*), natives of Gath, unconquered at the time of Joshua's death (Josh. 13:1-3). The Ark was deposited in a Gittite home (II Sam. 6:8-11). David's guard included 600 men of Gath (II Sam. 15:18). Goliath was a Gittite (II Sam. 21:19).

GITTITH (gĭt'īth, Heb. *gittîth*), a word found in the titles of Psalms 8, 81, 84. Its meaning is uncertain. It may denote some musical instrument made in Gath, or a melody or march popular in Gath.

GIZONITE (gĭ'zō-nīt). Hashem, one of David's valiant men, was described as a Gizonite (I Chron. 11:34). Probably an error for Gunite. He was probably the same as Jashen the Gunite (II Sam. 23:32).

GLASS, although a product known and used by man for ages, where its manufacture first arose is unknown. Pliny attributed it to the Phoenicians, but it was made in Egypt at least 2,500 years before Christ. It is supposed to have been discovered from lumps of glass found where large shocks of straw had burned, or through glaze appearing on pottery that was burned where sand and soda were present. By 1500 B.C. glass trinkets, as well as vessels, had come into general use in Egypt. No doubt Egyptian artisans introduced it to Nineveh, Phoenicia and other lands. As early as 750 B.C. Assyrians were making it, and Phoenicians had developed into a paying industry the making of glass beads.

The fact that glass does not seem to have been used to any degree by the Hebrews may be accounted for by their hatred of Egyptian products (Lev. 18:3), or else it was cheaper for them to produce pottery. Mirrors (Exod. 38:8) were made of polished bronze. The only direct reference in the OT to glass is Job 28:17, where gold and crystal (glass RSV) are compared with wisdom. The Hebrew word is *zekukith*, and may be translated *mirror*, hence the claim of some scholars that even this passage does not refer to glass. The glass mentioned by Paul (II Cor. 3:18), and that to which James referred (1:23,24) was evidently the customary mirror of polished bronze, as the Gr. word used, meant such. By the time of Christ the people of Palestine were familiar with glass. The figurative expressions, revealing the transparent nature of the Holy City, pictured by John in Revelation 21:18,21, refer to crystal glass.   J.D.F.

GLEAN (Heb. *lāqat, 'ālal*), the Hebrew custom of allowing the poor to follow the reapers and gather the grain that was left behind or the grapes which remained after the vintage (Judg. 8:2; Ruth 2:2, 16; Isa. 17:6). This custom was backed by one of the agricultural laws of Moses (Lev. 19:9; 23:22; Deut. 24:19-21). The word is also used figuratively to describe the utter destruction of Israel (Jer. 6:9; 49:9,10).

GLEDE (See Birds)

GLORY, the exhibition of the excellence of the subject to which it is ascribed. Concerning God, it is the display of His divine attributes and perfections. Concerning man, it is the manifestation of his commendable qualities, such as wisdom, righteousness, self-control, ability, etc. A connotation of splendor is included, such as "the glory of the moon and the stars" (I Cor. 15:41). In both Testaments there are references to the Shekinah glory of God, although not by name, for the word occurs in the Targums, not in the Bible. To avoid anthropomorphisms (ascription of physical characteristics to God) which might lead to erroneous doctrine, the Targum writers spoke of the glory of the Shekinah. This was actually the physical manifestation of the presence of God, as seen in the pillars of cloud and fire. NT references to the Shekinah glory are seen in John 1:4 and Romans 9:4. Glory is both physical and spiritual, as is seen in Luke 2:9 ("the glory of the Lord shone round about them") and John 17:22, where it refers to the glory of the Father, which Jesus gave to His disciples. As for the saints, glory culminates in the changing of their bodies to the likeness of their glorified Lord (Phil. 3:20).

GNASH (nǎsh, Heb. *hāraq*, Gr. *brugmós*). In the OT the expression "to gnash with the teeth" represents for the most part rage, anger, or hatred (Job 16:9; Pss. 35:16; 37:12; 112:10). In the NT it expresses disappointment rather than anger (Matt. 8:12; 13:42,50; 22:13; 24:51; 25:30; Luke 13:28).

GNAT (See Insects: Flies)

GOAD (gōd, Heb. *dōrevān, malmādh*, Gr. *kéntron*), an eight-foot wooden pole, shod at one end with a spade for removing mud from the plow and at the other with a sharp point for prodding oxen. It was a formidable weapon in the hands of Shamgar (Judg. 3:31). To "kick against the pricks" pictures oxen kicking against the goads — a figure of useless resistance to a greater power.

GOAT (See Animals)

GOATH (gō'ăth, Heb. *gō'âh*), a place (RV has *Goah*) the site of which is unknown, but apparently ly W of Jerusalem. Mentioned only once, in Jeremiah 31:39, in connection with prophecy concerning the restoration of Jerusalem. Referred to by Josephus as "the camp of the Assyrians."

GOB (gŏb, Heb. *gôv, pit, cistern*), a place mentioned in II Samuel 21:18 as the scene of two of David's battles with the Philistines. Here the brother of Goliath defied Israel but was slain by Jonathan, son of Shimei. The Septuagint calls it Gath, which is probably correct.

GOD (Heb. *'ĕlōhîm, ēl, 'elyôn, shaddāy, yahweh*; Gr. *theós*). Although the Bible does not contain a formal definition of the word "God," yet His being and attributes are displayed on every page. The greatest definition of the word in the history of Christendom, that is, in the culture in which the Bible has been a prevailing influence, is the definition found in the Westminster Shorter Catechism (Q.4): "God is a Spirit, infinite, eternal, and unchangeable, in his being, wisdom, power, holiness, justice, goodness, and truth." It is fair to say that this definition faithfully sets forth what the Bible constantly assumes and declares concerning God.

God is a Spirit. These words mean that God is a non-material personal being, self-conscious and self-determining.

In the differentia of the definition we have three adjectives each modifying seven nouns. The descriptive units in which these words are combined are not logically separable, but are inextricably woven together, so as to delineate the unity and the integrated complexity of God's attributes. The analysis cannot be exhaustive, but only descriptive.

Infinite. The infinity of God is not an independent attribute. If we were to say, "God is the infinite," without specification, the meaning would be pantheistic, equal to saying, "God is everything." In using the word "infinite" we must always be specific.

Infinite in His being. This doctrine is intended to teach that God is everywhere. The omnipresence of God is vividly brought out in such scriptures as Psalm 139. God is not physically, relatively, or measurably big. The word "immensity" is used by good theologians, but it conveys to some minds a false impression, as though God were partly here and partly there, like a giant, or an amorphous mass, or a fluid. The omnipresence of God means that wherever we are, even though we be like fleeing Jacob at Bethel (Gen. 28:16), God *Himself* is there.

It is easier to conceive of God's omnipresence by saying, "Everything everywhere is immediately in His presence." Finite creatures can act instantaneously in a limited area. Everything within one's reach or sight is immediately in His presence, in the sense that distance is no problem. So in an absolutely perfect sense, everything in the universe is immediately in the presence of God.

Infinite in His wisdom. This phrase designates God's omniscience. The Bible throughout regards His omniscience as all-inclusive, and not dependent upon discursive processes. God's knowledge does not increase or diminish as He knows when the temporal events of his redemptive program take place. He eternally knows what He has known in the past and what He will know in the future.

The words **Infinite in His power** point to His omnipotence, His ability to do with power all that power can do, His controlling all the power that is or can be.

Infinite in His holiness, justice and goodness. These words signify God's moral attributes. *Holiness* is regarded in the Bible as His central ethical character. Basic ethical principles are revealed by the will of God, and derived from and based upon the character of God. "Ye shall be holy for I am holy" (Lev. 11:44f. *et passim*). *Justice* refers to His administration of rewards and punishments among the personal beings of the universe. *Goodness* in this context indicates His love, His common grace toward all, and His special grace in saving sinners.

Infinite in His truth. This is the attribute which designates the basis of all logic and rationality. The axioms of logic and mathematics, and all the laws of reason, are not laws apart from God, to which God must be subject. They are attributes of His own character. When the Bible says that "it is impossible for God to lie" (Heb. 6:18; Titus 1:

2) there is no contradiction of omnipotence. How much power would it take to make two times two equal five? Truth is not an object of power.

There is no mere tautology in the Bible, as though the multiplication tables were true by mere divine fiat. As in ethics, so in rationality, the Biblical writers constantly appeal to the truth of God's immutable character. "He cannot deny himself" (II Tim. 2:13).

Just as the adjective "infinite," in the definition we are considering, applies to all the specified attributes, so the words "eternal" and "unchangeable" similarly apply to all.

Eternal in the Bible means, without temporal beginning or ending; or in a figurative sense, "eternal" may designate (as in the words "eternal life") a quality of being suitable for eternity.

That God existed eternally before the creation of the finite universe does not imply a personal subject with no object, for God is triune. (See TRINITY.)

The idea that eternity means timelessness is nowhere suggested in the Bible. This false notion doubtless came into Christian theology under the influence of Aristotle's "Unmoved Mover" (see Aristotle's *Physics*, book *Theta*, Ch. 6, 258b, 1.12, and *Metaphysics*, book *Lambda*, Ch. 7 *et passim*), the influence of which is strong in Thomas Aquinas.

That the Bible does not teach that God is timeless, is an objective, verifiable fact. The evidence is well set forth by Oscar Cullmann. See his *Christ and Time.*

Unchangeable, in Bible language, points the perfect self-consistency of God's character throughout all eternity. This is not a static concept, but dynamic, in all His relations with His creatures. That God brings to pass, in time, the events of his redemptive program is not contradictory. The notion that God's immutability is static immobility (as in Thomism) is like the notion of timelessness, and is contrary to the Biblical view. The God of the Bible is intimately and actively concerned in all the actions of all His creatures.

God is known by His acts. Supremely, "God has spoken in his Son" (Heb. 1:1ff). Further, His "invisible" being, that is, His "eternal power and divine character [*theiotes* as distinguished from *theotes*]" are "known" and "clearly seen" by "the things he has made" (Rom. 1:20). "The heavens declare the glory of God" (Ps. 19; Rom. 10:18). It is customary to distinguish between "natural revelation" and "special revelation," the Bible being identical with the latter.

God is known in fellowship. That by faith God is known, beyond the mere cognitive sense, in fellowship with His people, is one of the most prominent themes throughout the Bible. Moses, leading His people in the exodus, was assured, "My presence shall go with thee, and I will give thee rest." And Moses replied, "If thy presence go not with me, carry us not up hence" (Exod. 33:14f). The Bible abounds in invitations to seek and find fellowship with God. See Psalm 27, Isaiah 55, and many similar gracious invitations.

Other gods are referred to in the Bible as false gods (Judg. 6:31; I Kings 18:27; I Cor. 8:4-6), or as demonic (I Cor. 10:19-22). J.O.B.

GODLINESS (Gr. *eusébeia, theosébeia*), the piety toward God and rectitude of conduct which springs from a proper relationship with Him. It is not belief in itself, but the devotion toward God and love toward man which result from that belief. Religious faith is empty without godliness, for it is then but an empty form (II Tim. 3:5). The Gr. *eusébeia* is found fifteen times in the NT; it is translated fourteen times as *godliness* and once as *holiness*. It is the sum total of religious character and actions, and produces both a present and future state of happiness. It is not right action which is done from a sense of duty, but is that spontaneous virtue that comes from the indwelling Christ, and which reflects Him.   **B.P.D.**

GOLAN (gō′lăn, Heb. *gôlān*), a city in the territory of the half tribe of Manasseh in Bashan, E of the Jordan. It was one of the three cities of refuge, and assigned to the Gershonite Levites (Deut. 4:43). Probably an important city in its day, it was destroyed by Alexander Janneus after his army had been ambushed there. The site cannot definitely be identified, but the archaeologist Schumacher believes it was seventeen miles E of the Sea of Galilee, in present Syria, located in Gaulanitis, one of the four provinces into which Bashan was divided after the Babylonian captivity. It is a fertile plateau, 1000-3000 feet in elevation.

GOLD (See Minerals)

GOLGOTHA (gŏl′gō-thà, Gr. *Golgothá*, from Aram. *gulgaltā′, skull*), the place of our Lord's crucifixion. From the Heb. *gulgoleth*, which implies a *bald, round, skull-like mound* or *hillock*. The Latin name, *Calvarius* (*bald skull*) has been retained in the form *Calvary* (Luke 23:33). In the RV, it is simply, "the skull." Two explanations of the name are found: (1) It was a place of execution, and therefore abounded in skulls; (2) The place had the appearance of a skull when viewed from a short distance. The Gospels and tradition do not agree as to its location. Both Matthew (27:33) and Mark (15:22) locate it outside the city, but close to it (John 19:20) on the public highway, which was the type of location usually chosen by the Romans for executions. Tradition locates it within the present city.   **B.P.D.**

GOLIATH (gō-li′ăth, Heb. *golyāth*, Gr. *Goliáth, exile*), a gigantic warrior of the Philistine army, probably one of the Anakim (Num. 13:33; Josh. 11:22). Goliath's size was extraordinary. If a cubit is 21 inches, he was over eleven feet in height; if about 18 inches, he was over nine feet. The only mention made of Goliath is his appearance as a champion of the Philistines (I Sam. 17). The Philistines had ventured on another inroad into Israel's territory, and had taken a firm position on the slope of a hill, with Israel encamped on a hill opposite. From the Philistine camp Goliath made daily challenges to personal combat, but after forty days no one had accepted. David had been sent to his brothers with provisions. When he heard Goliath's challenge, he inquired its meaning. Upon being told, he went to face Goliath, armed only with a sling and five stones. Hit in the forehead, Goliath fell, and David cut off his head. When the Philistines saw that their champion was dead, they fled, pursued by victorious Israel. The Goliath of II Samuel 21:19 was probably the son of the giant whom David killed. He was slain by Elhanan, one of David's men. A discrepancy has been imagined, and some have thought that it was Elhanan who slew the giant.   **B.P.D.**

GOMORRAH (gō-mŏr′à, Heb. *'ămōrâh*, Gr. *Gomórra, submersion*), one of the five "cities of the plain" located in the Vale of Siddim at the S end of the Dead Sea. Zoar alone escaped the destruction by fire from heaven in the time of Abraham and Lot. The district where the five cities were located was exceedingly productive and well-peopled, but today traces of the punitive catastrophe abound. There are great quantities of salt, with deposits of bitumen, sulphur and nitre on the shores of the Dead Sea. The location was long a contention, but it definitely was established in 1924 by an archaeological expedition led by the late eminent archaeologist, Dr. Melvin Grove Kyle. "The Lisan is a kind of promontory that juts out from the eastern shore toward the western mountains and almost cuts the sea in two. Anciently, it manifestly separated the sea to the north of it from the low plain to the south of it. Thirty-five years ago, when I first saw the Dead Sea, it was so much lower than now that there was a beautiful island at the north end. Today, as we approach the Port of Jericho, we pass over the region of that island in several feet of water. The cities are clearly shown to have stood in front of Jebel Usdum, where they lie under the waters today. This region was found by geologists to be a burned-out area of oil and asphalt, of which there has been an accumulation which is now being exploited. Where these conditions exist, there is an accumulation of gases. Geologists admit that at some past time there was a great explosion, with first an upheaval and then a subsidence of strata. Salt, mixed with sulphur, was carried up into the heavens white hot and so rained down upon the cities of the plain, exactly as the Scriptures describe the rain of fire and brimstone from heaven" (Kyle, *Explorations at Sodom*, pp. 67,130,137-38). **B.P.D.**

GOPHER WOOD (gō′fẽr wŏŏd, Heb. *'ătsê ghō-pher*), the wood from which Noah's ark was made (Gen. 6:14). The word "gopher" is unknown elsewhere in Hebrew or allied languages. It may refer to some resinous wood, like pine, cedar, or cypress; or the reference may be to boats made of interwoven willow branches and palm leaves, coated on the outside with bitumen.

GOSHEN (gō′shĕn, Heb. *gōshen*, probably *mound of earth*). 1. The NE section of the Nile delta region is usually termed "the land of Goshen." Here the Israelites under Jacob settled, while Joseph was prime minister (Gen. 46). The district is not large, having an area of some 900 square miles, but because of irrigation is considered some of the best land of Egypt, excellent for grazing and for certain types of agriculture. The district had two principal cities, both built for the Pharaohs by the Hebrews. The one of greater importance had, at various times, at least three and possibly four names. Zoan, Avaris and Tanis were certainly its names, and archaeologists do not agree as to whether it also bore the name of Raamses. Some indicate a different location for Raamses. Under the name of Avaris, it was for 500 years the capital of the Hyksos. The other city, Pithom, is particularly interesting to the student of Biblical archeology because here is found a proof of Exodus 5:7-13, where the labor overseers were told to refuse the Hebrew workmen straw for making bricks, yet with no diminution of the assigned quota. In a building at Pithom are found three types of bricks, beginning at its foundation where straw was used. After the refusal of straw, the Hebrews desperately gathered all bits of straw and stubble they could find, and such bricks are found higher

IN THE LAND OF GOSHEN, where the Israelites settled under Jacob, while Joseph was prime minister of Egypt. In the distance are the famous pyramids of Gizeh; in the foreground, an irrigation canal.

in the building. It was completed with bricks devoid of straw.

2. A district of S Palestine, lying between Gaza and Gibeon, its name probably given in remembrance of Egypt (Josh. 10:41).

3. A town mentioned with Debir, Socoh and others, in the SW part of the mountains of Judah (Josh. 15:51).　　　　　　　　　B.P.D.

GOSPEL (gŏs'pĕl, Gr. *euaggélion, good news*). The English word Gospel is derived from the Anglo-Saxon *godspell,* which meant "good tidings" and, later, the "story concerning God." As now used, the word describes the message of Christianity and the books in which the story of Christ's life and teaching is found. This message is the good news that God has provided a way of redemption through His Son Jesus Christ. The Holy Spirit works through the Gospel for the salvation of men (Rom. 1:15,16). In the NT the word Gospel never means a book (one of the four Gospels), but always the good tidings which Christ and the apostles announced. It is called "the gospel of God" (Rom. 1:1; I Thess. 2:2,9); "the gospel of Christ" (Mark 1:1; Rom. 1:16; 15:19); "the gospel of the grace of God" (Acts 20:24); "the gospel of peace" (Eph. 6:15); "the gospel of your salvation" (Eph. 1:13; and "the glorious gospel" (II Cor. 4:4). The Gospel has to do entirely with Christ. It was preached by Him (Matt. 4:23; 11:5), by the apostles (Acts 16:10; Rom. 1:15), and by the evangelists (Acts 8:25). It was not until c. A.D. 150 that the word Gospel was applied to the writings concerning the message of Christ. Each of the four records was called a Gospel, and likewise the four together.　　　　　　　　　　　　　S.B.

GOSPEL, THE FOUR GOSPELS. The word *Gospel* is derived from the Anglo-Saxon *gōd spell,* or *good tidings,* and is a literal translation of the Greek *euaggélion,* which meant originally a reward for bringing good news, and finally the good news itself. In the NT the term is applied to the revelation of God's plan for reconciling man to Himself by forgiving his sin and by transforming his character. The Gospel is the story of God's gift of salvation through the person and work of Christ which the church has been commissioned to proclaim (Mark 16:15; Acts 20:24; Eph. 1:13). The impact of the life, death, and resurrection of Christ compelled His disciples to present His message to the public. By repeating the significant features of His ministry and His accompanying precepts, following the general order of His biography, they formulated a body of teaching which may have varied in detail with each recital, but which maintained the same general content.

The existence of this standardized message is confirmed by the NT itself. Paul, in the Epistle to the Galatians, mentioning a visit to Jerusalem which took place before A.D. 50, said: ". . . I laid before them the gospel which I preach among the Gentiles" (Gal. 2:2). In another passage he defined it clearly: ". . . the gospel which I preached unto you, which ye also received, wherein also ye stand, by which also ye are saved . . . For I delivered unto you first of all that which I also received: that Christ died for our sins according to the scriptures: and that he was buried; and that he hath been raised on the third day according to the scriptures; and that he appeared to Cephas . . ." (I Cor. 15:1-5). A similar presentation is afforded by the report of Peter's address in the house of Cornelius, the Gentile centurion. After sketching the baptism, life, death, and resurrection of Jesus, Peter concluded: "He [God] charged us to preach unto the people, and to testify that this is he who is ordained of God to be the judge of the living and the dead. To him bear all the prophets witness that through his name every one that believeth shall have remission of sins" (Acts 10:42,43).

From these samples of apostolic preaching one may conclude that the facts of Jesus' life constituted the Gospel, which was interpreted and applied to suit the occasion on which it was preached.

This Gospel, which was initially proclaimed in oral form, has been transmitted through the writings which are consequently called the "Gospels." Although Matthew, Mark, Luke, and John differ considerably in detail, they agree on the general outline of Jesus' career, on the supernatural character of His life, and on the high quality of His moral precepts. From the earliest period of the church they have been accepted as authoritative accounts of His life and teachings.

(continued on page 777)

THE FOLLOWING BIBLE NARRATIVE, *Jesus Spreads His Gospel,* was written by Curtis Mitchell. It is based upon the events related in the New Testament.

JESUS
Spreads His Gospel

HE MESSENGER stood at the doorway of the house in which Jesus rested. His mission was to invite Jesus to dine with a group of Pharisees. The low sun tinted the nearby hills with gold, and the songs of mountain larks bespoke a peaceful land. It provided a strange background for this ominous invitation.

"Shall we tell the Master?" a disciple asked.

"The Pharisees have sworn to kill Him. He must not go," another of His followers answered.

"Why must I not go? Why?" The deep voice was Jesus speaking from the doorway. "There's a time for caution and a time for boldness. We shall go."

As Jesus walked toward the home of the Pharisee, His mind reviewed their enmity with perfect understanding of why His doctrines were an affront. The Pharisees' leadership of the community depended on their knowledge of the letter of each of thousands of religious laws, and on their rigid discipline that kept violators in line. Already, His words in the Temple in Jerusalem had established a new authority when He said, "He who hears My word and believes in Me shall have everlasting life and shall not perish."

Earlier, He had healed a paralytic with the startling words, "Your sins are forgiven." Pharisees claimed that only God could forgive sins, so the act was called a sacrilege. He had also added to His Twelve a hated tax gatherer, a man whose calling was considered akin to extortion and even robbery; and He had refused to fast. Finally, He had violated the bewhiskered tradition that under *no* circumstances should work be performed on the Sabbath, offering the sensible substitute of "The Sabbath was made for man, not man for the Sabbath; so the Son of Man is Lord even of the Sabbath."

At the home of the Pharisee, Jesus was led to a table where other men were already gathered. His place was the honored one, on the first divan to the left of the host. Suddenly, angry words burst from two men at the host's right. They were priests arguing about whether a blessing should be said for every course of the meal, or would one suffice? The dispute was ages old, but small-minded rabbis could not let it rest. Red-necked, they screamed at each other, their gratitude to God forgotten.

When the matter was settled, a slave brought water for the ritual cleansing of the hands. Jesus deliberately waved the water aside, breaking His bread with hands unwashed. Gasps burst from every pair of lips. Surely, this Nazarene was blasphemous. He refused to wash before eating God's supreme gift of sustenance!

Jesus gazed at the critics, His eyes accusing. "You Pharisees," He cried, each word a sting. "You are careful to clean the outside of your cup and plate, but inside they are dirty; and so your own bodies are clean outside, but within you are full of greed and wickedness. You pay your tithes, yes, but what of your love of justice and God?"

As His host bristled, Jesus faced him. "Woe to you, Pharisee! You love too much to sit in the best seats in the synagogue. You love too much to be saluted in the marketplace. Woe to all of you! You are like unmarked graves over which men walk without even knowing it."

Across the table, a guest sprang up, shouting, "When You speak like this, You insult scribes, too."

Jesus said, "Woe to you also, you lawyers, for you load intolerable burdens on the backs of men and will not help with a single finger." The lawyer sputtered and sank back into his place.

Mercilessly, Jesus went on to expose further failings. "Woe to you lawyers, for you have taken away the key to knowledge. You have not entered yourself, but you have stopped those who wanted to enter!"

Jesus left the company and walked into the clean air, followed by the gabble of angry men. All the way home they dogged His heels, asking questions and laying snares to trap Him into saying something that would enable them to bear witness against Him in Jerusalem. But He held His tongue.

In these middle years of His ministry, Jesus was to spend much time engaged in controversy, often in Galilee, later in Phoenicia (feh-NISH-ih-uh) and the Decapolis (de-CAP-oh-lis), and finally in the great Temple on Mount Zion in Jerusalem. Proud Pharisees and students of the Law disputed with Him constantly. True, many people received His teaching with enthusiasm — but too often this enthusiasm was based on the hope of the people for an earthly deliverer. They were trying to fit Jesus into their dreams of national liberation from the hated Romans.

For a time, now, Jesus made His headquarters in the cool open porch of a friend's home. His disciples brought to Him the sick and needy who sought His aid. As He watched the disciples busying themselves among the seekers, His thoughts went back to the day He had named them as His helpers. . .

The Mission of the Twelve

THEY WERE RESTING beside a spring where two roads crossed in a valley. The hill country rose in tiers above them, spreading from the Valley of Jezreel (JEZ-ree-ell) to Mount Lebanon in the north. They had strolled through Judea and Samaria and done great works before huge crowds, but at that moment they were alone. Jesus judged the time ripe for a lesson.

He called the disciples around Him, having chosen twelve: Simon Peter and Andrew, his brother; James and John, the sons of Zebedee; Philip and Bartholomew; Thomas and Matthew, the tax collector; James, the son of Alphaeus (AL-fee-us), and Thaddaeus (THAD-ee-us); Simon of Cana and Judas Iscariot (JOO-dus iss-CARRY-ut).

He told them bluntly that the time had come for them to stand on their own feet, to do all that He was doing and to preach of the coming kingdom, to heal the sick and to serve their fellows. "Cleanse the lepers, raise the dead, and cast out demons," He ordered.

Their response told Him that they enjoyed the prospect. They saw themselves, perhaps, as leaders, as wise men to be invited to dinner, as worldshakers. Jesus' next words sobered them:

"But you will carry no money in your purses, nor even an extra coat, nor shoes nor staffs; for the laborer is worthy of his wages, and as you labor you shall be fed."

They were uncertain about His meaning. Jesus said, "I send you as sheep in the midst of wolves, so be wise as serpents and harmless as doves. But beware of men. They will try you before their courts and flog you in their synagogues. For My sake, you will be dragged before governors and kings. When this happens, do not worry, for the Spirit of God will tell you what to say."

Clear, indeed; but it was a grim partnership that Jesus offered, as He would later offer it to everyone. His hard words, though demanding, were inspiring: "Have no fear of those who oppose you. They can kill the body but not the soul. Rather, fear God who can destroy both. Two sparrows are sold for a penny, yet not one of them can fall without your Father knowing it. Indeed, the very hairs of your head are numbered. So fear not, for you are of greater value than many sparrows!"

He had never talked so freely of the dangers that faced those who would follow Him. His warning raked their ears. "Don't think the kingdom will be without conflict. My coming will set a man against his father and a daughter against her mother. But whoever loves his father or mother more than Me is not worthy of Me."

When they nodded unafraid, he added a promise: "He who receives you receives Me, and he who receives Me receives Him who sent Me. And he who loses his life for My sake will find it."

They had risen, flushed with determination. He looked into their hearts and knew how they would fare, and how one would cause Him pain and sorrow. And He sent them into the hills without money or a change of garments, to teach and heal.

After a while, He took Himself alone to a nearby city to meditate and pray.

The Great Sermon

NO AREA was so perfectly suited as the Middle East to become the birthplace of God's kingdom on earth. Ancients called it the Fertile Crescent, its lower horn resting on Egypt, running along the coast of Palestine and across Syria to turn the corner at Damascus, and then to follow the Tigris and Euphrates valleys to the Persian Sea. Bounded by water and wilderness, its paved Roman roads were conduits for merchandise and ideas. What men learned during their passage through Israel was discussed presently in caravansaries from Britain to India. All this ancient world was in a ferment of ideas and philosophies; and into this turbulent world the twelve helpers went forth with the message of redemption.

When the Twelve returned from their journey, they bubbled with stories. More important, they exuded confidence. Measuring their new competence, Jesus led them to their next lesson.

Beyond Capernaum (kuh-PUR-nay-um), where the hills rise out of the blue sea of Galilee, the twin peaks of a noble mountain stand astride a level place. Each June, this plateau is bright with wild anemones. Black boulders, rain-cracked and crumbling, are splotched with lichens. Here, tradition sets the scene of Jesus' greatest sermon. Here, centuries later, the last army of the Crusaders would be ground to bits by Saladin (SAL-uh-din).

The morning had started as did all mornings during that year of popularity. Even at sunrise, stragglers had come to beg for a cure, advance agents of the multitudes that would assemble later. But this morning, their number was greater than usual, as if they in some way sensed a great event to come. It was Jesus' habit to sleep in village or city and then to start walking during the cool of the morning, and now He led the way, followed by the disciples. Peter was the first to note their route. "No city lies up this mountain," he panted. "Does the Master plan a surprise?"

John said, "He prayed most of the night, more than I've ever heard."

At the level space between a pair of basalt peaks, Jesus stopped. His disciples sank to the earth a bit below Him, resting their legs. Further back, companies of pilgrims flung themselves down, their strength taxed to the utmost. Bird songs and wind suddenly died. A new sound flowed across the plateau, a voice so charged with quiet passion that every syllable sank into the consciousness of the listeners with the inevitability of pebbles sinking in a well. An ex-soldier turned to a crony. "This Jesus is a real man. I've heard generals give orders and I know." A student of law said, "This rabbi is wise. No judge in our courts uses such language."

Jesus was saying: "Blessed are you poor in spirit, for yours is the kingdom of Heaven. Blessed are you that hunger now for justice, for you shall be fed. Blessed are you that weep now, for you shall laugh. Blessed are you who, for My sake, are hated by others . . ."

He turned His tongue now against the world's darlings. "Woe to you who are rich, for you have received your reward. Woe to you that are full, for you shall hunger. Woe to you that laugh now, for you shall mourn and weep. And woe to you when all other men speak your praise!"

Then He told His listeners some of the precepts which should be observed by those who would follow Him: "Love your enemies, do good to those who hate you, bless those who curse you, pray for those who abuse you. . . As you wish that men would do to you, do so to them. . . Judge not and you will not be judged; condemn not, and you will not be condemned; forgive, and you will be forgiven; give, and it will be given to you; good measure — pressed down, shaken together, running over — will be put into your lap. For the measure you give will be the measure you get back. . .

"You have heard that it was said, 'An eye for an eye and a tooth for a tooth.' But I say to you, Do not resist one who is evil. But if anyone strikes you on the right cheek, turn to him the other also. . . Beware of practicing your piety before men in order to be seen by them; for then you will have no reward from your Father who is in Heaven. . .

"Do not lay up for yourselves treasures on earth, where moth and rust consume and where thieves break in and steal, but lay up for yourselves treasures in heaven. . . No one can serve two masters; you cannot serve God and mammon. . . Do not be anxious, saying, 'What shall we eat?' or 'What shall we drink?' or 'What shall we wear?' For the Gentiles seek all these things; and your Heavenly Father knows that you need them all. But seek first His kingdom and His righteousness, and all these things shall be yours as well. . . Not everyone who says to Me, 'Lord, Lord', shall enter the Kingdom of Heaven, but he who does the will of My Father who is in Heaven."

When He had filled His audience with all this wisdom and much more, He gave them a formula for successful living. "Whoever hears My words and does them," He said, "is like a man building a house, who dug deep in the earth and laid his foundation on solid rock; and when the floods came and the torrent broke against the house, it stood strong and unshaken because it had been founded on a rock."

An open square lay across their path and Jesus was the first to note its emptiness. A single figure stood in the sun, teetering on feet eaten by leprosy. That the man should be within the city at all was an affront to community pride. Lepers were banished to holes in the ground outside the town. Having heard of Jesus, this one dared to find a place on His route. "Lord, if You will, You can make me clean," he called.

"Be off!" a voice snapped furiously from the crowd. But Jesus approached the pariah, who stood rooted on his stumps. His ulcerated lips cried, "Lord, You can make me clean. . . ."

Jesus moved closer. "I will. Be thou clean!" He touched the leper's body with a gentle, lingering caress that all could see. The leper's hands rose to his face, exploring old wounds and found them healed. He hopped about on healed feet. Tears burst from his eyes. Jesus said, "Go to your synagogue and give thanks to God, as Moses commanded."

As the Master moved on toward the place where He would spend the night, the air was suddenly murmurous with hosannas.

The Feast at Simon's House

THE UPPER CLASS in Galilee — traders, merchants, landowners — first heard of Jesus from their servants, who were children of the despised folk who lived hand to mouth with their goats and patches of grain. Simon, a rich Pharisee, grew curious and invited Jesus to a feast.

The garden was unfenced and the house front was open to the street. A strange thing happened during the meal. A small crowd of the usual celebrity chasers had gathered along the thoroughfare. Jesus took His place at the table, His bare feet tucked behind Him as usual. Without warning, a sobbing young woman, who had waited among the loiterers, crossed the court to a spot immediately beside Jesus. Crouching above His feet, her warm tears fell on them and she used her hair as a towel to wipe them. Then she kissed each foot and uncorked an alabaster vial. Pouring its fragrant contents over Jesus' feet, she rubbed His ankles, filling the room with the smell of spice.

The host saw her and his face turned red. "What's this woman up to?" he demanded, knowing at once that she was a loose person despised by every virtuous housewife. And what of this Jesus who, without protest, was accepting her ministrations? No real prophet could fail to recognize such a sinner. As the Pharisee called his steward, Jesus spoke. "Simon, I have something to say to you."

"First I'll get rid of this slattern," Simon thought. "Her foulness disgraces my house. I'll run her out of town." He glimpsed lightning behind Jesus' eyes. "What would You say to me, Rabbi?" he muttered.

Jesus replied by telling a story of a creditor with two debtors, one owing a large sum, the other a small sum. When neither man could pay his debts, the creditor forgave them both. "Tell Me — which of those two would love the creditor more?" Jesus asked.

Simon weighed the problem. "The one who was forgiven more."

Jesus said, "Your judgment is good, so look now at this woman. I came here at your invitation, but you gave Me no water to wash My feet. You offered neither a kiss of welcome nor a drop of oil for My head. Now, this stranger has washed My feet with her tears, wiped them with her hair, and rubbed My feet with precious ointment. Because she has loved so much, her sins, which are many, are forgiven."

Simon thought, "To forgive a sin is to blaspheme against God, and He's doing it under my own roof. I'll carry this to the high priest!"

Jesus turned to the woman. "Go in peace, daughter. Your sins are forgiven."

The Pharisee gloated secretly at the weapon he had been given. Witnesses had heard the words, and would pass them along to the synagogue, to the Temple of Solomon, and to the Sanhedrin (SAN-heh-drin).

A Question from John

I N A DUNGEON to the south, John the Baptist pondered in his mind the tales he had been hearing of Jesus. John had been imprisoned through the plotting of the king's wife, Herodias (hee-ROE-dee-us). The wicked queen had left her husband and married his brother, Herod Antipas (HEH-rud AN-tih-pas). This action was a sinful violation of the sacred Law, and John had denounced her. The queen never forgave him. As the first step in her campaign to secure revenge, she persuaded her husband to throw John into jail.

As John sat in his cell, he turned over in his mind the work Jesus had been doing. In his preaching days, John had acclaimed Jesus as the Son of God whose coming had long been promised. There was every indication that Jesus had the approval of Heaven in His mission. He performed many miracles and healings. Many had come to hear Him. But — how was it that He had only twelve followers? Why were people not crowding to His banner by the thousands? Why did His kingdom not spread like wildfire? Perhaps these all-too-human doubts sometimes assailed the imprisoned prophet in the brooding darkness of his cell. In any event, he called two of his own disciples (King Herod still permitted him to have visitors) and instructed them to seek out Jesus and ask Him a question.

Jesus was preaching in the larger cities of Galilee, healing many and drawing large crowds, when John's deputation found Him. They arrived one evening as the multitude was collecting in a natural amphitheater in which Jesus would preach. When He heard of their presence, He summoned them at once.

They hurried to where He sat. The oldest of the ambassadors did the questioning. Without preamble he said: "Are you the Messiah (meh-SIGH-uh) who is to come, or shall we wait for another?"

Jesus said, "Go back to John and tell him the things you have just seen and heard: the blind receiving sight, the lame walking, lepers healed, the deaf receiving their hearing, the dead raised and the good news of the kingdom of God being preached to the poor."

Jesus knew John would recognize the prophet Isaiah's prediction of the Messiah being fulfilled in Him. No doubt John wanted one last communication before death that would also be a confirmation for *his* followers, who would soon be left without a leader. Knowing what would happen to John and Himself, Jesus injected one further bit of iron into these men and His own disciples: "Happy will be the man who never doubts me in spite of the outward circumstances."

Jesus went out to preach, choosing a new subject. "Let Me tell you about John the Baptist, whom many of you know. When you went into the wilderness to hear him, what did you expect to see? A reed shaken by the wind? Why did you go out at all? To see a man wearing silks and satins? Indeed, no! Such things are worn in palaces, not in a hermit's hut. Why, then? You went to see a prophet, yes, and *more* than a prophet, for of John it was written, 'Behold, I shall send a messenger . . . .' Truly, among men born of women, no one is greater than John the Baptist."

Then He told His hearers that they should face reality and make up their minds about the kingdom of God. Finally, He made his great claim of mediation. "All things have been delivered to Me by My Father; and no one knows the Son except the Father, and no one knows the Father except the Son, and anyone to whom the Son chooses to reveal Him."

No clearer claim was ever made. He, Jesus, was the only avenue to God, the appointed go-between. His great voice boomed as His arms invited their belief, "Come to Me, all who labor and are heavy-laden, and I will give you rest!"

Growing Opposition

OCCASIONALLY, sleek and clever rabbis would join the people who filled the valleys where Jesus preached. They made no outcry, no matter what He said, but talked earnestly within whatever group they joined, especially if it included some companion of Jesus.

"Why should we want to live under another kingdom?" they demanded. "True, the Romans aren't the best of masters. But are we so badly off? We worship as we please — in the same Temple that Solomon built. We have many privileges. Think twice before this Jesus persuades you to throw away your birthright by joining this 'kingdom' of His."

"After my tax, there's nothing left," a young peasant cried. "I'll take any kingdom but Rome's!"

Sometimes the rabbis' questions led to raging debate. Jesus felt the growth of uncertainty among His disciples. One hot afternoon, noting the strain in their faces, He called them to the shade of a giant sycamore. Speaking like a father, He comforted them for the lack of family life in their constant wandering, and the burden of living like a gypsy. But then He reminded them of the many other values:

"Your life is more than food and your body is more than clothing. Consider the least worthy of birds, the raven: it neither sows nor reaps; it has no storehouse and no barn, yet God feeds it. *You* are much more valuable than any raven."

They took the homely figure into their eastern minds, mulling over its truth. He added, "Consider the lilies of the field, how they grow; they neither toil nor spin; yet I tell you, even Solomon in all his glory was not arrayed like one of these!"

A disciple said, "Our robes are threadbare and our sandals tattered."

Jesus stepped into the center of the group. "If God so clothes the grass, which is alive and growing today and is burned in the stove tomorrow, how much more will He clothe you, O men of little faith? Don't worry about what you will get to eat or drink or wear. Instead, seek after the kingdom of God, and all these things will be given to you."

A cry floated across the fields, a warning. In the distance, a column of soldiers from the local garrison was approaching. Jesus gave an order and the Twelve melted into the hills. The soldiers advanced, alert eyes probing behind every boulder. The sun glanced off their swords, their armor, their helmets. Looking invincible, they were already defeated. Unknowing, they had become the adversaries of a new idea. When they passed the spot where Jesus had spoken, they did not even notice His footprints.

"What Manner of Man Is This?"

HIGH ADVENTURE overtook the followers of Jesus on the restless surface of the Sea of Galilee. Till now, He and the Twelve had moved among villages west of the great rift through which the Jordan flows. His decision

"Come Unto Me . . ."

CARL BLOCH

Christ the Comforter.

AUGUST JERNDORFF

The Sermon on the Mount.

DOMENICO MASTROJANNI

Jesus' Great Sermon.

HERMAN OLRICK

FERDINAND V. E. DELACROIX

Christ on Lake Gennesaret.

The Transfiguration (detail).

RAPHAEL

Christ restores the blind man's sight.

C. SCHLEISNER

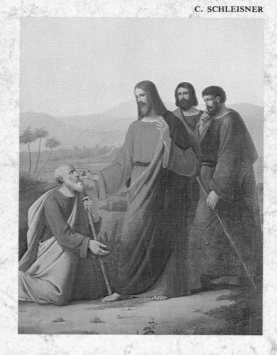

PHILIPPE DE CHAMPAIGNE

Supper at the house of Simon the Pharisee.

CHRISTIAN DALSGAARD

The Transfiguration.

Christ and the Adulteress.

JACOPO TINTORETTO

to cross to the lake's eastern shore raised the curtain on a new drama.

Thomas brought the news. "The Master plans to rest a while. We're to take ship and cross to a place on the other side of the lake."

A youthful disciple groaned. "We are always on the go!"

"You can always quit," Matthew shot back, remembering his own past with a shudder.

"But if we could only settle down somewhere. . ."

"You know what He says: 'The foxes have their holes and the birds their nests, but the Son of Man has no place to lay His head.' "

"When my father died, I should have buried him. Jesus told me, 'Let the dead bury their dead.' "

Peter moved into their midst. "No matter how much He asks from you, He asks more from Himself. He's even cut loose from His own family."

"That's true," the disciple admitted.

"Now, would *you* do as much?" Peter asked. "Mary and His brothers came to visit Him one day when He was preaching. He wanted to see them, I could tell, but His judgment was against it. He pointed at the crowds, at the scores lining up for healing, and He told me, 'Peter, *here* is My family. Whoever does the will of God is My brother, and My sister, and My mother.' "

The young man could not give up. "Without a family, you're nothing . . . nobody."

"We have Him, and we have each other."

"But we're only a handful of men, Peter."

"We are proclaiming the kingdom of God," Peter replied.

"Well said, My friend!" Jesus had joined the circle and listened to the argument. His voice was exultant, perhaps reflecting His joy at such splendid words. "With what shall we compare the kingdom of God? The kingdom is like a mustard seed which, when it is sown, is smaller than any other seed on earth. But when it grows up, it becomes the greatest of all shrubs and puts out branches where birds can nest and roost in the shade."

Presently, they went to the harbor and got into a boat and departed. Many among the crowd also rented vessels in order to follow. "How long is the crossing?" landsmen asked. "Is it dangerous?"

"Only a few hours," the sailors replied. "But the last half is the roughest part."

The craft bearing Jesus and the disciples flew before the wind for almost an hour. She was a snug ship and ably manned, and Jesus dropped off to sleep. In the lake's center, a tempest dropped out of the heights with such fury that their sails dragged in the water. Waves broke over the stern, filling the 'midships. Hanging to lines and cleats, the disciples looked for evidence that the squall would pass but saw only scudding foam and terrifying walls of water which, when they broke, revealed other craft in perilous attitudes.

Like children, they rushed to where Jesus slumbered and shook Him awake. "Master, don't You care if we die?"

Jesus lifted His tired body erect, swaying with the movement, shaping words that were torn from His lips by the blast. "Peace! Be still!" He commanded the elements.

And the wind ceased and the watery cliffs subsided.

Later, as passengers stretched their legs ashore, the story of what Jesus had done sped from group to group. Before their eyes, He had made the waves and wind obey. They asked each other, "What manner of Man can this be?"

The Demoniac

A MANIAC gave answer. Without warning, a giant of a man, naked except for broken chains which jangled from wrists and ankles, plunged from a cave at the top of a nearby cliff and flung himself down the slope. Sun had tanned and weathered his face until it was like sandal leather. Prostrate at Jesus' feet, he looked up and cried out, "What will You do with me, Jesus, Son of the Most High God?"

As Jesus recognized his sickness and prepared to heal it, a chorus of shrill cries made Him pause. The lunatic's lips were babbling, "Spare us, Master. Show Your mercy. Let us enter that herd of pigs on the mountain."

A city man asked, "What is this nonsense?"

A farmer replied, "He's full of demons. Unless they can go into some other living being, they fall into the abyss. Everybody knows that."

Jesus spread His hands and pressed them toward the giant. "Go into the swine," He said. "Leave this man now."

As the man wiped the froth of madness from his lips, the herd of pigs above began to move. In a moment, they were an avalanche of flesh; ahead of them, the granite slope ended in a precipice. When they reached it, they fell in a squealing mass, into the sea below.

Natives of that shore came running to face Jesus and the disciples with frightened and hostile looks. "Go home and leave us alone," they seemed to say. "What business have you with us?"

It was not a happy encounter, nor did the evangelists tarry, but returned to Capernaum.

Again, the sandy beaches of the western shore became their sanctuary. Again, people followed Him in His walks. He healed some of them: a woman who had been incurable for twelve years, and two blind men; and He brought back to life a teenage girl whose father was the ruler of the synagogue.

Only at night could He escape. If His place of sleeping was vacant, His disciples knew that He was sitting alone on some crag, staring across the lake. His manner worried Peter, who turned to John for information. "Is something amiss?"

"The Gentiles are much on His mind, especially since that day across the lake when they asked Him to go away."

"Gentiles are sinners. Gentiles are unclean," a disciple said.

John looked around the circle. "We may see some changes. Do you remember that Isaiah (eye-ZAY-uh) himself wrote 'The Gentiles will come to His light?' Maybe the prophet's words have a meaning for us."

One Sabbath morning, Jesus was absent from the breakfast table. "Where is He?" James asked.

"He's gone to Nazareth," replied Thomas.

The disciples cried out in perplexity. "Another strange journey, without an apparent reason."

When Jesus rejoined them that evening, He said nothing of His trip. Peter noticed that three Nazarenes were outside the house, looking up at the roof. He hurried out to them. "Have you followed the Master from Nazareth?"

"We hoped He would heal our sicknesses."

"I'll help you. But tell me first, what great works did He do in Nazareth?"

They said, "He spoke in our synagogue, but did nothing. There was no room, so we stood with the crowd outside, ready for anything. When He came out, He walked down the steps, looking at nobody."

The smallest man interrupted. "He looked at me, all right. He spoke to me, too, and strange words they were: 'A prophet is not without honor, except in his own country . . . .' "

" 'And among his own kin,' " the second man added.

" 'And in his own house,' " the third concluded.

"You have come to be healed," Peter said, "but remember, without faith, no works are possible. On the other hand, if you believe in Him, all things are possible."

"We believe," they said.

"Then come inside, and let Him touch you."

The Fate of John

JOHN the Baptist still languished in his prison cell. But his spirit was rejoicing, even in this dark hour. Through the message which his disciples had brought him, John knew that Jesus was indeed the One sent by God to bring in the kingdom. *Let them do with me what they will,* John exulted; *they cannot stay the hand of the Lord!*

As for his persecutor, Herodias, she too was happy in her evil, gloating way. She had him where she wanted him, this upstart of a prophet who had dared to denounce her sinful marriage. She preferred not to act too quickly; but when the king one day referred to his forthcoming birthday, she knew that the opportune moment had arrived.

The king's birthday would be an extraordinary festival with rare victuals and entertainment for members of the court and their foreign guests. Herodias laid her plans accordingly. When the day arrived, a feast was served that aped Greek extravagance. When each guest had been stuffed and wined, a troupe of jugglers from India charged into the room tossing around lighted torches and bowls filled with goldfish. Watching her husband from a curtained alcove, Herodias counted his drinks. "Keep his cup full," she told the steward. "Put no water in his wine."

Another performer, a huge Nubian, rode into the banquet hall astride a black-maned lion. His tricks so excited the crowd that Herod called him forward and presented a purse of coins. Next, musicians began to push harps and drums into a clearing between tables, and Herodias sped to the bedchamber of her daughter Salome (suh-LOW-me). Swiftly, she wrapped a swirl of veils about the girl's perfumed body. "Do you remember everything?" Herodias asked.

"You are a good teacher, Mother," Salome said.

The orchestra was playing a barbaric dance, strings and percussions throbbing wildly, when they returned. Salome poised at the top of a marble stairway, like a diver on a tower, and some magic of communication brought every eye toward her. Cries of delight rocked the hall. For a royal princess to dance was high tribute to the king's guests. Salome flung herself forward, descending like a whirlwind, spinning into her step-father's arms, and then, in recoil, bouncing away like a dervish.

Faster and faster she gyrated, as the drunken watchers clapped and stamped and uttered cries of encouragement.

When the dance was finally finished, Salome threw herself on the velvet cushion before Herod, amid deafening applause. The king was delighted. As a reward for her performance, he promised to give the girl anything she wanted.

"Anything?" she asked, wide-eyed.

"Anything at all!" he babbled. "Even a half of my kingdom, if you wish it!"

Salome excused herself for a moment and left the feasting chamber. She hurried to her mother and told her of Herod's offer. "Do you still want me to ask—" she began, hesitantly.

"Of course! You know what to say. Go and say it to the king!"

And so it was that Salome went back and asked the king to let her have *the head of John the Baptist on a platter*. Evil as he was, the king was shocked. But a promise was a promise. And so the wicked deed was done.

When John's disciples heard of it, they went to the prison and got the body, and sorrowfully buried it.

Then they told Jesus.

When Jesus had heard every detail, He left the Twelve, walking slowly toward a rocky place where He often sat and prayed. His movements were those of a man whose heart was heavy.

The Journey to Phoenicia

ONE BRIGHT MORNING the disciples found themselves on the road to Phoenicia — to the area of Tyre (TIRE) and Sidon (SIGH-dun).

John, the beloved disciple, told the others first of the impending journey. "We were walking along when, out of the blue, the Master asked me if I knew anything about the land of Phoenicia."

"The Phoenicians built King Solomon's fleet for him," Thomas said.

"They're Gentiles," put in another. "But they tithe, as we do. They are slaves of Rome, as we are. We farm the land, they farm the sea. We worship one God, they worship a thousand."

Peter interrupted. "I like this trip less and less."

James said, "Remember what happened at Gerasa across the lake. The Master healed their worst lunatic, but still the Gentiles were afraid and asked us to leave. This is not a good sign, if His teachings are to reach beyond Israel. On the other hand, Phoenicians have never feared anyone. They would listen."

Before the day was out, Jesus gave orders for the move, naming who of His company should go and who should remain behind. Tyre was a joyous city, according to an account in the ancient book of Isaiah, with shops, factories, and craftsmen of the highest order. Its most famous product was Tyrian (TIE-ree-an) purple, a precious dye made from a local shellfish and carried by merchants to every royal court in the world. Inland, a net of roads twisted through fissured foothills to Capernaum, Caesarea Philippi (SEZ-uh-REE-uh fil-LIP-eye), and Damascus.

The experience of travel in a foreign land was new to the disciples. The people they met were Canaanites (KAY-nan-ites), descendants of Israel's ancient enemies, but long since turned to commerce. Their faces were friendly and their hospitality unstinting. "We should stay here many days," Matthew suggested. "Roman patrols make these roads safe, and the people respect our privacy."

He was half right. That evening, as they sat at dinner in the garden of a newly won friend, a woman's voice shrilled from the road. "She's followed us half the afternoon," Judas said. "Shall I give her a penny and send her away?"

Her tremulous lips cried, "Have mercy on me, O Lord, Son of David. My daughter is sick to death."

The words stirred a memory in Jesus. Few indeed had called Him Lord, Son of David — and certainly no Gentiles (as this woman was). For it was a Jewish expression, reflecting the awareness that the coming Messiah would be a descendant of David. The disciples urged Jesus to send the woman away, for her cries annoyed them.

Jesus remembered other women with sick daughters whom He had healed. Now, a Gentile woman voiced an identical agony. Was I sent only to the lost sheep of Israel? he inquired of Himself. The woman darted into the garden and fell on her knees. "Lord, Lord, help me!"

He saw that she was young and that her garments were of poor stuff. "It's not fair to take children's bread and throw it to dogs." The disciples chuckled, thinking He referred to Jews as God's children and Gentiles as unbelieving dogs.

Her voice was desperate. "Yet even the dogs eat the crumbs that fall off their master's table!"

His eyes lighted in recognition of her conviction. "Woman, your faith is great. What you desire will be done for you."

She rose, taking backward steps and falling over her robe until she turned to race away to her daughter's sickbed. When she got there, the girl was well.

In Israel, Jesus had required those He healed to make thank-offerings according to Law, and asked them to tell no one of their experience. Invariably, they babbled wherever they went. The Phoenician woman was no different. The tale of a miracle performed by a wandering Hebrew who healed without even seeing His patients, raced across the northern hills.

Peter watched the sick and halt gather about the Miracle-worker. "If it's rest He wanted, it's ended now," muttered Peter, directing them into orderly groups according to their need.

Peter's Confession of Faith

AS THE SEASONS CHANGED, Jesus and His comrades moved their camp many times, talking with camel drivers and traders, shepherds and soldiers. After their stop in Phoenicia, they ranged the rich slopes of the Decapolis, an area surrounding ten Greek cities founded by colonists who had followed Alexander the Great three centuries earlier. Thousands of Gentile eyes saw Jesus and His wonders during those expeditions. Thousands of Gentile minds absorbed the simple points of His message. No matter how far He ventured, though, He detected spies in every audience. The Sadducees (SAD-yew-seez) had not forgotten Him.

In consequence, His public ministry continued as before, but His special tutoring of the Twelve, which had become His chief goal, was privately arranged through epigram, parable, and snatches of conversation. One exchange took place at the end of a hard day, on the trail south of Caesarea Philippi, that Gentile city in Israel's far north named by its prince to honor Rome's Tiberias Caesar. Where the serried rocks flattened, Jesus stopped so His party could catch its breath. Here, the earth was a riot of fissures and crags, as though it had boiled out of a giant cauldron and frozen hard. In the distance, the city lay among foothills, white and naked, reminiscent of its favorite god, Pan. A cave nearby held the buried spring whence the River Jordan sprang and where Pan's priestesses practiced secret rites.

Jesus studied His men, driven by a sudden wish to test them. Their bodies were like rawhide or they could not have stood those hard months. But what of their minds? What of their hearts? When other disciples had deserted Him, He offered a release which the loyal ones refused. Would they stand fast now? For a long moment, He studied them. Then His question burst in their ears.

"Who do men say that I am?"

The question echoed among the crags but their faces were composed. They had an answer, a half-dozen answers. "Some say John the Baptist."

"Elijah."

"Jeremiah."

He interrupted, intense and demanding, "But who do *you* say that I am?"

Now lips tightened across teeth with the labor of a decision that some had not achieved. Simon Peter brought his hairy eyebrows together, matching his Master's solemnity. "You are the Christ, the Son of the living God," he stated bluntly. Eleven other voices echoed his.

As if a load had been lifted from Him, Jesus straightened His tired back and flexed His arms. The crisis was over. God's plan could proceed. "Blessed are you, Simon, son of Jona, for no man told you this, but only My Father, who is in Heaven." Big Simon Peter nodded humbly. "And I say also that you are Peter, and on this rock I will build My church, and the gates of Hell shall not stand against it."

Teaching in Parables

NO CROWDS pressed about Jesus now; it was clear that the relentless Pharisees had turned many against Him. Synagogues which once had welcomed Him now barred their doors. So He preached in open fields to whoever would listen, with knoll or outcropping of rock for a pulpit.

He told many parables — homely stories that illustrated deep spiritual truths. There were parables of farmers and moneylenders, of weddings and candles and lost treasures. One parable, rebuking prejudice, told of a Jew who had been wounded by robbers, and how he was rescued by a kindly Samaritan — one of the hated enemies of the Jews.

At times, the Lord's spirit was heavy. The disciples were weighted with a sense of foreboding — especially when He spoke in terms of His going to Jerusalem and facing death there.

Peter said, "The heat and these endless journeys may have depressed Him — just as they have us. I'll speak to Him."

Later, he took Jesus aside to encourage Him. "God bless You, Master. None of these awful things will happen to You."

Jesus knew better — and He answered sternly: "Get thee behind Me, Satan! You understand nothing of matters that come from God."

The Transfiguration

ONE MORNING Jesus led Peter, James and John to the summit of a nearby mountain. The men were resting and watching Jesus, who had walked on a short way, when suddenly a cloud blocked their sight of the earth below. An eerie brilliance suffused the peak, transfiguring Jesus so that His face shone like the sun and His tunic sparkled as if with a million diamonds.

As the disciples gaped in wonder, two very old men joined the Lord. The disciples knew instantly that they were Moses and Elijah — who had been dead, lo these many centuries! Suddenly, the disciples heard a voice and hid their faces, for they knew its Author. "This is My beloved Son, with Whom I am well pleased."

Thus Moses and Elijah — representing the Law and the Prophets — paid the tribute of the Old Testament to the Lord of the New. And God the Father added His divine voice to heighten the solemnity.

On the way down the mountain, Jesus pledged them to silence. "Tell no man about the vision you saw," He ordered. "Say nothing until the Son of Man has been killed and has risen again from the grave."

To the disciples, it was another riddle.

The most colorful of all Hebrew festivals was the Feast of Tabernacles. It took place after harvest time, when autumn colors first stained pomegranate leaves and coolness braced the air. For seven carefree days, pilgrims from seventy heathen lands filled the streets of Jerusalem with garish costumes and the speech of Persia, Gaul, Media (MEE-dee-uh), Italy, and Africa. It was an ideal place and time for a leader to declare himself. The faction among Jesus' followers who sought a war against Rome begged Him to speak out. They could not understand that the kingdom He preached had neither armies nor politics.

Each of His previous visits to the Temple had caused trouble. During the first, He had evicted a horde of grafting money-changers. The second time, He had healed an infirm man on the Sabbath, and been attacked by the priesthood. This third festival, He thought, should begin peacefully. He would delay His arrival. "Go on," He told His brethren. "The time is not ripe for Me to depart."

His disciples were stubborn. "It does no good to perform Your works in Galilee," they maintained. "Go to Judea, where important people can see You. Show Yourself to the world."

But Jesus would not be moved, so they departed.

Jesus Returns to Jerusalem

THAT WEEK, thousands of men, women, and children roamed the streets of the Holy City from dawn till dusk, sleeping by night in "tabernacles" or huts made of branches. Their ancient book of Leviticus (leh-VIT-ih-kus) ordained that every good Jew should spend these seven days in the open, so the city's roofs, streets, and open spaces blossomed with myriads of edifices shaped like igloos, tepees, or lean-tos, made of pine and myrtle, olive and palm fronds. Even the wealthiest residents left their comfortable bedrooms to commemorate those great days when Israel's tribes awaited their destiny in the desert.

In the crowded Temple area, northerners met old friends from beyond the Jordan or the coast of Tyre, and invariably their chit-chat drifted to the works of Jesus of Nazareth. "He's a good man," some said, recalling the blind and maimed. Others shook their heads. "No, He's leading too many foolish people astray." Temple police, armed with truncheons, ambled through the volatile crowds ready to nip trouble in the bud.

Left alone in Galilee, Jesus walked over His beloved hills. His decision to delay was wise, but as the hours passed He felt an eagerness to face His critics. Three days later, dusty and travel-stained, He arrived in Jerusalem. But until the festivities were well underway He stayed in the background.

His advisers nagged Him again to show Himself. "Go to the Temple," they urged. "These pilgrims are ready to follow You."

"My time has not yet come," He repeated quietly.

The worshippers plodded to a famous well named Siloam, where the high priest filled a golden pitcher with holy water and returned to pour it, along with wine, into openings in the altar built to God. It was a symbolic act their forefathers had practiced for a thousand years.

The celebration was half over before He chose His moment to speak. His first discourse in the Temple was an almost spontaneous outpouring of thoughts long held, uttered as He sat among friendly country people. But it gained instant attention, for He spoke as they had never heard anyone speak before.

A city priest spoke for his profession, saying, "How can this ignorant countryman have such knowledge? How can He speak with authority — without study?"

The Beautiful Gate of the Temple towered above Jesus, a sophisticated contrast to His sunburned skin and rough robe. He proclaimed, "My doctrine is not Mine, but His Who sent Me." That sounded as if, once again, He was saying that God was His Father. It was the beginning of a rousing argument. A lawyer with a long memory charged Him with having violated the Law by healing a man on the Sabbath.

Jesus retorted that orthodox Jews themselves circumcised their sons on the Sabbath — which surely, in God's eyes, made the repair of a man's whole body no less creditable. "Yet you talk of trying to kill Me!" He concluded, eyes blazing.

As one discussion led to the next, many people grew indignant, demanding His arrest. Others cried, "Let Him talk. He'll hang *Himself.*"

Jesus accused them of blindness and ignorance. The longer He talked, the louder grew the hubbub. At last, an enraged rabbi lurched forward, reaching for a hold on His robe. A foot wearing a shepherd's sandal tripped him. Men rose up, fists swinging, oaths sputtering. But the disciples and their friends behaved like a trained unit. They made a cordon of their oaken bodies and passed Jesus through it to safety.

The Leaders Plot

A HUNDRED YARDS AWAY, in an inner chamber, old Annas was shaking a yellow finger under the nose of his son-in-law, the high priest Caiaphas. "That Galilean is dangerous, I tell you. His tongue is mightier than a legion of soldiers. The foolish already think He's the Messiah promised by our prophets."

Caiaphas snorted. "Idiots may believe it, but tradition says the Messiah will come suddenly, out of nowhere. We've known this man for years. His father was a carpenter. Nobody would follow Him."

Annas shrilled, "His inner circle is already twelve strong. Last summer, He trained and sent out seventy others to get recruits in Samaria." He clapped his hands and two Temple policemen stepped smartly through a curtained doorway. "What are they doing in the Temple?"

An officer rubbed his grizzled chin. "Fighting among themselves, as usual, sir. But mostly, they're for Jesus. They say that if *He's* not the real Messiah, what other miracles could the real Messiah perform?"

"What do you think, captain?"

The other officer squared his shoulders. "He speaks with sincerity. The crowd likes that."

Annas cried out, "Hear that, foolish husband of my daughter. Must this rascal overturn the altar before you act? Gag Him quickly, or He'll stir up such trouble that Pontius Pilate will strip us of all our authority. Your job, my son, is to keep down unrest as well as to make burnt offerings."

"Relax," said Caiaphas. "In time I'll trap this Galilean, but the way must be prepared." He turned to the officers. "I want to question Him tomorrow. When He comes to the Temple, bring Him to me."

On the morrow, the captain of police returned alone. He had placed himself in the crowd about Jesus, with every intention of arresting Him, but the Master's words checked him. Full of amazement, he broke from the knot of listeners and hastened to the high priest. "No man ever spoke like this," he reported with feeling.

Caiaphas turned livid with anger. "You know well that not one man of learning supports Him. Not one official, nor any rabbi. As for that mob around Him, they're stupid."

Rich old Nicodemus (nik-oh-DEE-mus) lay in a corner, stretched full length on a golden lounge. He had talked to Jesus one dark night, and now he screwed up his courage. "Your judgment is too severe, Caiaphas. Our law doesn't judge a man without giving him a hearing. Be fair."

The high priest beat his chest. "Are you a Galilean, too? Then read your Scriptures. Read them from beginning to end. You'll find that no prophet is to come out of Galilee."

Nicodemus withdrew. He had done his best. Caiaphas dismissed the captain. "Go back to your post and keep your eyes open. I've had second thoughts on how to deal with this pretender."

The Woman Taken in Adultery

THE LAST DAY of the feast was a time for more fun and less ceremony; and a time for looseness. After a night with His disciples on the Mount of Olives, Jesus returned to the Temple area. "This day is My last with these people," He reminded Himself, measuring matters still unsaid against the time that remained. Taking a seat, He began to talk.

His theme was shocking. He said flatly that He was God's messenger, that the only way for men to reach God was through His intercession.

As He spoke, Annas, Caiaphas, and a knot of Sadducees strode through the Temple gate. Two of their party pulled along an olive-skinned girl, hair loose, feet unshod, youthful cheeks alight with terror. Caiaphas pointed at Jesus. "Stand her before Him."

Annas whispered, "This trap is neat. I commend you."

The people around Jesus drew their skirts close as the high priest and his retinue pushed to a place only a few feet away. Caiaphas smiled an oily smile. "Master, if You speak in behalf of God, as I've heard, help us solve this problem." He prodded the girl. "This shameless woman was caught in adultery, in the very act!" A moan rose from the crowd; they knew the penalty. "Now, in the Law that Moses gave us, he commanded that such as she be stoned until dead. Master, what do You say?"

As if He had heard nothing, Jesus leveled a place on the sandy floor until its surface was like parchment. With one finger, He began to write. Caiaphas spoke again, interrupting. "Give me Your answer, Jesus. I, the high priest of Judah, demand Your reply!"

He smiled arrogantly, anticipating triumph. If Jesus said that the Law of Moses should be disobeyed, He would antagonize every decent Jew. If He said the girl should be killed, He would set aside Rome's firm edict that no Jewish life should be taken without the Empire's approval. Either way, He was trapped.

Jesus straightened up, towering over them all, His eyes regarding them with a penetrating gaze. With great clarity, He addressed the Sadducee party: "He that is without sin among you, let *him* first cast a stone at her." He sat again, deliberately, adding more words to His dusty message.

Annas' eyes followed His finger for a long moment. Then he sighed, and hobbled away on his old man's legs. A Sadducee elder followed closely, and another, and finally Caiaphas himself — with none uttering a single word. When only Jesus and the woman and His original audience were left, He looked at her for the first time, saying, "Woman, where are your accusers? Does no man stay to condemn you?"

Her young cheeks were wet. "No man, Lord."

Jesus said, "Neither do I condemn you. Go now, and sin no more."

Her head lifted, her spine straightened, she backed away, suddenly radiant with the new life that had come through His forgiveness.

"I Am the Light of the World"

WHEN she had gone, Jesus looked into the veiled eyes of those around Him. Tomorrow they would be dispersed. This instant demanded His immediate revelation, His personal involvement with them, with all who sinned, with all who looked beyond the grave. They knew of His works; they had heard Him raise the issue of adultery above politics and the Law to that of personal morality. To their deepest instincts, He began to address His invitation.

"I am the Light of the world," He began. "Whoever follows Me will not walk in darkness, but will have the light of life."

Two young men whispered at the crowd's fringe. "He bested them all. What could He have written to make old Annas run?"

"Maybe a list of Annas' own sins."

"It was long enough, as I could see. But how would this Nazarene know?"

Jesus' voice reached them, low but clear. "For a while longer, I will be with you, and then I go to My Father Who sent Me."

A voice said, "Truly, this is the Prophet."

Another spoke, "I think He's the Christ who comes after the Prophet."

But they were still divided, and some Pharisees who had been sitting with them began to argue, asking, "Wise man, where is Your Father?" His answer did not please them. Noisy and impertinent, they challenged each statement and mocked His logic.

Jesus looked at the faces in the group about Him. Time was short and these were God's enemies. No turning back, no soft tongue and gentle manner now. Instead, He thrust and cut with all His strength. "*Your* father is the devil, who was a murderer from the beginning," He asserted. "You would perform his lusts by killing Me. You are no sons of God, as you claim, because if you were you would understand God's words when He speaks through Me."

They retaliated, calling Him a Samaritan, their most insulting epithet. They charged Him with being controlled by a demon. "You're full of lies and will be till Your death."

Jesus said, "If a man keeps My sayings, he will never see death."

They cried, "Our father Abraham and the prophets are dead! Are You greater than Abraham and the prophets?"

Jesus replied, "Before Abraham was, *I am.*"

The enormity of this assertion struck them like a sudden thunderclap. How could any man claim that he had existed before Abraham — thousands of years ago? Surely, this was a lunatic, a sorcerer, a heretic. The court's roadway was paved with polished stones. Now the Pharisees tore them loose with thrusting, bloodied fingers.

Jesus turned His back, speaking now to those who believed. "Continue in your understanding of My teachings, and you are My disciples. For you shall know the truth, and the truth shall make you free."

Free! The sound of the word exploded in the mind of every listening Hebrew who hated Rome and slavery and taxes. If Jesus could set them free, if Judah could rise to greatness . . . . Zealots from Galilee and plain people from everywhere rose to thrust themselves between the enraged Pharisees and their Victim.

Meanwhile, Jesus passed swiftly through their midst and went out of the seething Temple.

His time had come at last. In the fateful months ahead, He would proclaim the Fatherhood of God, and His own divine Sonship, again and again, despite every pressure and punishment, even through the final agony on the Cross at Calvary Hill. The kingdom of God was at hand!

(continued from page 756)

Character: Reduced to writing, the Gospel message constitutes a new type of literature. Although it is framed in history, it is not pure history, for the allusions to contemporary events are incidental, and the Gospels do not attempt to develop them. They contain biographical material, but they cannot be called biography in the modern sense of the word, since they do not present a complete summary of the life of Jesus. The Gospels are not sufficiently didactic to be called essays; they conceal rather than reveal the direct opinions of their writers. The chief purpose of the Gospels is to create faith in Christ on the part of their readers, who may or may not be believers. Nothing exactly like them can be found either in the OT, to which their writers referred frequently, nor in the Hellenic and Roman literature contemporary with them.

Of the numerous accounts and fragments that were composed to perpetuate the ministry and teaching of Jesus, only four are accorded a place in the NT: Matthew, written by Jesus' disciple Matthew Levi, the tax-gatherer; Mark, from the pen of John Mark, an inhabitant of Jerusalem and a companion of Barnabas and Paul; Luke, the first half of a history of Christianity in two volumes by an associate of Paul; and John, a collection of select memoirs by John, the son of Zebedee. Although the authorship of all of these Gospels has been disputed, there has been an increasing tendency to revert to the traditional views stated above. Other Gospels, such as the Gospel of Peter, or the Gospel of Thomas, are later productions of the second and third centuries, and usually represent the peculiar theological prejudices of some minor sect.

Origin of the Gospels: The existence of the oral Gospel is attested by Papias, one of the earliest of the church fathers, who lived at the close of the first century. A quotation from the preface to his "Interpretation of our Lord's Declarations" preserved in Eusebius indicates that he still depended on the transmission of the Gospel content by the living voice. "But if I met with any one who had been a follower of the elders anywhere, I made it a point to inquire what were the declarations of the elders ... for I do not think that I derived so much benefit from books as from the living voice of those that are still surviving" (quoted in Eusebius: *Historia Ecclesiae,* III. 39). In Papias' time not more than two or three of the original band of Jesus' disciples would still be living, and he would be compelled to obtain his information from those who had heard the apostles. Nevertheless, he preferred the oral testimony to written record. Irrespective of the value of Papias' judgment, his words indicate that the content of the apostolic preaching was independently transmitted by word of mouth two generations after the crucifixion, simultaneously with the use of whatever written records existed.

A clue to the transition from oral preaching to written record is provided by explanatory statements in the Gospels of Luke and John. In the introduction to his Gospel, Luke asserts that he was undertaking to confirm by manuscript what his friend Theophilus had already learned by word of mouth (Luke 1:1-4). He spoke of facts which were taken for granted among believers, and indicated that there had already been numerous attempts to arrange them in orderly narratives. Since his use of the word "narrative" (Gr. *diēgēsis*) implies an extended account, there must have been a number of "gospels" in circulation which he considered to be either inaccessible or else unsatisfactory. If his use of language permits deduction by contrast, these rival gospels were the opposite of his own. They were partial in content, drawn from secondary sources, and perhaps were not organized by any consecutive line of thought. They may have been random collections of sayings or events which had no central theme, or they may not have contained enough biographical material to afford an adequate understanding of Jesus' life.

Luke affirmed on the contrary that he had derived his facts from those who "from the beginning were eye-witnesses and ministers of the word" (1:2). Not only had his informants shared in the events of which they spoke, but also they had been so affected that they became propagandists of the new faith. Luke had been a contemporary of these witnesses, and had investigated personally the truth of their claims, that he might produce an orderly and accurate record of the work of Christ.

John also committed his Gospel to writing that he might inculcate faith in Christ as the Son of God (John 20:30,31). He did not profess to give an exhaustive account of Jesus' activities, but took for granted that many of them would be familiar to his readers. The selective process that he employed was determined by his evangelistic purpose and theological viewpoint.

Although Matthew and Mark are less explicit concerning their origins, the same general principles obtain. The introduction of Matthew, "The book of the generation of Jesus Christ, the son of David, the son of Abraham" (Matt. 1:1), duplicates the phraseology of Genesis (Gen. 5:1) to convey the impression that, like Genesis, it is giving a significant chapter in the history of God's dealing with man. Mark's terse opening line, "The beginning of the Gospel of Jesus Christ, the Son of God," is a title, labeling the following text as a summary of current preaching. Neither of these two offers any reason for its publication, but one may deduce fairly that all of the Gospels began in an attempt to preserve for posterity what had hitherto existed in the minds of the primitive witnesses and in their public addressses.

There has been some question whether the Gospels were first published in Aramaic, the language of Palestine, where the church began, or in Greek. Eusebius quoted Papias' statement that Matthew composed his history in the Hebrew dialect and everyone translated it as he was able (Eusebius, *Historia Ecclesiae,* III, 39). Without the original context, these words are ambiguous. Papias does not make clear whether "Hebrew" was the speech of the OT, or whether he really meant Aramaic. He does not specify whether Matthew's contribution was simply collected notes from which others composed a Gospel, or whether he had already formed an organized narrative that was translated. He does imply that before the Gentile expansion had made the literature of the church Greek, there was a body of material written in Hebrew or Aramaic.

Papias' statement has aroused a great deal of controversy. There are Aramaisms in the Gospels such as *Ephphatha* (Mark 7:34), *Talitha cumi* (Mark 5:41), and the cry from the cross, *Eloi, Eloi, lama sabachthani* (Mark 15:34), which reflect Jesus' use of His mother tongue and the perpetuation of His language in the memoirs of His followers. These, however, do not necessitate that the Gospels were written originally in Aramaic. C. C. Torrey (*Our Translated Gospels.* New York, Harper, 1936) contended that all four Gospels were translations, but there is no agreement on the evidence. If they were translations, they must have been composed prior to the middle of the first century, when the churches were predominantly Palestinian. It is more likely that the Gospels originated in the evangelistic preaching to the Gentile world, and that they were written in Greek, although they contained an Aramaic background.

Composition of the Gospels: The personal reminiscences of the apostolic band, plus the fixed content of their preaching constituted the materials from which the Gospels were constructed, and the purpose of the individual writers provided the method of organization. Both Luke (1:1-4) and John (20:30,31) pledge accuracy of historical fact before they proceed with interpretation, and the same may safely be predicated of Matthew and Mark. All the Gospels were composed for use in the growing movement of the Church; they were not written solely for literary effect. Matthew obviously wished to identify Jesus with the Messiah of the Old Testament by pointing out that He was the fulfilment of prophecy and that He was intimately related to the manifestation of the kingdom. Mark, by his terse descriptive paragraphs, depicted the Son of God in action among men. Luke employed a smoother literary style and a larger stock of parabolic stories to interest a cultured and perhaps humanistic audience. John selected episodes and discourses which others had not used in order to promote belief in Jesus as the Son of God.

The Publication of the Gospels: Where and when these documents were first given to the public is uncertain. The earliest quotations from the Gospel material appear in the letters of Ignatius, in the *Epistle of Barnabas,* the *Teaching of the Twelve Apostles,* and the *Epistle of Polycarp.* All of these are related to Antioch of Syria, and their quotations or allusions bear a stronger resemblance to the text of Matthew than to that of any other Gospel. If, as Papias said, Matthew was first written for the Hebrew or Aramaic church in Jerusalem, it may have been the basis for a Greek edition issued from Antioch during the development of the Gentile church in that city. It would, therefore, have been put into circulation some time after A.D. 50, and before the destruction of Jerusalem in A.D. 70.

Clement of Alexandria (A.D. 200) described the writing of the Gospel of Mark: "When Peter had proclaimed the word publicly at Rome, and declared the gospel under the influence of the Spirit; as there was a great number present, they requested Mark, who had followed him from afar, and remembered well what he had said, to reduce these things to writing, and that after composing the Gospel he gave it to those who requested it of him. Which, when Peter understood, he directly neither hindered nor encouraged it." (Eusebius, *Historia Ecclesiae,* VI, 14.) Irenaeus (c. A.D. 100), Clement's contemporary, confirmed this tradition, adding that Mark handed down Peter's preaching in writing after his death. If the second Gospel represents the memoirs of Peter, it is pos-

sible that its content did not become fixed in literary form until A.D. 65 or later.

The Gospel of Luke may have been a private document, sent first of all to Luke's friend and patron, Theophilus. The adjective "most excellent" (Luke 1:3) implies that he probably belonged to the aristocracy, and that the dual work which Luke wrote was calculated to remove any lingering doubts that he may have entertained concerning the historical and spiritual verities of Christian faith. It can hardly have been written later than A.D. 62, since it must have preceded Acts, which was written about the end of Paul's first imprisonment.

The last chapter of John's Gospel attempts to correct a rumor that he would never die. Obviously the rumor would have no basis unless he had attained an advanced age at the time when the concluding chapter was written. It is possible that it can be dated before A.D. 50, but most conservative scholars place it about A.D. 85. Traditionally it has been ascribed to the apostle John, who ministered at Ephesus in the closing years of the first century.

Synoptic Problem: The three Gospels of Matthew, Mark, and Luke are called *synoptic* from the Greek word *synoptikos,* which means "to see the whole together, to take a comprehensive view." They present similar views of the career and teaching of Christ, and resemble each other closely in content and in phraseology.

The numerous agreements between these Gospels have raised the question whether the relationship between them can be traced to common literary sources. Almost the entire content of the Gospel of Mark can be found in both Matthew and Luke, while much material not found in Mark is common to the other two Gospels. On the other hand, each Gospel has a different emphasis and organization. The "Synoptic Problem," as it is called, may be stated as follows: If the three Gospels are absolutely independent of each other, how can one account for the minute verbal agreements in their text? If they are copied from each other, or compiled freely from common sources, how can they be original and authoritative? Are they, then, truly the product of inspired writers, or are they merely combinations of anecdotes which may or may not be true?

Numerous theories have been propounded to account for these phenomena. The most popular in recent years has been the documentary theory, which assumes that the Gospels were derived from Mark and a hypothetical document called "Q" (from the German *Quelle,* meaning *source*), containing chiefly sayings of Jesus. According to this theory Matthew and Luke were composed independently by combining these two sources. Canon B. H. Streeter (*The Four Gospels,* New York, Macmillan, 1936) suggested also the addition of two special sources, *M* for Matthew and *L* for Luke, embodying the private knowledge or research of the two writers.

While this hypothesis seemingly solves the problem of the verbal resemblances, it is not entirely satisfactory. The existence of "Q" is at best only a probability; no copy of it has ever been found. R. M. Grant has pointed out that extant collections of the "Sayings of Jesus" dating from the second and third centuries should probably be assigned to the Gnostics, who, in turn, were dependent either on oral tradition or upon the canonical

Gospels for their text (R. M. Grant, *The Secret Sayings of Jesus*, New York, Doubleday, 1960, pp. 29,40-61). These documents which have been considered analogous to "Q," and therefore as justifying the hypothesis of its existence, are themselves secondary. It is more likely that the coincident didactic passages of Matthew and Luke are drawn from utterances that Jesus repeated until they became fixed in the minds of His disciples, and were reproduced later in the Gospels.

In recent years the school of historical criticism, called *Formgeschichte,* has advanced another alternative. In an attempt to penetrate the development of the Gospel story before the Gospels, it has suggested that they were composed out of individual reminiscences of Jesus' deeds and bits of His teaching that were first preserved and circulated by His followers. Through repetition and selection these stories took permanent shape, and were incorporated into a general sequence that constituted the Gospel narratives. Advocates of *Formgeschichte* have separated the unitary sections of the Gospels into various classes: the *Passion story* of Jesus' last days; the *Paradigms,* stories of Jesus' deeds that illustrate the message; *Tales* of miraculous occurrences told to interest the public; *Legends* of saintly persons that are morally edifying; *Sayings* of Jesus that preserve His collected teachings in speeches or in parables.

This modification of oral tradition injects a greater uncertainty into the process of literary history. If the Synoptic Gospels are merely different arrangements of independent blocks of text, the problem of origins is multiplied. While sections of the Gospels may have been used for illustrative purposes, and while certain parts of them, like the Sermon on the Mount, might have once been a separate collection of sayings (or deeds, as the case may be), the fact that they were composed in the first century by trustworthy disciples of Jesus precludes fraud or unreliability.

Perhaps the best solution of the Synoptic Problem is the fact that all three Gospels are dealing with the life of the same Person, whose deeds and utterances were being continually preached as a public message. Constant repetition and frequent contact between the preachers tended toward fixing the content of the message. From the day of Pentecost the "teaching of the apostles" possessed some definite form, for it was used in instructing inquirers (Acts 2:42). As the church expanded, the written accounts were created to meet the demand for instruction, and they reproduced the phraseology and content of the oral teaching. Each Gospel, however, was shaped to its own purpose and audience, so that the variations in wording reflected the differences of interest and environment. Matthew was written for Christians with a Jewish background; Mark for active Gentiles, probably Romans; Luke for a cultured and literary Greek. All three, however, bear united witness to the supernatural character and saving purpose of Jesus Christ.

The Johannine Problem: The Fourth Gospel differs markedly in character and in content from the Synoptics. Excluding the feeding of the five thousand and the Passion narrative, there are few points of agreement with the others. So radical are the differences that the veracity of the Gospel has been challenged on the grounds that if it is historical, it should coincide more nearly with the Synoptics.

For this reason some have held that the Fourth Gospel was written in the second century as the church's reflection on the person of Christ, phrased in terms of the Greek *Logos* doctrine. The discovery of the Rylands Fragment, a small scrap of papyrus on which a few verses of John were written, demonstrated that by the beginning of the second century the Gospel of John was circulated as far as southern Egypt. Since the handwriting of the fragment can be dated about 125 A.D., the Gospel must have been written earlier. It could not have been a late product of church tradition.

The language of the Gospel does not necessitate a Hellenistic origin. The existence of the concepts of light and of darkness, truth and falsehood, living waters, and others in the Dead Sea Scrolls show that John need not have drawn his vocabulary from Hellenism, but that many of his terms were a part of contemporary Judaism (William LaSor, *The Amazing Dead Sea Scrolls,* Chicago, Moody Press, 1953, pp. 211-214). The Gospel of John is the account of an eye-witness, writing in his later years and interpreting the person of Christ in the perspective of his Christian experience.

Canonicity: The Gospels were among the first writings to be quoted as sacred and authoritative. There are quotations or allusions from individual passages in Ignatius of Antioch (c. A.D. 116), the *Epistle of Barnabas,* and the *Shepherd of Hermas,* which were written in the early part of the second century. Justin Martyr (c. A.D. 140) mentions the Gospels explicitly, calling them "Memoirs of the Apostles" (*First Apology,* LXVI). Marcion of Sinope (c. A.D. 100), a Gnostic, edited a compilation of Scriptures in which he included a mutilated Gospel of Luke. Tatian, (c. A.D. 150) an Assyrian who was converted in Rome under the ministry of Justin, and later became a Gnostic, produced the first harmony of the Gospels, called the *Diatessaron.* It included only the familiar four, weaving their text together into one continuous narrative. Only a few traces of the *Diatessaron* are still available in translations or in commentaries, but its existence proves that Matthew, Mark, Luke, and John were already the chief sources of information concerning the life and works of Jesus in the first half of the second century.

Growing intercommunication between the churches and the need for strengthening their defenses against heresy and the attacks of pagan critics promoted their interest in a canon of the Gospels. By A.D. 170 the four Gospels were securely established as the sole authorities. According to Irenaeus' contention, "It is not possible that the Gospels can be either more or fewer in number than they are. For since there are four zones of the world in which we live and four principal winds . . . it is fitting that she [the church] should have four pillars, breathing out immortality on every side . . ." (*Against Heresies,* III, xi, 8). Irenaeus' reasons are not very cogent, but the fact that he acknowledged only four indicates the sentiment of his times. The Muratorian Canon, a fragmentary manuscript of the seventh or eighth century containing a list of accepted books earlier than A.D. 200, included in its original form the four Gospels; and they were used by Tertullian of Carthage (c. A.D. 200), Clement of Alexandria (c. A.D. 200), Origen of Alexandria (c. A.D. 250), Cyprian of Carthage (c. A.D. 250); and they appear in the manuscript texts of the Chester

Beatty Papyri and of the Old Latin version, both of which were in existence before A.D. 300. Eusebius (c. A.D. 350) and the fathers following him exclude all other Gospels from their official list, leaving these four the undisputed supreme authorities for knowledge of the life and work of Jesus Christ. See MATTHEW, Gospel of; MARK, Gospel of; LUKE, Gospel of; JOHN, Gospel of; CANON, N.T.   M.C.T.

GOVERNOR (gŭv'êr-nôr), one who governs a land for a supreme ruler to whom he is subordinate. The word governor in the ERV is the rendering of a large variety of Hebrew and Greek words, and is used to represent men holding a number of official governmental positions. For example, Joseph, the prime minister of Egypt, was called its governor (Gen. 42:6; 45:26); Gedaliah, left in Judah to rule the conquered Jews after the destruction of Jerusalem, was called governor (Jer. 40:5; 41:2). In the NT the term occurs chiefly in reference to the Roman procurators of Judea — Pilate, Felix, and Festus. In the 1st century A.D., Roman provinces were of two kinds: imperial and senatorial. The first were ruled by procurators appointed by the emperor; the second, by proconsuls appointed by the senate. Judea was an imperial province. Pontius Pilate was the fifth of the governors of Judea; Felix, the eleventh; and Festus the twelfth. Procurators were directly responsible to the emperor for their actions, and ruled for as long as he willed.

GOZAN (gō'zăn, Heb. *gôzān*), a city located in NE Mesopotamia, on the Habor River, a tributary of the Euphrates. Here the Israelites were deported by the Assyrians following the fall of Samaria, the capital of the northern kingdom, (II Kings 17:6; 18:11; 19:12; II Chron. 5:26). The Assyrians called the city Guzanu, (the Guzanitis of Ptolemy). In 1911 Baron Von Oppenheim discovered a new culture at Tell Halaf, the modern name for Gozan. The relics of pottery are thought to date back to as far as 4000 B.C.

GRACE (Heb. *hēn*, Gr. *cháris*), a term employed by the Biblical writers with a considerable variety of meaning: (1) Properly speaking, that which affords joy, pleasure, delight, charm, sweetness, loveliness; (2) Good will, loving-kindness, mercy, etc; (3) the kindness of a master toward a slave. Thus by analogy, it has come to signify the kindness of God to man (Luke 1:30). The NT writers, at the end of their various epistles, frequently invoke God's gracious favor upon their readers (Rom. 16:20, 24; Phil. 4:23; Col. 1:19; I Thess. 5:28; *et. al.*). In addition, the word "grace" is frequently used to express the concept of kindness bestowed upon someone undeserving thereof. Hence, undeserved favor, especially that kind or degree of favor bestowed upon sinners through Jesus Christ. "For God who is rich in mercy for his great love wherewith he loved us, even when we were dead in sins hath quickened us together in Christ — by grace we are saved" (Eph. 2:4,5). Grace, therefore, is that unmerited favor of God towards fallen man, whereby, for the sake of Christ — who is the only begotten of the Father, full of grace and truth—(John 1:14) He has provided for man's redemption. He has from all eternity determined to extend favor towards all who exercise faith in Christ as Lord and Saviour.

The relationship between law and grace is one of the major themes of the Pauline writings (Rom.

5:1; 15-17; 8:1,2; Eph. 2:8,9; Gal. 5:4,5). Grace is likewise without equivocation identified as the medium or instrument through which God has effected the salvation of all believers (Titus 2:11). Grace is also regarded as the sustaining influence enabling the believer to persevere in the Christian life (Acts 11:23; 20:32; II Cor. 9:14). Thus, it is not merely the initiatory act of God in grace which secures the believers' eternal salvation, but also that which maintains it throughout the entirety of the Christian life. It is also used as a token or proof of salvation (II Cor. 1:5, RV "benefit"). A special gift of grace is imparted to the humble (I Pet. 5:5; James 4:6). Grace can also refer to the capacity for the reception of divine life (I Pet. 1:10). There are likewise several secondary senses in which "grace" is used: a gift of knowledge (I Cor. 1:4); thanksgiving or gratitude expressed for favor (I Cor. 10:30; I Tim. 1:1,2). Grace is employed at least once in the sense of "reward or recompense" (Luke 6:32), for which Matthew substitutes the term *misthos*, or *wages* (Matt. 5:46).

GRAFF, GRAFT, a horticultural process by which the branches of the wild olive tree in eastern lands are cut back so that branches from a cultivated olive may be inserted and grafting take place. Paul makes use of this practice in reverse (Rom. 11:17-24) where the opposite process is envisioned as happening; *i.e.,* the wild branches, the Gentiles, are thought of as "grafted in" to the good stock of the parent tree, the children of Israel. This deliberate inversion, certainly not a foolish mistake, heightens rather than mitigates the picturesque figure of speech conveying the eternal truth of the rejection of Israel and the status of the church.

GRAIN (See Plants)

GRANARY (grăn'êrē, Heb. *māzû*, Gr. *apothéke*, derived from a Hebrew word meaning *to gather* (Ps. 144:15), or Heb. *ôtzār, storehouse* (Joel 1:17). In the NT the term is sometimes rendered *barn*, and sometimes *garner* (Matt. 3:12; Luke 3:17). The Egyptians had storehouses for grain, liquor, armor, provisions, jewels, etc. Joseph, during the years of famine in Egypt, had authority over the storehouses (Gen. 41:56).

GRAPE (See Plants)

GRASS. There are a great many species of true grasses in Palestine, but actual turf is virtually unknown. The word "grass" is used in a somewhat comprehensive sense in the English version and is the rendering of a number of Hebrew terms and one Greek term. Genesis 1:11,12 divides the vegetable kingdom into three great classes: grass, herbs, and trees. The word is used in a figurative sense, too, as when man's brief exile is compared to grass (Ps. 103:15,16; Matt. 6:30; Luke 12:28).

GRASSHOPPER (See Insects)

GRATE (Heb. *resheth*), a copper network, moved by a copper ring at each corner and placed under the top of the great altar (Exod. 27:4; 35:16; 38: 4,5). It reached halfway up the altar and was doubtless to catch the ashes from the burning sacrifices.

GRAVE (Heb. *qěvěr, she'ôl,* Gr. *mnemeíon*), a place for the interment of the dead; a tomb, a sepulchre. Graves and accompanying burial customs differed in Biblical times from country to country. The pyramids were used for burial of members of the royal house. The Egyptians were meticulous in the construction of their graves because of their ardent belief in a future life. The rich were buried in a *mastaba,* or a rectangular structure of brick placed above the grave itself. In the neighborhood of Gizeh near the pyramids and at Saqqarah a number of these mastabas have been discovered. The very poor were interred clothesless and coffinless in the dry, sandy soil of Egypt. In later centuries, the rock tomb was substituted for the mastaba. Examples of these are the rock-hewn tombs of Thotmes III and Tutankhamon. Tutankhamon's tomb consisted of a passage cut into a hill of rock leading to a hall supported by columns where the sarcophagus of the pharaoh lay. Bas-reliefs in bright colors were frequently depicted on the walls of these tombs. Sumerian practice demanded that the royal dead be accompanied by the living, human beings and animals, forming a ghastly entourage. Queen Shu-ad of Ur, Abraham's city, was interred in this style with her husband. Three of the great kings of Persia cut their tombs out of the rocks near Persepolis. Among the Hebrews, graves were sometimes mere holes in the earth (Gen. 35:8; I Sam. 31:13); natural caves or grottos; or artificial tombs hewn out of the rock (Luke 7:12, John 11:30). In such a sepulchre, provided through the kindness of Joseph of Arimathea, the body of Jesus was laid. Flat stones were placed upon the graves as markers to warn passers-by that they should not contract ceremonial defilement by unwittingly trespassing. These stones were white-

ONE OF THE TOMBS of the Kings in Jerusalem, showing a rolling stone at the opening. Hebrew graves consisted of holes in the earth, natural caves or grottos, or artificial tombs hewn out of the rock.

ROMAN sarcophagi of Antioch, along the Orontes River. The ancient Greeks and Romans made their tombs of limestone.

washed annually in the month of Adar. This was the underlying figure of speech behind Jesus' stinging rebuke of the Pharisees, "Ye are like unto whited sepulchres" (Matt. 23:27). There were some traces still extant in the days of Christ (Matt. 8:28) of the idea that tombs were the dwelling places of demons.   J.F.G.

GRAVE CLOTHES (Gr. *keiría, winding sheet*). Preparatory to burial, the body was washed, and frequently anointed with spices, then stretched out on a bier until it was ready to be buried (Acts 5:7). After the washing and anointing, the corpse was wrapped in a linen winding sheet, the hands and feet were bound with grave-bands, and the face covered with a napkin (John 11:44; 19:40).

GRAVEN IMAGE, an image of wood, stone, or metal, shaped with a sharp cutting instrument as distinguished from one cast in a mold (Isa. 20:22; 44:16,17; 45:20). Images were, however, sometimes cast and then finished by the graver (Isa. 40:19). Such images were used by the Canaanites (Deut. 7:5), by the Babylonians, and by others (Jer. 50:38; 51:47,52). The Israelites were forbidden by the Decalogue to make them (Exod. 20:4).

GREAT OWL (See Birds)

GREAVES (See Arms, Armor)

GRECIA, GRECIANS. Grecia is Greece, the home of the Hellenes. Greeks and Grecians, however, are to be distinguished. Greeks are generally those of Hellenic race (e.g. Acts 16:1; 18:4 and probably John 12:20), but the word may be used to indicate non-Jews, foreigners and aliens (Rom. 1:16). Grecians were Greek-speaking Jews, folk of the Dispersion, from areas predominantly Greek (Acts 6:1; 9:29). Greece and its associated island groups form the SE end of southern Europe's mountain system, a rugged peninsula and archipelago, not rich in fertile or arable land, which was the terminus of the southward movement of the Indo-European-speaking tribes who became the Greek people. These tribes, or their predecessors, had established ordered life in the peninsula and islands by the twelfth century before Christ.

Their civilization vanished before the end of the second millennium, in a dark age of destruction and invasion occasioned by further waves of wandering tribes, just as Celt, Roman, Saxon, Dane, Norman, ripples of the same folk-movement of related peoples, made a succession of construction and destruction in Britain. Out of four centuries of chaos emerged the complex of peoples on island and mainland who are called the Greeks. Their own generic name was Hellenes, but Graecia was a portion of the land which, lying in the NW, naturally came first into the ken of Rome. After the common fashion of popular nomenclature (see under 'Palestine'), the name of the part which first claimed attention was extended to include the whole. Mediated through Rome, the term Greece was applied to all Hellas, and all Hellenes were called Greeks by western Europe. Geography, as always, played a part in the history of the people. The city state was a natural consequence of the isolated plain or river valley ringed by precipitous terrain. So was sea-faring. And from sea-faring and the dearth of fertile land in a rugged peninsula, sprang colonization, and the spread of Greek colonies which marked the first half of the pre-Christian millennium. As early as the eighth century before Christ, Greek ports and trading posts were scattered from the Crimea to Cadiz. In these same centuries began the first flowering of Greek thought and poetry. In Ionia, the foundations of scientific and philosophical thought were laid. On Lesbos, in those same years, Sappho and Alcaeus wrote supreme lyric poetry. In short, the active, inquisitive, brilliant, inventive Greek race was visible in full promise round the eastern end of the Mediterranean before the bright flowering of fifth-century Athens. That century was one of the great golden ages of man. Greece, interpreted by the dynamic people of Attica, in one brief noon-tide of the human spirit, made immortal contributions to literature, art, philosophy and political thought. Everything Greek in all future centuries was deepened and colored by Athens' achievement. Hellenism, which had centuries of dynamic life ahead of it, was shaped by Athens in the short years of its spiritual supremacy. Athens' glory faded, and her strength was sapped in lamentable war with the dour and uncreative autocracy of Sparta. On the ruins of a Greece fatally weakened by internecine strife, Philip of Macedon, in the mid-fourth century before Christ, built his empire. His son Alexander, in one of the strangest acts of conquest in all history, took that empire to India, swept the vast state of Persia out of existence, and, as his father had unified Greece, brought under his single rule the great complex of states and kingdoms which lay between the Dardanelles and the Indus, the Caspian and the Nile. When Alexander died in Babylon at the age of thirty-three in 323 B.C., his generals divided the world (vid. sub *Seleucids, Ptolemy*), and out of the division arose the Oriental kingdoms which the Romans conquered when their empire rounded the Mediterranean Sea. The Greek language, Greek thought, Greek culture, in the wake of Alexander, provided a unifying element in all the Middle East. Without the vast flow of the Greek tide eastwards, the NT could not have been born. Greek provided its language and fashion of thought. Hellenism was a stimulus to the human mind. To reason, question, speculate, was a habit with the Greeks. Hence the logical

RUINS of the Theater and the Temple of Apollo at Delphi, a cultural center of ancient Greece, near Mt. Parnassus. Delphi is also the site of the celebrated oracle of Apollo.

mind of Greek-speaking Paul of Tarsus, heir of both Hellenism and Judaism. Hence the 'Grecians' of the NT, Stephen, for example, and Philip, who sweep fresh, bold, and vigorous into the story of the early Church, ready to reform, and to rethink old concepts. Paul needed his Greek education, as he needed the Judaism of Gamaliel. Paul's synthesis of the covenants, so compelling in its logic, so fundamental in Christian theology, was the work of a Greek Jew. It was thought trained in the Hellenism of Tarsus which solved the problem of the Testaments, and brought out from the stores of Judaism the wares which Christians could recognize and use.   E.M.B.

GREEK LANGUAGE was a major branch of the Indo-European language which is the presumed parent of all the languages of Europe except Basque, Finnish and Hungarian, and of Sanskrit and the languages which derive from the Sanskrit stock in India. From Ireland to Pakistan this linguistic kinship can be demonstrated from vocabulary, morphology, and syntax. No monuments of the original Indo-European language exist, but the wide diffusion of demonstrably related tongues is strong argument for some form of early unity. The pattern of folk-wandering, which spread the Indo-European languages so widely, was a longer and more complex process than was imagined in the nineteenth century. This century has demonstrated the Indo-European basis of Hittite, and in 1953 Michael Ventris showed that the language of the Pylos tablets was a primitive Greek, thus proving that the language was spoken in the Peloponnesus several centuries before the time once favored for the arrival in the area of the Hellenic tribes. The piecemeal nature of their southward infiltration, and the firm geographical subdivisions of the area they occupied, led to the survival into literary times of several dialects, *Attic-Ionic,* spoken in Attica, and the Ionic areas of Asia Minor, with associated islands; *Achaean,* which included the Aeolic of Lesbos, and the dialects of Thessaly and Boeotia, together with the undocumented dialect of the Arcado-Cyprian; and thirdly what L. R. Palmer calls *West Greek,* including under that name the dialects of Phocis, Locris, Elis, and Aetolia, together with the Doric of the Peloponnesus, the Peloponnesian colonies, and Magna Graecia. Of these dialects, Attic achieved the supreme position because of the worth and greatness of the incomparable literature in which it found its expression. Attic Greek was one of the major achievements of the human mind. The richness and subtlety of its syntax, its flexibility, the delicacy of its particles, these and other linguistic features make Attic the most expressive medium ever developed for human thought. The dialects passed with the city states and the unification of Greece, and were followed by a basic Greek which developed in the form of a simplified Attic. This, spread by Alexander's conquests throughout the eastern end of the Mediterranean, was called the *Koine* or Common Dialect. It was the speech of the LXX and the NT, and the major influence in bringing the contributions of Palestine, Greece, and Rome into that partnership which determined the form and shape of the NT, the global Gospel of Paul of Tarsus, the Christian Church, and modern Europe.   E.M.B.

GREEK VERSIONS. 1. The first and most famous of the Greek Versions of the OT, and the only one to survive in its entirety, is the Septuagint or "Version of the Seventy." This is the version most frequently quoted in the NT, for it became the Bible of the Hellenistic Jews, as the Vulgate became the Bible of the Latin world. The Vulgate was, in fact, in direct succession, being a translation of the Septuagint. Legend has gathered around so remarkable an achievement of translation, but it is possible to disengage some essential facts. It seems certain that the Septuagint was published in the time of Ptolemy II Philadelphus (295-247 B.C.), the Golden Age of Greek Alexandria. The city was always remarkable for its large colony of Jews, and the Greek Version of the Scriptures was probably a nationalistic gesture, designed to demonstrate, in what was becoming the world's second language, the worth of Jewish literature. It is doubtful whether the suggestion emanated from the king himself, interested though he was in all literature . The story of the 72 elders sent from Jerusalem, and the 72 days taken to complete the work, is legend. The Septuagint is written in the common dialect, but tinged by Hebraisms. The quality of the language and style varies, but on the whole the Greek is odd and undistinguished. It prompts knotty questions of criticism, to the solution of which the Dead Sea Scrolls have provided a little material. They have demonstrated, for example, that the Septuagint followed an older Hebrew text than that which survived in the traditional OT.

2. The acceptance of the Septuagint as the Bible of Greek-speaking Christianity, prompted orthodox Jewry to produce its own version distinct from it. Hence the version of Aquila of Hadrian's day (A.D. 117-138). The version of which only fragments exist, was in the worst "translation Greek," which followed slavishly the Hebrew forms and syntax.

3. Theodotian, an Ephesian of the second century, and an Ebionite Christian, produced a version which could be described as a RV of the Septuagint. It found favor with the Christian community. It was a freer translation than that of Aquila.

4. Symmachus, of unknown date, produced, perhaps at the end of the second century, a Greek version which appears to have been the best of all the translations, a rendering into idiomatic Greek.
                                                  E.M.B.

GREYHOUND (See Animals)

GRIND (Heb. *tāhan,* Gr. *alétho, grind with a hand mill*), the grinding of grain into flour when pulverized between two heavy stones, a domestic art usually performed by women; hence, the import of Christ's parable: "Two women shall be grinding at the mill . . ." (Matt. 24:41; Luke 17:35).

GROVE (Heb. *ăshērâh,* Gr. *álsos,* mistranslated *grove* in the KJV following the LXX and the Vulgate). Although one gains a rather confused picture from the mere reading of the Scripture, the sum total of information affords a rather full and horrible panorama of iniquitous idolatry. The equipment for such worship, presumptively Phoenician in origin, were the "high places," (Heb. *bāmôth*), the altars crowning them, the standing pillars and the images of the Ashera. The worship was interwoven with the concept of the fertility of the land, and so became a fertility cult. The chosen symbol of the cult was the trunk of a tree. This explains the prohibition against the planting of trees by the altar of Jehovah (Deut. 16:21; Judg. 6:25,28,31). The goddess of the cult was Asherah, who also appears as mistress of the sea. A long risqué poem describes the journey of Lady Asherah to obtain permission from El to erect a temple (see Pritchard: *Archaeology and the Old*

EXCERPT from the Septuagint, a fragment of the Sinaitic Greek translation of the Old Testament, photographed from one of the scraps found at Mount Sinai.

Testament, pp. 112f). The prophets of Israel roundly condemn the worship of Asherah and congratulate those kings who destroyed them (I Kings 15: 13f; II Kings 17:10; 21:3; 23:4). Allied with the idea of fertility, Asherah has her counterpart in the Babylonian Ishtar, the goddess of love, and as such the goddess of human productivity.

GUARD, the rendering of a number of Heb. and Gr. words: 1. *tabbāh, slaughterer,* used of Potiphar (Gen. 37:36, etc.), Nebuzaradan (II Kings 25:8, etc.; Jer. 39:9, etc.), and Arioch (Dan. 2: 14). The term may refer to a member of the king's bodyguard, who also had the duty of "slaughtering" anyone who tried to harm the king. 2. *rûts, runner,* trusted foot soldiers of a king, who performed various functions (I Kings 14:27,28; II Kings 10:25). 3. *mishmār, watch* (Neh. 4:22). 4. *mishma'ath, guard* (II Sam. 23:23). 5. *spekoulátor, guard, a spy* (Mark 6:27). 6. *koustodía, watch* (Matt. 27:65).

GUDGODAH (gŭd-gō'dȧ, Heb. *gudgōdhâh, cleft, division*), a place in the wilderness journeys of the children of Israel (Deut. 10:7), corresponding to Hor-haggidgag of Numbers 33:32. Identification still uncertain.

GUEST CHAMBER (Heb. *lishkâh,* in I Sam. 9:22 of KJV "parlor", *katáluma, inn, room in which to eat*). The *lishkâh* may have been a room in which the sacrificial feasts were held. *Katáluma* often means "inn," but in Mark 14:14 and Luke 22:11 it means a room in which to eat.

GUILT is the deserving of punishment because of the violation of a law or a breach of conduct. In the OT law the conception of guilt is largely ritualistic and legalistic. A person could be guilty as the result of unwitting sin (Lev. 5:17). Israel, moreover, is viewed as an organic whole, so that what one does affects all. There is collective responsibility for sin, as when Achan sinned and all Israel suffered. With the prophets, the ethical and personal aspects of sin and of guilt are stressed.

God is less interested in ritual correctness than in moral obedience.

In the NT Jesus stressed the importance of right heart attitude as over against outwardly correct acts, and taught that there are degrees of guilt, depending upon a person's knowledge and motive (Luke 11:29-32; 12:47,48; 23:34). Paul also recognized differences of degree in guilt (Acts 17:30; Eph. 4:18). Theologians differ as to whether Paul in Romans 5:12-21 teaches that Adam's guilt was imputed to all his posterity; and if it was, just how it was done.   S.B.

GUNI (gū'nī). 1. The name of a family clan of the tribe of Naphtali (Gen. 46:24; Num. 26:48; I Chron. 7:13).

2. The head of a Gadite family (I Chron. 5:15).

GUNITE (gū'nīt), the family of Guni, son of Naphtali (Num. 26:48).

GUR (gûr), a rising ground, not definitely identified, but thought to be near Jenin; roughly, about 12 or 13 miles NE of Samaria. The place where Ahaziah received his mortal wound while fleeing from Jehu, after the slaughter of Joram (II Kings 9:27).

GUR-BAAL (gûr'bā'ăl, *sojourn of Baal*), a small colony town of Arabs, against whom Uzziah of Judah was given divine aid (II Chron. 26:7); perhaps in the desert S of Beer-sheba.

GUTTER (gŭt'têr, Heb. *tsinnôr, pipe, spout, conduit*), the channel or tunnel (AV Gutter) through which David's soldiers are inferred to have marched to wrest the city of Jerusalem from Jebusite rule (II Sam. 5:8), at the fountain of Gihon (q.v.), site of the later tunnel which Hezekiah constructed (II Kings 20:20) connecting the spring at Gihon with the pool of Siloam. It was 1800 ft. long and 6 ft. high. It was dug out as a far sighted measure so that the city's water supply would not be imperiled during the impending siege at the hands of Sennacherib of Assyria.

H

HAAHASHTARI, HAASHTARI (hā'à-hăsh'tà-rī, hā-ăsh'tà-rī, *the Ahashtarite*), a man of Judah, mentioned in I Chronicles 4:6. Probably a muleteer, son of Naarah.

HABAIAH (hà-bā'yà, *Jehovah has hidden*), ancestor of some priests in Zerubbabel's time (Ezra 2: 61); called Hobaiah in Nehemiah 7:63 RV.

HABAKKUK (hà-băk'ŭk, Heb. *hăvaqqûq, embrace*), the name of a prophet and of the eighth book of the Minor Prophets, which is entitled "The oracle which Habakkuk the prophet saw" (1:1). Of the man Habakkuk nothing is known outside of the book which bears his name. Legendary references to him (in the apocryphal *Bel and the Dragon* and elsewhere) appear to have no historical value. The musical references in Chapter 3 have led some to believe that he was a member of a Levitical musical guild; even this is uncertain.

Most traditional scholars believe the book to be a unity, the work of Habakkuk, produced in Judah during the Chaldean period. The reasons for this view are found in the book itself. The temple still stands (2:20; 3:19) and the rise of the Chaldean power is predicted (1:5,6). The argument here depends upon the understanding of the Hebrew word *kasdîm*, translated Chaldeans. Some recent scholars emend the word to *kittîm*, meaning Cy-

priots, and understand it to refer to the Macedonian Greeks under Alexander the Great. They therefore date the book to this much later period. There is no good reason to make this emendation. *Kasdîm* clearly means Chaldeans.

The Neo-Babylonian or Chaldean empire first came to prominence when the Babylonian king Nebuchadnezzar defeated the Egyptians at the battle of Carchemish in 605 B.C., and re-established Babylon as the seat of world power. The prophecy of Habakkuk could hardly have been given before 605 B.C. Jerusalem fell to Nebuchadnezzar in 587 B.C. The book must be placed somewhere between these dates, probably during the reign of the Judean king Jehoiakim. Some date the book earlier, believing that the Chaldeans were known to Judah before Carchemish and emphasizing the unexpectedness of the attack mentioned by Habakkuk (1: 5). Still, a date soon after 605 B.C. seems to be preferred.

In modern times the unity of the book has been questioned. The psalm of Chapter 3 is certainly somewhat different in style from the rest of the book, but this is hardly sufficient reason to deny it to Habakkuk. The theory that all psalms were post-Exilic in Israel is now discredited. The theme of the prose part (chs. 1,2) is the same as that of the psalm. And there are real similarities of

FRAGMENT of the Habakkuk Commentary from the Dead Sea Scrolls. The Commentary sought to show that the religious situation foretold in the Book of Habakkuk was realized in the author's day. The Commentary was found in the caves at Qumran. © Shrine of the Book, Jerusalem.

language. Chapter 3 is specifically ascribed to Habakkuk (3:1), and there seems to be no good internal indication that he was not its author.

Chapters 1 and 2 set forth Habakkuk's prophetic oracle or burden. Twice the prophet is perplexed and asks divine enlightenment; twice he is answered. First he is concerned over the violence and sin of his people, the Judeans. Why are these wicked men not punished (1:2-4)? God answers that He is about to send the Chaldeans to judge Judah (1:5-11). This answer plunges Habakkuk into a greater perplexity: How can a righteous God use the wicked Chaldeans to punish Judah, which, although it has become apostate, is still better than the Chaldeans (1:12-17)? God's answer is that the proud conquerors will themselves be punished (2:1-20). The Chaldeans are puffed up with self-sufficient pride, but in this hour of national calamity the righteous will live by His faithfulness, i.e., by His constancy, abiding in God although all of the helps given to the OT believers (the nation, the temple and its ritual) are swept away (2:4). This statement naturally becomes important to the NT writers and is quoted in Romans 1:17, Galatians 3:11, and Hebrews 10:38. The second answer to Habakkuk concludes with a series of woes against the Chaldeans (2:5-20).

Chapter 3 is called "a prayer of Habakkuk the prophet" (3:1). In a moving lyric poem the prophet records his final response to God's message of judgment. He describes the divine revelation in terms of a stormy theophany (3:2-15), but concludes that no matter what comes he will trust in God (3:16-19).

The commentary on Chapters 1 and 2 recently found at Qumran near the Dead Sea casts little light on the meaning of these chapters, although it enables us to know how the Essene community there in the first century B.C. understood the book.
J.B.G.

HABAZINIAH (hab'a-zĭ-nī'a), ancestor of the Rechabites of the time of Jeremiah. Mentioned only in Jeremiah 35:3.

HABERGEON (hăb'êr-jŭn, Heb. *tahărā'*), a jacket of mail to defend the breast and neck (II Chron. 26:14; Neh. 4:16). Job 41:26 has "pointed shaft," with "coat of mail" in the margin. Habergeon is also used to render a different Heb. word of uncertain meaning in Exodus 28:32; 39:23.

HABIRU (hà-bī'rū), the name of a people first made known in the Amarna letters (15th century B.C.), where they are mentioned among those who are intruders of Palestine. Since then the name has appeared in Babylonian texts and documents from Mari (18th century B.C.), the Hittite records from Boghaz-keui and the Hurrian texts from Nuzi (14th century B.C.). The same name appears in Egyptian records as "Apiriu" as late as the 12th century B.C. Abraham is the first person in the Bible to bear the name Hebrew, 'Ibri (Gen. 14: 13). Some scholars philologically equate the names Habiru and 'Ibri. The fundamental meaning of Habiru seems to be "wanderers." It is not an ethnic designation, for the Habiru of these various texts are of mixed racial origin, including both Semites and non-Semites. The name Habiru therefore has a wider connotation than the people known as Hebrews, although it became associated with them particularly. The patriarchal movements of Genesis appear to be parts of a larger movement of peoples known as the Habiru, with the Hebrew

conquest of Canaan as only one of these. The connection, if any, of the Hebrews with the Habiru still remains obscure.
S.B.

HABOR (hā'bôr, Heb. *hāvōr*), a river of Gozan, the region in the northern part of Mesopotamia to which Shalmanezer, king of Assyria, banished the northern tribes of Israel after Hoshea, the last king, had rebelled against him (II Kings 17:6; 18: 11). To this same region, Tiglath-pilezer (Tilgath-pilneser) had carried the tribes E of Jordan (I Chron. 5:26).

HACHALIAH (hăk'à-lī'à, in ASV, *Hacaliah*), the father of Nehemiah, governor of the Jews (Neh. 1:1; 10:1).

HACHILAH (hà-kī'là), a hill in the wilderness SE of Hebron, near Ziph and Maon (I Sam. 23:19; 26:1,3)). Here David hid from Saul, but was discovered, and here Saul encamped, seeking David.

HACHMONI (hăk'mō-nī, Heb. *hakhmônî, wise*), the father of Jehiel, an associate of David's sons (I Chron. 27:32) and of Jashobeam, one of David's mighty men (I Chron. 11:11). Cf. "Tachmonite" in II Samuel 23:8. The text is obscure.

HADAD (hā'dăd, *sharpness, fierceness*). 1. A grandson of Abraham through Ishmael (Gen. 25: 15; Hadar in KJV; I Chron. 1:30).

2. An early king of Edom, whose capital was at Pau or Pai (I Chron. 1:50). In Genesis 36:39 he is called "Hadar."

3. An earlier king of Edom, a son of Bedad, who smote Midian in the field of Moab (Gen. 36: 35; I Chron. 1:46).

4. An Edomite of royal descent whose life had been saved in his early childhood by flight from David's devastating attacks. Hadad went to Egypt, where Pharaoh received him and his men, gave him a house, and highly favored him. Hadad became brother-in-law to Tahpenes, queen of Egypt, but later when he learned that Joab had died, he went back to Edom and became an adversary to Solomon (I Kings 11:14-25).

5. The supreme God of Syria, whose name is found in proper names like Ben-hadad and Hadadezer. In Assyrian inscriptions he is identified with their air-god Ramman, i.e., Rimmon.

HADADEZER, HADAREZER (hăd'ăd-ē'zêr, hăd'-ăr-ē'zêr, *Hadad is a help*), a king of Zobah, twice defeated in battle by David, king of Israel (II Sam. 8:3ff; 10:1-19; I Chron. 18:3ff). Zobah was a kingdom lying NE of Damascus and between the valleys of the Orontes and the Euphrates.

HADAD-RIMMON (hā'dăd-rĭm'ŏn, *Hadad and Rimmon, two Syrian divinities*), a place in the valley of Megiddo, where Josiah, king of Judah, was mortally wounded (II Kings 23:29,30), and where later there was a memorable mourning for him as recorded in Zechariah 12:11. It is now called Rummaneh, i.e. "place of pomegranates."

HADAR (hā'dàr). 1. According to Genesis 25:15 in KJV a son of Ishmael, but the Hebrew and ASV unite in calling him Hadad and I Chronicles 1:30 supports Hadad.

2. The last of the ancient kings of Edom (Gen. 36:39) but in I Chronicles 1:50,51 he also is called Hadad. "Hadar" and "Hadad" are easily confused in Hebrew.

HADASHAH (hà-dăsh'à, *new*), a town of Judah in the low plain in Joshua's time (Josh. 15:37).

HADASSAH (hà-dăs'à, *a myrtle*), daughter of Abihail, who became Esther, queen of Xerxes, i.e. Ahasuerus (Esth. 2:7,15).

HADATTAH (hà-dăt'à, *new*), a town in the S of Judah. In Joshua 15:25 KJV makes it seem to be a separate town, but the Hebrew and ASV make it clear that "Hadattah" is simply a description of Hazor. It may be that there were an old and a new Hazor.

HADES (hā'dēz, Gr. *Haídes, not to be seen*), the place or state of the dead, as contrasted with the final punishment of the wicked. In the NT Greek, the word occurs ten times and is uniformly rendered "hell" in KJV. In the TR from which KJV was translated, the word occurs also in I Corinthians 15:55 and is rendered "grave," but in the better texts the Greek has *thanate* and ASV "death," which is correct. The NT word is taken over from the Greek mythology, where *Hades* was the god of the lower regions. Although the word was taken from heathen myths, the concept is from the OT word *Sheol. Sheol* occurs 65 times in the Hebrew OT and is rendered in KJV as "hell" 31 times, "the grave" 31 times, and "the pit" three times; but in ASV it is uniformly transliterated *Sheol,* even as *Hades* in the ASV is a transliteration rather than an attempt to translate the Greek. The word "hell" in English always has an unpleasant connotation and is properly thought of as the final destiny of the wicked when it translates *geenna,* which occurs 12 times and is always rendered "hell."

For the most part, the NT does not give very definite light on Hades. In Matthew 11:23 (cf. Luke 10:15) our Lord says that Capernaum will go down into Hades. The preposition "down" points to the OT teaching that Sheol is inside the earth (Amos 9:2; Ps. 139:8, etc.) and the following verse (Matt. 11:24) puts the day of judgment for both Sodom and Capernaum later than the stay in Hades. In Matthew 16:18, "the gates of hell" seem to be a reference to Satan's headquarters, as the great enemy of the Christian Church. In the parable of the rich man and Lazarus (Luke 16:19-31) the rich man is pictured as being tormented in Hades, but able to see in the distance Abraham with Lazarus in his bosom. He asks for a drop of water to cool his tongue and for a message to be sent to his five brethren who are still alive on earth, and in each case his request is denied. In the first Christian sermon Peter quotes (Acts 2:25-31) from Psalm 16:8-11 proving from it that our Lord arose from the dead and was not left in Hades. In Revelation "death and Hades" are four times associated (1:18; 6:8; 20:13,14), being treated as almost synonymous terms. In the last verse mentioned, death and Hades are to be cast into the lake of fire, i.e. doomed to utter destruction. See GEHENNA.   A.B.F.

HADID (hā'dĭd, Heb. *hādhîdh, sharp*), a village in Benjamin named with Lod (Ezra 2:33; Neh. 7:37; 11:34). It was located about three miles E of Lydda.

HADLAI (hăd'lī, *ceasing, forbearing*), the father of Amasa, an Ephraimite chief, mentioned only in II Chronicles 28:12.

HADORAM (hà-dō'răm, Heb. *hădhōrām*). 1. A son of Joktan (Gen. 10:27; I Chron. 1:21) and probably an Arab tribe of that name in Arabia Felix.

2. Son of the king of Hamath whom his father sent to congratulate David on his victory over Hadadezer (I Chron. 18:9-11). In II Samuel 8:9, 10 the name is written as Joram.

3. Rehoboam's superintendent of the men under taskwork (II Chron. 10:18). The children of Israel stoned him when Rehoboam sent him to them, presumably to collect taxes or to raise a levy of workers. (Perhaps the same as Adoniram of I Kings 4:6.)

HADRACH (hā'drăk, Heb. *hadhrākh*), a country associated with Damascus and Hamath and mentioned only in Zechariah 9:1. Gesenius guesses that it lay E of Damascus.

HAGAB (hā'găb, Heb. *hāghāv, locust*), ancestor of some temple servants who returned with Zerubbabel (Ezra 2:46).

SARAH, DESPAIRING OF GIVING ABRAHAM an heir, prevailed upon him to take her maidservant, Hagar, for his concubine. When Hagar learned that she was with child by Abraham, she felt mightier than her mistress, and taunted Sarah cruelly.

HAGAR (hā'gàr, Heb. *hāghār, emigration, flight*), an Egyptian handmaid to Sarai, wife of Abram (Gen. 12:10-20). God had promised to him a son who would be his heir (Gen. 15:4), but Sarai was barren, and so, following the marital customs of the times, she gave Hagar to her husband as her substitute (Gen. 16:1-16). Nuzi documents which

787

LAHAI-RIO SPRING at Mt. Seir, traditional spot where Hagar and her son Ishmael found water after the Lord's intercession.

have been discovered stipulate that if a wife is barren, she must furnish her husband with a slave wife.) When Hagar saw that she had conceived, she despised her mistress, causing trouble in the household. Hagar was driven out, but the angel of the Lord appeared to her and sent her back to her mistress (Gen. 16:7-14). When Ishmael, her son, was 14 years old, his father 100 and Sarah 90, Isaac was born. At a great feast held in connection with Isaac's weaning, Ishmael scoffed at the proceedings (Gen. 21:9), and as a result Sarah insisted that Hagar and her son be cast out, which Abraham unwillingly did. God told Abraham that Ishmael's descendants would become a nation. Hagar is last seen taking for her son a wife out of the land of Egypt, her own land (Gen. 21:1-21). Paul made the story of Hagar an allegory of the difference between law and grace (Gal. 4:21-5:1).

HAGARENES, HAGARITES (hă′gȧr-ēnz, hă′gȧr-īts, in ASV "Hagrites"), an Arab people with whom in the days of King Saul, the tribe of Reuben made war (I Chron. 5:19,20). The Hagarites were so strong that Reuben won the victory only by crying to God in the battle. Psalm 83 tells how the Hagarenes were leagued not only with Moab and the Ammonites E of the Jordan, Edom, the Ishmaelites and Amalek to the S, but also with Gebal, Tyre and Philistia along the coast against Israel, and Asaph prays that God for His own name's sake will defeat them utterly.

HAGGAI (hăg′ā-ī, Heb. *haggay, festal*), prophet of the Lord to the Jews in 520 B.C. Little is known of his personal history. He lived soon after the

HAGGAI DENOUNCED THE PEOPLE for building ornate houses for themselves and for failing to finish the primary task of rebuilding the Temple. Their neglect of God's house, Haggai now told them, was the reason for the barrenness of their crops.

Captivity, and was contemporary with Zechariah (cf. Hag. 1:1 with Zech. 1:1).

After the return from the Captivity the Israelites set up the altar upon its base, established daily worship, and laid the foundation for the second temple; then they were compelled to cease building for some years. However, though times were hard they were able to build fine ceiled houses for themselves (Hag. 1:4). Meanwhile kings succeeded one another in Persia. Cyrus, favored of God and friend of the Jews (Isa. 44:28; II Chron. 36:22) passed away in 529 B.C.; then his son Cambyses (the "Ahasuerus" of Ezra 4:6) reigned 529-522 B.C., followed for only seven months in 522 by the Pseudo-Smerdis (a usurper); then arose Darius Hystaspes (Ezra 4-6; Hag., Zech. 1-6), who helped and encouraged the Jews to go ahead, and who commanded the hinderers to desist. In the second year of Darius (520 B.C.) Haggai fulfilled his brilliant mission of rebuking and encouraging the Jews. The five short messages which make up his books are all dated, occupying only three months and 23 days; and in those few weeks the whole situation changed from defeat and discouragement to victory. Zechariah assisted Haggai in the last month of his recorded ministry (Zech. 1:1-6).

In order to make the dates clearer to modern readers, we shall give the months their approximately equivalent names in our calendar. On "Sept." 1, 520 B.C. the Lord spoke through Haggai, and instead of addressing the people at large, the prophet went straight to "headquarters," i.e., to Zerubbabel the prince and to Joshua, the high priest. The people stopped building the Lord's house though they were quite able to build their own, and God's message was "Consider your ways." The punishment for their neglect had been futility; they labored much but produced little; and so God used "weather judgments" to bring them to their senses. The leaders heeded the message and with the best of the people, they began immediately to build and on "Sept." 24 God's short message was "I am with you" (Hag. 1:13). A month later, they were tempted to be discouraged when they contrasted their present effort with the former magnificent temple and so God told them that "the glory of this house shall be greater than the former" (2:9). This message was delivered on "Oct." 21 and it contained the notable statement, that "the silver is mine, and the gold is mine." The fourth and fifth messages came in one day "Dec." 24, 520 B.C. In the fourth, Haggai said that holiness is not contagious, though evil is, and Israel's change in attitude would cause God to change chastening into blessing. In the last message (2:20-23) God predicts a shaking of the nations but at the same time a great reward to Zerubbabel. One wonders if this is connected with the fact of Zerubbabel's becoming an ancestor of our Lord in both the royal line (Matt. 1:13) and the Lucan line (Luke 3:27).   A.B.F.

HAGGERI (hăg'ĕ-rī, *wanderer*), the father of Mibhar, one of David's heroes (I Chron. 11:38), ASV "Hagri."

HAGGI (hăg'ī, *festal*), a son of Gad, and grandson of Jacob (Gen. 46:16); patriarch of the Haggites (Num. 26:15).

HAGGIAH (hă-gī' à, *a festival of Jehovah*), a Levite of the family of Merari, mentioned only in I Chronicles 6:30.

HAGGITH (hăg'ĭth, *festal*), wife of David (II Sam. 3:4) and mother of Adonijah (I Kings 1:5-31).

HAGIOGRAPHA (hăg'ĭ-ŏg'rà-fà, *holy writings*), a name applied to the third division of the OT by the Jews, the other two being the Law and the Prophets. Sometimes they were called the "Writings." They comprise 11 books, in the following order: Psalms, Proverbs, Job, Song of Solomon, Ruth Lamentations, Ecclesiastes, Esther, Daniel, Ezra, Nehemiah, I and II Chronicles (The Alexandrian canon contains also: Tb., Jdt., BS., WS., Bar., 1-2 Mach. and additional parts of Daniel and Esther).

HAI (hā'ī, *the heap*). 1. A town E of Bethel and near Beth-aven (Gen. 12:8; 13:3). Because of the sin of Achan, the Israelite attack on it failed; but after he was punished, it was taken (Josh. 7,8). In Joshua the name is spelled Ai in the KJV.
2. A city of the Ammonites (Jer. 49:3).

HAIL. 1. Hail storms sometimes take place in the Near East in the spring and summer and do considerable damage to crops, sometimes even injuring property and endangering life. Plagues of hail are mentioned in Exodus 9:23,24 and Joshua 10:11. The prophets speak of hail as a means of punishing the wicked (Isa. 28:2; Ezek. 38:22; Rev. 8:7; 11:19).
2. An interjection found only in the Gospels as a translation of *chaíre,* used as a greeting or salutation.

HAIR, the natural head-covering common to man and to most mammals. It varies in length, color and structure among the different races and seems to be intended of God for protection, for beauty and for identification. The peoples of the Bible lands were generally black-haired, though red-haired individuals are fairly common among the people of Israel. Hebrews and Arabs (cf. Rev. 9: 8) wore their beards long as a mark of dignity but the Egyptians were clean-shaven (Gen. 41:14).

The quick-whitening of hair was one of the symptoms of leprosy (Lev. 13:3,10), but if the leprosy and the white hairs covered the body and there was no raw flesh, the leprosy was no longer contagious (Lev. 13:13). Thin yellow hair appearing in the head or beard was a symptom of scall or scurf, related to leprosy (Lev. 13:29-37).

The men of Israel were not to mar the corners of the beard (Lev. 19:27) and this prohibition explains the "prayer-locks" in front of the ears of Jewish men today. The word "hair" is used in several figurative senses: e.g., in marksmanship some Benjamites could "sling stones at a hair-breadth and not miss" (Judg. 20:16); or in meaning complete safety — "there shall not one hair of his head fall to the ground" (I Sam. 14:45); or to indicate multiplicity — "my iniquities are more than the hairs of my head" (Ps. 40:12); or to show age or dignity — "the hair of his head like pure wool" (Dan. 7:9). Hair was a mark of beauty and sometimes of pride. Absalom's hair (II Sam. 14:26; 18:9), of which he was inordinately proud, caused his death. In Samson's case, his uncut hair was a symbol of his Naziritic dedication, and when he lost his hair, his strength went with it (Judg. 13:7; 16:17-20). In NT times the length of the hair was one mark of distinction between the sexes (I Cor. 11:14-16).   A.B.F.

HAKKATAN (hăk'à-tăn, *the little one*), father of Johanan who returned with Ezra (Ezra 8:12).

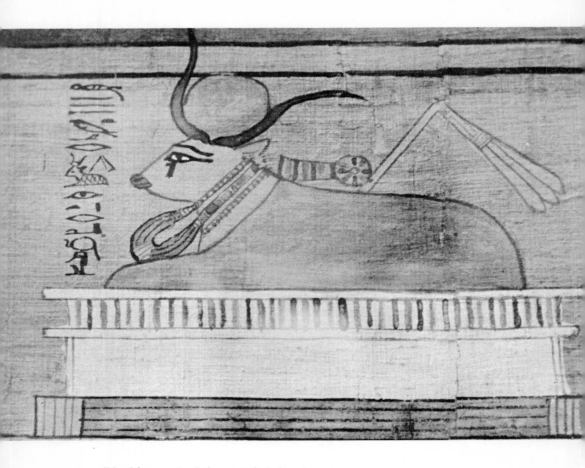

"And he received them at their hand,
and fashioned it with a graving tool,
after he had made it a molten calf:
and they said, These be thy gods, O Israel,
which brought thee up out of the land of Egypt."

(EXODUS 32:4)

Calf worship entered into the religious practice of most ancient
Semitic peoples. Its prevalence in Egypt undoubtedly influenced
the actions of Aaron when he set up the Golden Calf at Mount
Sinai. Here the Egyptian goddess Hathor is depicted on a
papyrus (*ca.* 1300 B.C.).

"Now therefore take, I pray thee,
thy weapons, thy quiver and thy bow,
and go out to the field,
and take me some venison...."
(GENESIS 27:3)

This painting is from a tomb near Thebes and dates back to *ca.* 1400 B.C. The painting depicts two Egyptians enjoying the hunt. They are accompanied by their wives and their slaves, represented in descending size, according to their lower stations in life.

HAKKOZ (hăk'ŏz, *the nimble*, KJV sometimes has Koz, once Coz). 1. A descendant of Aaron whose descendants returned with Zerubbabel from the captivity (I Chron. 24:10; Ezra 2:61; Neh. 3:4,21). 2. A man of Judah (I Chron. 4:8).

HAKUPHA (hà-kū'fà, *bent, bowed*), father of some of the Nethinim who returned with Zerubbabel from Babylon (Ezra 2:51; Neh. 7:53).

HALAH (hā'là), a district in Media to which many of the captive Israelites were taken by Shalmanezer and by Tiglath-pilezer (II Kings 17:6; 18:11; I Chron. 5:26). It is about 80 miles W by N of the famous Behistun rock.

HALAK (hā'lăk, *smooth*), a mountain that marked the southern limit of the conquests of Joshua; perhaps the chalk cliffs crossing the Arabah about six miles S of the Dead Sea (Josh. 11:17; 12:7).

HALHUL (hăl'hŭl), a town in the hill country of Judah (Josh. 15:58) about four miles N of Hebron. It retains its ancient name, and contains a mosque dedicated to the Prophet Jonah.

HALI (hā'lī, *ornament*), a town on the southern boundary of the tribe of Asher (Josh. 19:25).

HALL, in the KJV denotes: (1) the court of the high priest's palace (Luke 22:55); (2) the official residence of a Roman provincial governor. It was called the praetorium (Matt. 27:27; Mark 15:16).

HALLEL (hă-lāl, *praise*). Psalms 113-118, which were read on Passover day, were called the "Egyptian Hallel"; Psalm 136 is an antiphonal Psalm of praise and is sometimes called "the Hallel." Psalms 120-136 are often called the "Great Hallel."

HALLELUJAH (hăl'ē-lōō'yà, Heb. *hallelû-yâh, praise ye Jehovah*), a word which is found in most of the languages into which the Bible has been translated. Like "Amen," it is nearly a universal word. It is found dozens of times, principally in the Psalms, often at the beginning and the end, as in Psalm 150:1,6.

HALLOHESH (hă-lō'hĕsh, *the whisperer*), in Nehemiah 3:12, father of Shallum, a ruler, and in Nehemiah 10:24 one of the covenanters, perhaps the same man.

HALLOW (hăl'ō, *to renaer or treat as holy*). The prime idea in this as in the kindred words "holy," "sanctify," etc., is the setting apart of a person or a thing for sacred use; to hold sacred; reverence as holy.

HAM (hăm, Heb. *hām,* perhaps *hot*). 1. The youngest son of Noah, born probably about 96 years before the Flood; and one of the eight persons to live through the Flood. He became the progenitor of the dark races; not the Negroes, but the Egyptians, Ethiopians, Libyans and Canaanites (Gen. 10:6-20). His indecency, when his father lay drunken, brought a curse upon Canaan (Gen. 9: 20-27).

2. A city of the Zuzim, E of the Jordan (Gen. 14:5). This is not the same word as the son of Noah.

3. The descendants of the original Ham (Ps. 78:51; 105:23; 106:22). In these passages "Ham" is used as another name for Egypt as representing Ham's principal descendants.

ON ONE OF THE OCCASIONS when Noah had succumbed to the temptations of drinking too much, he was discovered by his son Ham. Noah had fallen asleep in his tent without covering himself, and when Ham saw the nakedness of his father, he called his brothers Shem and Japheth.

K ING AHASUERUS was pleased
with Haman, the slender, dark-
eyed young man who had recently
come to the court. Haman seemed
to be more concerned about the
king's mood than all the others. He
always knew in advance the king's
own wishes.

HAMAN (hā′măn, Heb. *hāmān*), the great enemy
of the Jews in the days of Esther. He is called
"the Agagite," undoubtedly because he came from
Agag, a territory adjacent to Media. "Ahasuerus"
or Xerxes, as he is known in secular history, had
promoted Haman to a high position in the court,
but Mordecai, the noble Jew, refused to do him
obeisance, and so Haman plotted to destroy the
Jewish race, but God intervened. Esther foiled Haman's plot (Esth. 7) and Haman died on the gallows he had made for Mordecai.

HAMATH (hā′măth, Heb. *hămāth, fortification*),
one of the most ancient surviving cities on this
earth, located in upper Syria on the Orontes river
from which it derives its water by means of immense undershot water wheels driven by the current. The "entrance of Hamath" (Num. 34:8) was
to be the northern limit of Israel, but God left some
of the Hivites in that neighborhood to be a test
to the faithfulness of Israel (Judg. 3:3). In the
days of David, Hamath had a king of its own (II
Sam. 8:9). Jeroboam II, the last powerful king of
the northern tribes (II Kings 14:23-28), recovered Hamath to Israel. It has had for thousands
of years a checkered history. For a time it was
under the power of Assyria (II Kings 18:34), later
under Babylonia (Jer. 39:5); and still later Antiochus Epiphanes of Syria (c. 175-164 B.C.) re-
named it Epiphaneia after himself. Today it is
largely Moslem, but with a large admixture of
Christians. The city is dominated by its citadel hill
which no doubt contains layers of many different
civilizations.

HAMATH-ZOBAH (hā′măth-zō′bà), mentioned
in II Chronicles 8:3, but the reference is uncertain. It could mean the neighbor kingdoms of Hamath and Zobah, or some place called Hamath,
belonging to the kingdom of Zobah; or, to avoid
confusion with the Zobah in the Hauran (II Sam.
23:36), Hamath may have been mentioned in connection with it.

HAMMATH (hăm′ăth, *hot spring*). 1. One of the
fortified cities assigned by lot to the tribe of Naphtali in the division of the land under Joshua (Josh.
19:35). It lay close to the shore of the Sea of
Galilee, only a mile or so S of the city of Tiberias,
and even today three of these hot springs send up
sulphurous water at the southern extremity of the
ancient ruins. Gesenius thinks that it is probably
the same as the Hammoth-dor of Joshua 21:32,
and Hammon of I Chronicles 6:76.

2. The founder of the house of Rechab (I
Chron. 2:55). Hemath in KJV.

HAMMEDATHA (hăm′ē-dā-thà), father of Haman the Agagite, the villain in the book of Esther
(Esth. 3:1, etc.).

HAMMELECH (hăm′ē-lĕk, *the king*), father of
Jerahmeel and Malchiah (Jer. 36:26; 38:6). The
KJV wrongly translates it as a proper name; it
should be rendered "the king," as in ARV.

HAMMER. There are two chief words for "hammer" in the OT, *pattîsh,* a tool for smoothing
metals and for breaking rocks (Isa. 41:7; Jer. 23:
29), and *maqqeveth,* a mallet to drive tent-pins
into the ground (Judg. 4:21; I Kings 6:7), for
building and for making idols (Isa. 44:12; Jer.
10:4). The word "hammer" is sometimes used
figuratively for any crushing power, as Babylon
(Jer. 50:23) or God's word (Jer. 23:29).

HAMMOLEKETH (hă-mŏl′ē-keth, *the queen*), a
sister of Gilead (I Chron. 7:18). "Hammolecheth"
in KJV.

HAMMON (hăm′ŏn, *hot spring*). 1. A place in
Asher about 10 miles S of Tyre (Josh. 19:28).

2. A city of Naphtali (I Chron. 6:76). See
HAMMATH, which may be the same place (Josh.
19:35).

HAMMOTH-DOR (hăm′ŏth-dôr, *warm springs of
Dor*), a city in Naphtali, appointed as a city of
refuge (Josh. 21:32). See HAMMATH.

HAMMURABI (hàm'ŏŏ-rà'bē), the king of the city of Babylon who brought that city to its century-and-a-half rule over southern Mesopotamia known as the Old Babylonian Kingdom. He was an Amorite, the name given to a Semitic group which invaded the Fertile Crescent about 2000 B.C., destroying its civilization and establishing their own Semitic culture. There has been considerable difference of opinion about the date of his reign, recent scholars favoring 1728-1686 B.C.

Hammurabi made Babylon one of the great cities of the ancient world. Archaeologists have discovered that in his city the streets were laid out in straight lines which intersect approximately at right angles, an innovation which bears witness to city planning and strong central government, little known in Babylon before this time. Marduk, the god of Babylon, now became the head of the pantheon and his temple, Etemenanki, one of the wonders of the ancient world. Many letters written by Hammurabi have been found. These show his close attention to the details of his realm, and enable us to call him an energetic and benevolent ruler.

Hammurabi began the first golden age of Babylon — the second being that of Nebuchadnezzar, over a thousand years later. He systematically unified all of the old world of Sumer and Akkad (southern Mesopotamia) under his strongly centralized government. The prologue to his famous law code describes his administration: "Anu and Enlil (the sky and storm gods) named me to promote the welfare of the people, me, Hammurabi, the devout, god-fearing prince, to cause justice to prevail in the land, to destroy the wicked and the evil, that the strong might not oppress the weak, to rise like the sun over the black-headed (people), and to light up the land. Hammurabi the shepherd, called by Enlil, am I; the one who makes affluence and plenty abound . . . the one revived Uruk, who supplied water in abundance to its people; the one who brings joy to Borsippa; . . . who stores up grain for mighty Urash; . . . the savior of his people from distress, who establishes in security their portion in the midst of Babylon . . . that justice might be dealt the orphan and the widow . . . I established law and justice in the language of the land, thereby promoting the welfare of the people."

By far his most famous claim to fame is Hammurabi's law code. It is inscribed on a magnificent stele of black diorite, eight feet high, found at Susa in 1902. Formerly it had stood in Babylon, but the Elamites carried it off when they conquered Babylon in the 12th century B.C. It is now in the Louvre in Paris. At the top of the stele is a finely sculptured scene showing Hammurabi standing before the sun god Shamash (the patron of law and justice) who is seated and is giving to Hammurabi the laws. Beneath in 51 columns of text are the laws, in beautiful cuneiform characters.

It is now known that Hammurabi's was not the first attempt to systematize the laws of Babylonia. Fragments of several previous law codes have been found. Ur-nammu of Ur and Lipit-Ishtar of Isin both promulgated earlier codes and another was known in Eshnunna. But Hammurabi's is the most complete expression of early Babylonian law, and undoubtedly incorporates many laws and customs which go back to far earlier times. Hammurabi did not invent these laws; he codified them.

The monument contains not only the code, but Hammurabi added a prologue and epilogue, which narrated his glory (a portion was quoted above) and that of the gods whom he worshiped, blessed those who should respect his inscription and cursed future vandals who should deface it. The whole inscription is translated in *Ancient Near Eastern Texts Relating to the OT* (edited by James B. Pritchard, Princeton, Princeton University Press, 1950, pp. 163-180) and should be read by students interested in the subject.

The law code itself included nearly 300 paragraphs of legal provisions touching commercial, social, domestic and moral life. There are regulations governing such matters as liability for (and exemption from) military service, control of trade in alcoholic drinks, banking and usury, the responsibility of a man toward his wife and children, including the liability of a husband for the payment of his wife's debts. Hammurabi's code was harsher on upper-class offenders than on a commoner committing the same offense. Death was the penalty not only for homicide, but for theft, adultery, and bearing false witness in cases involving the accused's life. But the graded penalties show a great advance on primitive laws, and contemporary legal texts show that the harsher penalties were rarely exacted.

Women's rights were safeguarded. A neglected wife could obtain a divorce. A concubine who had become a mother was entitled to the restitution of whatever she had brought with her, or a pecuniary indemnity appropriate to her social position. If a house fell on its owner, or a doctor injured his patient, the man who built the house, or treated the patient, might suffer death, mutilation, or at least a heavy fine.

Students of the Bible are especially interested in the comparison of Hammurabi's code with the Mosaic legislation of the Bible. There are many similarities. In both a false witness is to be punished with the penalty he had thought to bring upon the other man. Kidnapping and house-breaking were capital offenses in both. The Biblical law of divorce permits a man to put away his wife, but does not extend to her the same right as did Hammurabi. Both codes agree in prescribing the death penalty for adultery. The principle of retaliation upon which a number of Hammurabi's laws were based is vividly stated in Exodus 21:23-25.

How are these similarities to be explained? It is obvious that Hammurabi's could not have borrowed from Moses, for the Hebrew lawgiver lived several centuries after the Babylonian. Direct borrowing in the other direction also seems very unlikely. Most scholars today agree that the similarities are to be explained by the common background of the Hebrews and Babylonians. Both were Semitic peoples inheriting their customs and laws from their common ancestors. At first this explanation would seem to run counter to the Biblical claim that Moses' law was given to the legislator by divine revelation. A closer examination of the Pentateuch will show that the Hebrews before they came to Sinai followed many of the regulations set forth in the law (e.g. penalties against murder, adultery, fornication, Gen. 9:6; 38:24; the levirate law, Gen. 38:8; clean and unclean animals, Gen. 8:20; Sabbath, Gen. 2:3; Exod. 16:23,25-29). Moses' law consists of things both old and new. What was old (the customs the Hebrews received from their ancient Semitic ancestors) was here formally incorporated into the nation's constitution. Much is new, especially the high view of the nature of Jehovah and the idea that law is an expression of this nature (Lev. 19:2).

Formerly many scholars identified the Amraphel, king of Shinar, whose invasion of Transjordan is described in Genesis 14:1-12 with Hammurabi king of Babylon. Recently this identification has generally been given up. The two names are not the same and the chronological problems raised by the new low date for Hammurabi makes their equivalence very unlikely.   J.B.G

HAMONAH (hȧ-mō'nȧ, *multitude*), prophetic name of a city near the future burial place of Gog (Ezek. 39:16).

HAMON-GOG, VALLEY OF (hā'mŏn-gŏg, *multitude of Gog*), a place E of the Dead Sea which will be set apart for the burial of the "multitude of Gog" (Ezek. 39:11-15), after God's destruction of the northern host which will invade Israel in "the latter years" (Ezek. 38:8).

HAMOR (hā'môr, Heb. *hămôr, an ass*), father of Shechem who criminally assaulted Dinah, a daughter of Jacob, as a result of which both father and son were killed in revenge by her brothers Simeon and Levi (Gen. 34:1-31).

HAMUEL (hăm'ū-ĕl, *warmth of God*), a Simeonite mentioned only in I Chronicles 4:26. In ASV more properly Hammuel.

HAMUL (hā'mŭl, *pitied, spared*), a grandson of Judah, and son of Perez (Gen. 46:12), head of the family of Hamulites.

HAMUTAL (hȧ-mū'tal, *father-in-law is dew*), mother of two kings of Judah, Jehoahaz (II Kings 23:31) and Zedekiah (24:18).

HANAMEEL (hăn'ȧ-mĕl), mentioned only in Jeremiah 37:7-12, was a cousin of Jeremiah the prophet, who while in prison bought from Hanameel a field, when real estate values were low because of the Chaldean invasion, to encourage the Jews to believe that the captivity would not be permanent and that restoration was certain. In ASV, Hanamel.

HANAN (hā'năn, Heb. *hānān, gracious*). 1. A Benjamite of Jerusalem (I Chron. 8:23).
2. A son of Azel, a descendant of Jonathan (I Chron. 9:44).
3. One of David's mighty men, son of Maachah (I Chron. 11:43).
4. One of the Nethinim, or temple-servants who returned with Zerubbabel (Ezra 2:46; Neh. 7:49).
5. An interpreter of the Law (Neh. 8:7).
6. Three covenanters with Nehemiah (Neh. 10: 10,22,26).
7. An influential Jew in Jerusalem (Jer. 35:4).

HANANEEL (hȧ-năn'ē-ĕl, Heb. *hănan'ēl, God is gracious*), a tower in the wall of Jerusalem (Jer. 31:38; Zech. 14:10) on the N side between the sheep gate and the fish gate (Neh. 3:1; 12:39).

HANANI (hȧ-nā'nī, Heb. *hănānî, gracious*). 1. A son of Heman, David's seer who served in music (I Chron. 25:4,25).
2. Seer in Asa's time who rebuked Asa and was imprisoned (II Chron. 16:7-10).
3. A priest who had married a foreigner (Ezra 10:20).
4. Brother of the great Nehemiah. (Neh. 1:2; 7:2). It was he who brought to Nehemiah in Shushan, the news of Jerusalem's sad state, and Nehemiah later gave to him and to Hananiah, governor of the castle, authority over Jerusalem.

5. One of the musical priests whom Nehemiah appointed for the celebration at the dedication of the wall of Jerusalem (Neh. 12:36). Ezra was the leader of this band.

HANANIAH (hăn'ȧ-nī'ȧ, Heb. *hănanyâh, Jehovah is gracious*). 1. A son of Heman, David's seer (I Chron. 25:4,23) who headed the 16th course of musical Levites.
2. A captain of Uzziah's army (II Chron. 26: 11).
3. Father of Zedekiah, who was one of Jehoiakim's princes (Jer. 36:12).
4. The grandfather of Irijah who arrested Jeremiah for alleged treason (Jer. 37:13).
5. Father of a Benjamite household, who dwelt at Jerusalem (I Chron. 8:24).
6. The Heb. name of Shadrach, one of the three who survived the furnace of fire (Dan. 1: 6,7).
7. A son of Zerubbabel (I Chron. 3:19,21).
8. A returner with Ezra (Ezra 10:28) who married a foreign woman.
9. A perfumer in the time of Nehemiah (Neh. 3:8).
10. Another repairer of the wall (Neh. 3:30).
11. A governor of the castle in Jerusalem, a faithful man who feared God (Neh. 7:2).
12. One of the chief covenanters, perhaps the same as the preceding (Neh. 10:23).
13. Head of a priestly house in the days of the high priest Joiakim (Neh. 12:12,41).
14. A false prophet of Gibeon in the tribe of Benjamin in the days of Zedekiah, the last king of Judah (Jer. 28). In the year 594 B.C. he stood up against Jeremiah, God's prophet who had been pronouncing the doom of Judah and Jerusalem, and prophesied that within two years Nebuchadnezzar would bring back the vessels of the temple, would restore to power Jehoiachin who had reigned for three months in 597 B.C., and would bring back the Jewish captives. Jeremiah rebuked him. Jeremiah had been wearing a yoke of wood to symbolize the coming captivity. Hananiah broke it off and he was told that a yoke of iron would take its place. The Lord slew him that year.

HAND, one of the most frequently used words in Scripture, occurring over 1,600 times. Besides its literal use, it occurs in many figurative senses as well. It very often stands for power, as in Genesis 9:2,5. "Into your hand are they delivered" would make nonsense if taken literally; and "at the hand of every beast will I require it" does not prove that beasts have hands. To "put one's hand under the thigh" as in Genesis 24:2,9; 47:29 meant to take a solemn oath; to "put one's hand upon the head" meant blessing, as in Genesis 48:14, and signifies ordination, as in I Timothy 4:14 and II Timothy 1:6. To "kiss one's own hand" can be a mark of adoration, as in Job 31:27; while to kiss the hand of another is one of the usual marks of respect in the East, though this custom is not mentioned in Scripture.

The Hebrew expression "to consecrate" would be literally "to fill the hand," thus intimating that without consecration we have little or nothing to offer to God. God, being a spirit, neither has nor needs hands, yet we read of the "hand of God" in several connections, all of which are easily understood. "The hand of God was very heavy there" (I Sam. 5:11) refers to a plague which the Philistines suffered. "By stretching forth thy hand to heal" (Acts 4:30) shows God's powerful mercy. "No man is able to pluck them out of my Father's hand" (John 10:29) indicates God's omnipotent protection of His own. To be placed at the right hand of royalty is a high honor and, of course, at "the right hand" of Deity is incomparably higher. "Jehovah said to my Lord, Sit thou at my right hand —" (Ps. 110:1) shows the supreme position of the Son of God. When He judges the nations (Matt. 25:31-46), separating the "sheep" from the "goats," "he shall set the sheep on his right hand, but the goats on the left," showing that the left hand is equally the place of dishonor. The Hebrew word for "north" is the same as for "the left hand" and for "south" the same as for the right hand. In a trial, the accuser stood at the right hand of the accused, as is shown in Zechariah 3:1, where Satan is the accuser; but our Advocate stands also at our right hand to defend us (Ps. 109:31; 16:8).

A.B.F.

HANDICRAFT, a trade requiring manual skill, the art of using one's hands gainfully. Among some rich and decadent nations, the crafts and trades were left to slaves, but the Jews trained every boy to a trade; so Paul was a tent-maker (Acts 18:3) and even our Lord learned the art of carpentry (Mark 6:3). Some handicrafts go back to extreme antiquity; e.g. the making of musical instruments and smithery to antediluvian days (Gen. 4:21, 22). Bezalel was called of God to his trade (Exod. 31:2).

HANDKERCHIEF. The Gr. *soudárion* is a transliteration of the Latin word *sudarium*, which was a cloth intended to wipe sweat from the face. Handkerchiefs were brought from Paul's body for healing purposes (Acts 19:12); the wicked servant (Luke 19:20-23) kept his lord's money in a napkin; the face of dead Lazarus was enclosed in a napkin — the same word —(John 11:44), as was also the face of our Lord (John 20:7).

HANDLE, found only in Song of Solomon 5:5 referring to the door knob. The Hebrew word has over a dozen meanings.

HANDMAID or **HANDMAIDEN,** a female slave or servant. When used of one's self, it indicates humility, as Ruth, speaking to Boaz (Ruth 3:9); Hannah praying to the Lord (I Sam. 1:11) and speaking to Eli (1:16); Mary speaking to Gabriel (Luke 1:38) and singing (Luke 1:48).

HANDS, IMPOSITION OF, a ceremony, the idea behind which varies, but the fundamental sense seems to be that of transference, but sometimes accompanied by the ideas of identification and of devotion to God. It appears in the ritual of sacrifice (Exod. 29:10,15,19, etc.), in the act of blessing(Gen. 48:14) and of witness-bearing in capital offenses (Lev. 24:14).

On the great day of atonement (Lev. 16:21) Aaron was to lay all the sins of Israel upon the head of the scape-goat who would carry them away. Jacob put his hands of blessing upon both the sons of Joseph (Gen. 48:13-20); Peter and John laid hands on the Samaritan Christians who then received the Holy Spirit (Acts 8:14-17); Paul ordained Timothy (II Tim. 1:6) who also received a gift through ordination by the presbytery (I Tim. 4:14). The act was accompanied by prayer (Acts 6:6).

HANDSTAFF, a rod carried in the hand, mentioned only in Ezekiel 39:9. Probably a weapon.

HANES (hā'nēz), a place in Egypt mentioned only in Isaiah 30:4. From its association with Zoan, and the context, it would seem to have been in the Delta, though some associate it with Heracleopolis Magna, W of the Nile and far up the river.

HANNAH, whose heart had overflowed with longing for a child, was full to bursting with joy and gratitude. She knew that the child she bore her husband was the gift of God, sent for God's purpose.

MARCO BASAITI

The Calling of James and John.

CARL BLOCH

The Last Supper.

The Calling of St. Matthew.

JUAN DE PAREJA

The Evangelists.

JACOB JORDAENS

DOMENICO FETI

The multiplication of the loaves and fish.

The Institution of the Holy Communion.
KONSTATIN HANSEN

Pentecost.
EL GRECO

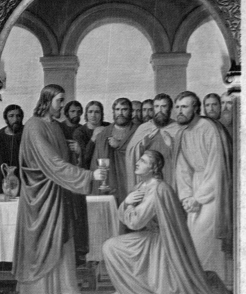

CASPAR DE CRAYER

The miraculous draught of fishes.

FRIEDRICH OVERBECK

The revival of Lazarus.

Christ washing the feet of His disciples.

BERNHARD STRIGEL

HANGING, or death by strangulation, was not a form of capital punishment employed in Bible times. Where the word is used in Scripture, except in the two cases of suicide by hanging (Ahithophel, II Sam. 17:23; Judas, Matt. 27:5), it refers to the suspension of a body from a tree or post after the criminal had been put to death. This was practiced in Egypt (Gen. 40:19,22), by the Israelites (Deut. 21:22), and by the Persians. Hanging added to the disgrace. The body was buried before nightfall (Deut. 21:23, Josh. 8:29).

HANGINGS (Heb. *kelā'îm, māsākh*), those parts of the tabernacle and its court which were so hung as to preserve the privacy and the sacredness of that which was within. Some were more or less permanent, but others could be removed to permit passage of a person. Of the first class were the 280 cubits of fine twined linen, five cubits wide which enclosed the court (Exod. 27:9-19) and the curtains of the tent itself (Exod. 26:1-14); and of the second class the screen of the court (Exod 27:14-16), the hanging screen at the door of the tent (Exod. 26:36), and the veil which shut out from vulgar view the most holy place (Exod. 26:31-35). It was the veil corresponding to this that was rent of God from top to bottom at the crucifixion of our Lord (Matt. 27:51, Heb. 9:8, 10:19,20).

HANIEL (hăn'ĭ-ĕl, Heb. *hannî'ēl, grace of God,* ASV Hanniel). 1. A prince of Manasseh who helped in dividing the land among the tribes (I Chron. 34:23).

2. An Asherite, son of Ulla (I Chron. 7:39).

HANNAH (hăn'à, Heb. *hannâh, grace, favor*), one of the two wives of Elkanah, a Levite who lived at Ramathaim-zophim, a village of Ephraim. It was otherwise known as Ramah (cf. I Sam. 1:1 with 1:19). Peninnah, the other wife of Elkanah (I Sam 1:2), had children, but Hannah was for a long time barren, and as is common in polygamous households, "her rival provoked her sore" (1:6). The fact that Elkanah loved Hannah and gave her a double portion (1:5) only increased the hatred and jealousy in Peninnah's heart. But Hannah was a godly woman and she prayed for a son and vowed to give him to the Lord as a perpetual Nazirite. Eli saw Hannah's lips moving in silent prayer, and rebuked her for what he thought was drunkenness. She replied very humbly and Eli apologized; the family returned home; she conceived and became the mother of Samuel the great prophet of Israel and the last of the judges. Hannah's praise (2:1-10) shows that she was a deeply spiritual woman. Her song resembles Mary's song, "the Magnificat" (Luke 1:46:55) when she, too, was expecting a baby in miraculous circumstances. Each woman rejoiced in the Lord, and each gave in marvelous fashion God's way of dealing with the proud and with the humble. Cf. 1:8 with Luke 1:52,53 and Ps. 113:7-9.)   A.B.F.

HANNATHON (hăn'nà-thŏn, Heb. *hannāthôn, gracious*), a city on the northern boundary of Zebulon (Josh. 19:14). It is mentioned in the Amarna Letters.

HANNIEL (han'ĭ-ĕl, Heb. *hannî'ēl, the favor of God*). 1. Son of Ephod, the prince of the tribe of Manasseh, appointed by Moses to help in dividing the land (Num. 34:23).

2. Son of Ulla, and a descendant of Asher (I Chron. 7:39).

HANOCK (hăn'nŏk, Heb. *hănôkh, initiation*). 1. A grandson of Abraham by Keturah through their son, Midian (Gen. 25:4, I Chron. 1:33; KJV has *Henoch*).

2. Eldest son of Reuben (Gen. 46:9; Exod. 6:14, I Chron. 5:3'), he was the head of the family of the Hanockites (Num. 26:5).

HANUN (hā'nŭn, Heb. *hānûn, favored*). 1. King of Ammon who, having mistaken David's friendly servants for spies, mistreated them, thus bringing on a war in which the Ammonites lost their independence (II Sam. 10; and I Chron. 19).

2. A man who, with the help of the inhabitants of Zanoah, built the valley gate setting up the doors, locks and bars of it in the wall of Jerusalem (Neh. 3:13).

3. Son of Zalaph, who helped repair the wall of Jerusalem (Neh. 3:30).

HAPHRAIM (hăph-rā'ĭm, ASV Hapharaim, Heb. *hăphāraîyim, two pits*), a city located near Shumem in Issachar (Josh. 19:19). Modern *Et-Taiyibeh.*

HARA (ha'rà, Heb. *hārā',* mountain country, a place named in I Chronicles 5:26, along with Halah, Habor and the river Gozan, as the destinations of the tribes of Reuben and Gad and the half-tribe of Manasseh when they were carried away by the Assyrians. But such a place as Hara is unknown. The LXX omits it in this verse, as also do II Kings 17:6 and 18:11 in naming the destinations of the captive nation, Israel. Both these latter references add the phrase "in the cities of the Medes"; LXX has "mountains of the Medes". Some scholars think Hara should read Haran; others believe the text is corrupt.

HARADAH (hàr-ā'dà, Heb. *hărādhâh, terror*), one of Israel's encampments in the wilderness wanderings at which they tarried after leaving Mount Shepher (Num. 33:24). The site is unknown, but its name suggests it was a mountain.

HARAN (hā'răn, Heb. *hārān, mountaineer*). 1. Youngest brother of Abram and father of Lot, Abram's nephew. He died in Ur before his father, Terah, departed with his family from that city (Gen. 11:27,28).

2. A son of Caleb by his concubine, Ephah. This Haran had a son named Gazez (I Chron. 2:46).

3. A Gershonite Levite who lived in the time of David, he was the son of Shimei (I Chron. 23:9).

HARAN or **CHARRAN** (hā'răn, chär'răn, Heb. *hārān,* Gr. *charhrán*), a city located in northern Mesopotamia, on the Balikh river, a branch of the Euphrates, to which Terah, the father of Abram, emigrated with his family (Gen. 11:31). After his father's death Abram departed from this city to go into the land of Canaan (Gen. 12:4). His brother Nahor remained there. Abraham later sent his servant to find a wife for his son Isaac among his relatives there (Gen. 24:4). After that Jacob, at the request of his father, Isaac, came to this same area in search of a wife (Gen. 29:4,5). In the time of Hezekiah, Rabshakeh, an officer of Sennacherib, when delivering a propaganda lecture to the people of Jerusalem, mentioned Haran, along with other cities in the same area, as conquered by Assyria (II Kings 19:12; and Isa. 37:12). Ezekiel mentions this city as one of those which carried on trade with Tyre (Ezek. 27:23).

Haran is frequently referred to in Assyrian and Babylonian records under the form of *harranu,* Anglicized as Harran. This term means *road,* probably because this city was located at the intersection of the trade routes from Damascus in the S and that going E and W between Carchemish and Nineveh. A center of worship of the moon-god, Sin, was established there in very early times. The city and temple were wrecked in the wars of the Assyrian kings. After the fall of Nineveh in 612 B.C., some Assyrian refugees fled to Harran and held out there until 610 B.C. Nabonidus, king of Babylon, who delighted in restoring old temples, rebuilt the city and temple and reinstated the worship of the moon-god there about 75 years later. This city is mentioned in Mari documents in the form of Nakhur, probably from Nahor, Abram's brother. The Romans knew it as Carrhae, famous as the place where the Parthians defeated Crassus in 53 B.C. It is still in existence as Harran, near the original site in southern Turkey. The present day Moslems who live in the area have many traditions concerning Abraham.   C.E.H.

HARARITE (hā'rà-rīte, Heb. *hărārî, mountain dweller*), an area in the hill country of either Judah or Ephraim. This term occurs only in the catalog of David's mighty men. Shammah, the son of Agee, a Hararite (II Sam. 23:11,33); Jonathan, the son of Shagee the Hararite (I Chron. 11:34); Ahiam, the son of Sacar the Hararite (I Chron. 11:35).

HARBONA, HARBONAH (här-bō'nà, här-bō'nà, Heb. *harevônā', harevônâh, ass driver*), one of the seven chamberlains of Ahasuerus, king of Persia (Esth. 1:10; 7:9).

HARETH, HERETH (hā'rĕth KJV, Hē'rĕth ASV, Heb. *hereth*), occurs only in I Samuel 22:5 as the name of a forest in Judah where David stayed.

HARHAIAH (här-hā'ja, Heb. *harhăyâh, meaning unknown*), father of Uzziel, a goldsmith, who repaired a portion of the wall of Jerusalem (Neh. 3:8).

HARHAS (här'hăs, Heb. *harhas,* meaning uncertain), grandfather of Shallum, husband of Hulda the prophetess (II Kings 22:14). In II Chronicles 34:22 this name is Hasrah.

HARHUR (här'hûr, Heb. *harhūr, fever*), head of one of the families which returned from exile with Zerubbabel (Ezra. 2:51, Neh. 7:53).

HARIM (hā'rīm, Heb. *hārim, consecrated or slit-nosed*). 1. A priest assigned to the third course in David's time (I Chron. 24:8).
2. A family which returned from Babylon with Zerubbabel (Ezra 2:32, Neh. 7:35).
3. A family of priests which returned from exile with Zerubbabel (Ezra 2:39, Neh. 7:42; 12:15). Members of this family married foreign wives (Ezra 10:21).
4. Another family who married foreign wives (Ezra 10:31).
5. Father of Malchijah, a worker on the wall (Neh. 3:11). This man may have been the same one who entered into a covenant with the Lord under Nehemiah (Neh. 10:5).
6. Another man who covenanted with the Lord under Nehemiah (Neh. 10:27).

HARIPH (hā'rīf, Heb. *harîph, autumn*), a family which returned to Judah from Babylon with Zerubbabel (Neh. 7:24). (The corresponding place, Ezra 2:18, has Jorah). A man of this name was among those sealed in the covenant with God (Neh. 10:19).

HARLOT, a prostitute, which kind of woman is designated by four terms in the OT: (1) *zônâh,* the regular word for harlot and the most frequently used; (2) *qedēshâh,* a special kind of harlot, a religious prostitute, that is, a priestess of a heathen religion in which fornication was part of the worship. Mentioned only four times, but three of those references are early (Gen. 38:21,22, and Deut. 23:17; (3) *'ishshâh zârâh,* or *zārah* alone, a "strange woman," occurs only in the Book of Proverbs, and the way it is used there shows that a harlot is meant; (4) *nokhrîyâh,* a foreign (or strange) woman, found, in this form, also only in the Book of Proverbs, and it obviously means harlot.

The first two of the above terms were sometimes translated *whore,* other times *harlot* in the KJV. In ASV *zônâh* is consistently rendered *harlot* and *qedēshâh, prostitute.*

The NT word for harlot is *pórnē,* which in KJV is inconsistently sometimes *whore* and sometimes *harlot,* but in ASV is always *harlot.*

Some legal measures were in force concerning harlots. Parents were not to force their daughters to become harlots (Lev. 19:29; 21:7,14), priests were not to marry harlots (Lev. 19:29), the wages of harlotry were not to be brought into the temple to pay a vow (Deut. 23:18). These prohibitions were necessary to keep the worship of the Lord free from the impurities of the sin of harlotry.

The actual punishment of harlots was severe when enforced. In Genesis 38:24 Judah ordered Tamar to be burned for being a harlot. Leviticus 21:9 commanded burning for a priest's daughter who became a harlot. Deuteronomy 22:21 ordered stoning for a bride found to have played the harlot.

Such a common sin needed to be guarded against. It is not surprising to find that the Book of Proverbs, which mentions every term for harlot except *qedēshâh,* teaches about and warns against harlots by admonitions and illustrations. The situation in the Corinthian Church was such that the Apostle Paul had to give the Christians there special warnings against fornication with harlots (I Cor. 6:15,16).

The words harlot and harlotry are used very often, especially in the prophetic books, to describe idolatry. This figurative use was evidently based on the idea that the Lord was the husband of the nation of Israel (see Jer. 3:20). When the people took their allegiance from Jehovah and gave it to idols instead, He called it "going a whoring after other gods" (KJV) or "playing the harlot with other gods" (ASV). This expression occurs rather frequently in the prophetic books, and a few times in other books. Also, this spiritual harlotry is mentioned several times in the Book of Revelation, chapter 17.   C.E.H.

HAROD (hā'rŏd, Heb. *hârōdh, trembling*), a spring, or well, beside which Gideon and his men encamped one morning. The Lord reduced his army there to 300 men with whom he routed the Midianites that night (Judg. 7:1). It was located in the Mount Gilboa area about four miles SE of the city of Jezreel. The modern name of the spring is *Ain Jalud.*

HARODITE (hā'rŏd-īt, Heb. *hărōdî, belonging to Herod*), patronymic of two of David's mighty men, Shammah and Elika (II Sam. 23:25). In the parallel place in I Chronicles 11:27 this name is given as "Harorite", a scribal error for "Harodite".

HAROEH (hȧ-rō'ĕ, Heb. *hārŏ'eh, the seer*), a son of Shobal, and grandson of Caleb, son of Hur (I Chron. 2:52).

HAROSHETH OF THE GENTILES (hā-rō'shĕth, Heb. *hārōsheth haggôyim*), a town near the Kishon river in N Palestine. It was the home of Sisera, the captain of the army of Jabin, king of Canaan (Judg. 4:2,13,16). The significance of the phrase "of the Gentiles" is unknown but suggests mixed races lived there. It has been identified with modern Teil 'Amr in the Mt. Carmel Kishon area.

HARP (See Music)

HARROW (hă'rō, Heb. *sādhādh*), occurs three times, always as a verb. Job 39:10 translated "harrow." In Isaiah 28:24 and Hosea 10:11 it is rendered "break up the clods." From the root meaning of the word it seems to mean dragging or leveling off a field.

HARROWS (Heb. *hārîts*), a sharp instrument made of iron with which David cut conquered peoples (II Sam. 12:31, I Chron. 20:3). It has no connection with the verb rendered "harrow."

HARSHA (hȧr'shȧ, Heb. *harshā', dumb, silent*), the head of family of the Nethinim which returned under Zerubbabel from exile (Ezra 2:52, Neh. 7: 54).

HART (See Animals)

HARUM (hā'rŭm, Heb. *hārum, made high*), a descendant of Judah mentioned as the father of Aharhel (I Chron. 4:8).

HARUMAPH (hȧ-roo'maf, Heb. *hărûmaph,* perhaps *slit-nosed*), the father of Jedaiah, a worker helping to repair the wall (Neh. 3:10).

HARUPHITE (hȧ-roo'fīt, Heb. *harûphî,* or *hărî-phî*). Shephatiah, one of the men who joined David's forces in Ziglag, was called the Haruphite or the Hariphite (I Chron. 12:5). If this latter form is the correct one, then this man may be connected with the Hariph clan (Neh. 7:24).

HARUZ (hā'rŭz, Heb. *hārûts, diligent*), father-in-law of Manasseh, king of Judah (II Kings 21:19).

HARVEST (hȧr-vĕst, Heb. *qātsîr,* Gr. *therismós*). The economy of the Israelites was strictly agricultural. Harvest time was a very significant event for them. They had three each year. The barley reaping (Ruth 1:22) came in April-May; the wheat harvest (Gen. 30:14) was about six weeks later in June-July, and the ingathering of the fruits of tree or vine took place in September-October.

Grain crops were reaped with sickles, and the cut stalks were laid in bunches which were carried to the threshing-floor. Some laws governed these simple harvest operations. The corners of the fields were not to be reaped, and the scatterings of the cut grain were not to be picked up. The part of the crop thus left was for the poor people to use (Lev. 23:22). The owner was required each year to present the first-fruits of the crop as an offering to God before he could take any of it for his own use (Lev. 23:10,14). Stalks of grain which grew up without being sown could not be harvested (Lev. 25:5). With a new orchard

SUMMER HARVESTING SCENE on the threshing floors at the ancient village of Sepphoris. Herod Antipas made Sepphoris his capital before he moved to Tiberias. After the city revolted against Rome in A.D. 6, it was razed, but was rebuilt soon afterward.

or vineyard the fruit could not be gathered for three years, and the fourth year's crop had to be given entirely to the Lord. So the owner had to wait until the fifth year to get any fruit for himself (Lev. 19:23-25).

The Lord fitted the three main religious feasts which He prescribed for the people into this agricultural economy. The Passover came in the season of the barley harvest (Exod. 23:16). Seven weeks later at time of the wheat harvest occurred the feast of Pentecost (Exod. 34:22). The feast of Tabernacles was observed the seventh month, which was the period of the fruit harvest (Exod. 34:22).

In the New Testament, most of the time the term harvest is used figuratively for the gathering in of the redeemed saints at the end of the age (Matt. 13:39).   C.E.H.

HASADIAH (hă-à-dī′á, Heb. *hăsadhyâh, Jehovah is kind*), a son of Zerubabbel (I Chron. 3:20).

HASENUAH (hăs-ē-nū′à, Heb. *hassenu'âh,* the word is *senuah* with the definite article prefixed, meaning *the hated one*). 1. An ancestor of Sallu, a Benjamite who returned from exile (1 Chron. 9:7). In ASV "Hassenuah."

2. The father of Judah, the assistant overseer of Jerusalem in Nehemiah's time (Neh. 11:9). In KJV Senuah (q.v.).

HASHABIAH (hăsh-à-bī′à, Heb. *hăshavyâh, whom Jehovah esteems*). 1. An ancestor of Ethan, a Levite and temple singer in David's time (I Chron. 6:45).

2. An ancestor of Shèmaiah, a Levite, who returned from Babylon (I Chron. 9:14) and lived in Jerusalem (Neh. 11:15).

3. A son of Jeduthun, a musician in David's time (I Chron. 25:3).

4. A civil official in David's time (I Chron. 26:30).

5. Overseer of the tribe of Levi in David's time. (I Chron. 27:17).

6. A chief of the Levites in Josiah's time (II Chron. 35:9).

7. A Levite teacher whom Ezra brought with him (Ezra 8:19).

8. A chief priest in Ezra's company (Ezra 8:24).

9. Ruler of the half tribe of Keilah, a worker on the wall (Neh. 3:17).

10. A priest, head of the family of Hilkiak (Neh. 12:21).

11. An ancestor of Uzzi, the overseer of the Levites at Jerusalem in Nehemiah's time (Neh. 11:22).

12. A chief of the Levites who sealed the covenant (Neh. 3:17) and was appointed to praise God (Neh. 12:24).

HASHABNAH (hà-shăb′nàh, Heb. *hăshavnâh*), one of those who sealed the covenant with Nehemiah (Neh. 10:25).

HASHABNIAH (hăsh′ăb-nē-ī′à, Heb. *hăshavneyâh*). 1. The father of Hattush, a worker on the wall (Neh. 3:10). ASV Hashabneiah.

2. One of the Levites who prayed at the confession of sin (Neh. 9:5). ASV Hashabneiah.

HASHBADANA (hăsh-băd′à-nà, Heb. *hashbaddā-nâh*), a man who stood on the left of Ezra as he read the law to the people (Neh. 8:4).

HASHEM (hā′-shěm, Heb. *hāshěm*), a man whose sons were among David's mighty men (I Chron. 11:34). The parallel passage (II Sam. 23:32) has Jashen.

HASHMANNIM (hăsh′-măn-nǐm, Heb. *hashman-nîm,* meaning unknown), a Hebrew word that occurs only in Psalm 68:33 and is translated *heaven of heavens.* But it may be a textual error for *bashmannim,* which means "with oils or ointment."

HASHMONAH (hăsh-mō′nà, Heb. *hashmōnâh*), a station where the Israelites encamped in the wilderness (Num. 33:29,30). The site is unknown.

HASHUB (See Hasshub)

HASHUBAH (hà-shōō′bà, Heb. *hăshuvâh, consideration*), a son of Zerubbabel (I Chron. 3:20).

HASHUM (hā′-shŭm, Heb. *hāshum*). 1. A family that returned from exile under Zerubbabel (Ezra 2:19; 10:33; Neh. 7:22).

2. A priest who stood at the left of Ezra as he read the law to the people (Neh. 8:4).

3. A chief of the people who sealed the covenant (Neh. 10:18). Maybe the same as 2.

HASHUPHA (hà-shōō′fà, Heb. *hăsûphā'*), a family that returned from exile under Zerubbabel (Ezra 2:43; Neh. 7:46), ASV Hasupha.

HASMONAEANS (See Maccabees)

HASRAH (hăs′-rà, Heb. *hasrâh,* meaning uncertain), grandfather of Shallum, the husband of Hulda the prophetess (II Chron. 34:22). In the parallel place (II Kings 22:14) this name is given as Harhas.

HASSENAAH (hăs-ē-nā′-à, Heb. *hassenā'âh,* the word is *sena'ah* (q.v.) with the definite article prefixed, meaning *the hated one*). Father of the sons who built the fish gate in the wall of Jerusalem (Neh. 3:3).

HASSHUB (hăsh′ŭb, Heb. *hashshûv, considerate*). 1. The father of Shemaiah, a Levite who returned from exile (I Chron. 9:14). He dwelt in Jerusalem (Neh. 11:15. KJV Hashub.

2. A worker on the wall of Jerusalem (Neh. 3:11).

3. Another worker on the wall (Neh. 3:23). KJV Hashub.

4. One who sealed the covenant (Neh. 10:23). KJV Hashub. May be identical with 2 or 3.

HASUPHA (See Hashupha)

HAT (See Dress)

HATACH (hā′tăk, Heb. *hăthākh,* meaning uncertain), a chamberlain of the king of Persia appointed to attend upon Esther (Esth. 4:5-10).

HATHATH (hā′-thăth, Heb. *hăthath, terror*), a son of Othniel, the first judge of Israel (I Chron. 4:13).

HATIPHA (hà-tī′fà, Heb. *hătîphā',* meaning uncertain), head of family of the Nethinim which returned from exile under Zerubbabel (Ezra 2:54; Neh. 7:56).

HATITA (hà-tī′tà, Heb. *hătîtā', exploring*), an ancestor of a family of Levitical porters which returned from exile under Zerubbabel (Ezra 2:42; Neh. 7:45).

HATSI HAM MENUCHOTH (hă-tsī-hăm-měn-ū′-kōth, Heb. *hătsî hammenûhôth, half of the Menuhoth*), a marginal reading on I Chronicles 2:54 in KJV which is eliminated in ASV.

HATTIL (hăt′-ĭl, Heb. *hattîl, waving*), a family which returned from exile under Zerubbabel (Ezra 2:57; Neh. 7:59).

HATTIN, HORNS OF (hăt′tēn, *hollows*), a peculiar form of a hill near the village of Hattin, which tradition dating from the 13th century holds as the scene of Christ's Sermon on the Mount.

The crater-like top of this hill has a grassy knoll about 60 feet high on each end of it which is called the Horns of Hattin. This phrase is not mentioned in the Bible but it may denote the "mountain" of Matthew 5:1.

HATTUSH (hăt'-ŭsh, Heb. *hattûsh,* meaning unknown). 1. A descendant in the royal line of Judah in the fifth generation from Zerubbabel (I Chron. 3:22).

2. A descendant of David who returned from Babylon with Ezra (Ezra 8:2).

3. A worker on the wall (Neh. 3:10), may be the same as 2.

4. One of those who sealed the covenant (Neh. 10:4), may be the same as 2 or 3.

5. A priest who returned with Zerubbabel (Neh. 12:2).

HAURAN (hȧ'ōō-rȧn, Heb. *hawrān,* probably *black* or *black land*), the modern name of a great plain situated on a plateau 2000 feet high E of the Jordan river and N of the land of Gilead. In ancient times it was called Bashan. Its soil is of volcanic origin and is very rich, making the region famous for its wheat crops. The name Hauran is mentioned only by Ezekiel in his description of the boundaries of the land of Israel in the Millennial age (47: 16,18).

The Israelites never had a very great hold on this area. Its openness to the E made it a frequent prey to robbers from the desert. Under the Romans, Herod ruled over it as part of his realm, and he greatly encouraged settlement by stopping the robber raids. It was then known as Auranitis. Christianity flourished there from the second century A.D. until the seventh century, when it was overthrown by the Moslems. Today Hauran is an integral part of Syria.

HAVILAH (hăv'-ĭ-lȧ, Heb. *hăwîlâh, sand-land*). 1. A son of Cush, a descendant of Ham (Gen. 10:7; I Chron. 1:9).

2. A son of Joktan, a descendant of Shem (Gen. 10:29; I Chron. 1:23). These names are generally taken to mean tribes or nations. If both references refer to the same area, it pertained to both Hamitic and Semitic peoples. It is generally thought to have been located in southern Arabia.

3. A land encompassed by the river Pishon which flowed from a source in the Garden of Eden; it contained gold and other minerals (Gen. 2:11, 12). Probably located in Armenia or Mesopotamia, although actual location is uncertain.

4. A land mentioned as one of the boundaries of the dwelling of the Ishmaelites "from Havilah unto Shur that is before Egypt." This Havilah is probably the same as 2 in southern Arabia (Gen. 25:18). Saul conquered the Amalekites in this same area "from Havilah as thou goest to Shur that is before Egypt" (I Sam. 15:7).

HAVOTH-JAIR (hā-vŏth-jā'-îr, Heb. *hawwŏth-yā'îr,* [ASV Havvoth-jair] *villages of Jair*), a group of villages which Jair, son of Manasseh, took (Num. 32:41). The word *hawwah* means a village of tents; it is used only in connection with these towns of Jair. This group consisted of 30 villages (Judg. 10:4; I Chron. 2:22,23). Jair captured both Gilead and Bashan, this latter district evidently contained 30 more towns (Deut. 3:14; Josh. 13:30; I Kings 4:13; I Chron. 2:23). The phrase Havoth-jair applied only to the villages in Gilead.

HAZAEL (hăz'-ā-ĕl, Heb. *hăzā'ēl, God sees*), a high official of Benhadad, king of Syria, whom, when the king was sick, he sent to inquire of the prophet Elisha concerning his recovery from this illness. Elisha told Hazael the king would certainly recover, but he would surely die. Previously God had instructed Elijah to anoint Hazael king of Syria (I Kings 19:15). Hazael pretended to be surprised by Elisha's statement that he would become king. He returned and suffocated Benhadad, and seized the throne for himself (II Kings 8: 7-15).

This usurpation is confirmed by an inscription of Shalmaneser III which states that Hadadezer of Damascus (that is, Benhadad) perished and Hazael, a son of nobody, seized the throne. This phrase "a son of nobody" means he was not in the royal line of descent.

The date of Hazael's reign can be ascertained as at least 43 years in length (841-798 B.C.); very likely it was a few years longer. Ahaziah, king of Judah, reigned only one year (II Kings 8:26). That year was 841. During that year he fought with Joram, king of Israel against Hazael (II Kings 8:28). In the annals of Shalmaneser III, king of Assyria (858-824), for his 14th year (844), he recorded a battle against Hadadezer (Benhadad) of Damascus. In his 18th year (840) Shalmaneser said he encountered Hazael at Damascus. So Hazael usurped the throne during the period (844-841). He reigned at least until 798, the date of the death of Jehoahaz, king of Israel, for Hazael oppressed Israel all the days of this king (II Kings 13:22.) He died shortly afterwards (II Kings 13: 24).

Hazael greatly punished Israel, as Elisha had foreseen (II Kings 8:12). He wounded Jehoram, son of Ahab, at Ramoth-gilead (II Kings 8:29). During the reign of Jehu, Hazael took all the territory E of the Jordan valley from Israel (II Kings 10:32). While Joash was ruling in Judah, Hazael captured Gath and threatened Jerusalem, but Joash induced him to retire by paying tribute (II Kings 12:17,18). He continually raided Israel during the reign of Jehoahaz (II Kings 13:3). As previously mentioned, he oppressed Israel all the days of this king (II Kings 13:22). Shalmaneser III records two attacks on Hazael in which the Assyrian king claims great victories with severe damage to the Syrian countryside.   C.E.H.

HAZAIAH (hȧ-zā'yȧ, *Jehovah sees*), member of a family of Shiloh whose great-grandson lived in Jerusalem 444 B.C. (Neh. 11:5).

HAZAR (hā'zȧr, Heb. *hătsar, a settlement*), often the first element in Heb. place names.

HAZAR-ADDAR (hā'zȧr-ăd'ȧr), a place on the southern boundary of Judah, W of Kadesh-barnea and E of Azmon (Num. 34:4). In Joshua 15:3 it is called simply Addar (KJV Adar).

HAZAR-ENAN (hā'zȧr-ē'năn, *village of fountains*), the NE corner of the land of Canaan as promised of the Lord to the people of Israel (Num. 34:9,10; cf. Ezek. 47:17).

HAZAR-GADDAH (hā'zȧr-găd'ȧ, *village of good fortune*), a town in the south of Judah, very close to the boundary of Simeon (Josh. 15:27).

HAZAR-HATTICON (hā'zȧr-hăt'ĭ-kŏn, *middle-village*), mentioned only in Ezekiel 47:16 as being near Damascus and on the border of Hauran. Exact location uncertain.

801

SITE OF HAZOR, chief city of Canaan. The city was fortified by King Solomon, as it had a strategic location in the hills.

HAZARMAVETH (hā′zar-mā′vĕth, *village of death*), found in the "Table of the nations" (Gen. 10:26 and I Chron. 1:20); apparently a son of Joktan, but probably representing the people or the district of modern Hadramut.

HAZAR-SHUAL (hā′zar-shōō′ăl, *village of the jackal*), a town in the south of Judah (Josh. 15: 28) later bestowed upon Simeon (Josh. 19:3). After the captivity held by Simeonites (I Chron. 4: 28) and Judah (Neh. 11:27).

HAZAR-SUSAH (hā′zar-sū′sa, *village of a mare*), a town given to Simeon out of Judah (Josh. 19:5), but called "Hazar-susim," i.e. "village of horses" in I Chronicles 4:31. Site uncertain.

HAZAZON-TAMAR (hăz′a-zŏn-tā′mer, *Hazazon of the palm trees*), ancient name of a town on the W coast of the Dead Sea, occupied in Abraham's time by the Amorites (Gen. 14:7), but smitten by the four great kings of the East. KJV Hazezontamar.

HAZEL (hā′z'l), found in Genesis 30:37, KJV, where it renders the Heb. *luz,* which the RV better translates "almond tree."

HAZELELPONI, ZELELPONI (hăz′e-lĕl-pō′nī, zĕlĕl-pō′nī, ASV Hazzelelponi), a Jewish woman mentioned only in I Chronicles 4:3.

HAZERIM (ha-zē′rĭm, *villages*), the ancient homes of the Avvim near Gaza in southern Palestine (Deut. 2:23). RV properly translates "villages."

HAZEROTH (ha-zē′rŏth, *courts* or *villages*), a station on Israel's journeys in the wilderness, about 40-45 miles from Mt. Sinai, northeastward toward the Gulf of Akabah. The people seem to have stayed there for some time after the terrible plague at Kibroth-hattaavah (Num. 11:35). It was here that Aaron and Miriam made their rebellion against Moses (Num. 12). The identification of the place is uncertain.

HAZEZON-TAMAR (hăz′e-zŏn-tā′mer), another spelling for Hazazon-tamar, *q.v.*

HAZIEL (hā′zĭ-ĕl, *God sees*), a Gershonite Levite in the latter days of David (I Chron. 23:9).

HAZO (hā′zō), a son of Nahor and uncle of Laban and Rebekah (Gen. 22:22).

HAZOR (hā′zôr, Heb. *hātsôr, an enclosed place*), the name of at least five towns mentioned in the Bible: 1. An important town in northern Palestine, ruled in the days of Joshua by Jabin (Josh. 11:1, 10). Palestine at the time was a conglomeration of little city-states or kingdoms, and of various groups united by tribal ties. For the former, see Joshua 11:1, and for the latter Joshua 11:3. This Hazor was reckoned as "the head of all those kingdoms" in Joshua's day, and Jabin led them against Joshua, who almost annihilated them. Nearly two centuries later, another Jabin (Judg. 4) reigning at Hazor was reckoned as king of Canaan, but God, using Deborah and Barak, subdued and destroyed him. Hazor, having a strategic location in the hills, about five miles W of the waters of Merom, was fortified by Solomon (I Kings 9:15). Its Israelite inhabitants were carried away into captivity (II Kings 15:29) in Assyria by Tiglath-pileser about the middle of the eighth century B.C.

2. A town in the extreme south of Judah, mentioned only in Josh. 15:23.

3. Another town in the south of Judah (Josh. 15:25). Its name "Hazor-hadattah" means simply "new Hazor" and indicates that some of the inhabitants of Hazor (2) had removed to a new location. KJV in Joshua 15:25 makes it seem that Hazor and Hadattah were separate places but cf. ASV.

4. A town N of Jerusalem, inhabited by Benjamites in the restoration (Neh. 11:33).

5. A region in the south of Arabia against which Jeremiah pronounced a "doom" (Jer. 49:28-33).

HAZOR-HADATTAH (hā′zôr-ha-dăt′a, *new Hazor*), see No. 3 in the article on Hazor. Joshua 15: 25 in KJV makes it seem like the names of two villages.

HE (hā), the fifth letter of the Hebrew alphabet, pronounced like English *h.* It was also used for the number 5.

HEAD (hĕd, Heb. *rō′sh*, Gr. *kephalé*). The word "head" occurs about 433 times in Scripture and the Hebrew word for "head" occurs 592 times, being translated "head" 349 times, "chief" 90 times, "top" 75 times, "company" 12 times, "beginning" 14 times, "captain" 10 times, "chapter" 4 times, etc. There are many figurative uses: "the hoary head" (Prov. 16:31), expressing old age; "heads over the people" (Exod. 18:25); "round the corners of your heads" (Lev. 19:27, referring to a heathen custom of trimming the beard); "heads of the people" (Num. 25:4, probably meaning "chiefs"; cf. ASV); "his blood shall be upon his head" (Josh. 2:19, meaning "we shall not be responsible for his life"); keeper of mine head" (I Sam. 28:2 i.e. "my protector"); "Am I a dog's head" (II Sam. 3:8 i.e. "Am I utterly contemptible?"); "yet will I not lift up my head" (Job 10:15, i.e. "yet will I not be self-assertive"); "his head reached unto the clouds" (Job 20:6, i.e "he be highly exalted"), etc.

HEAD OF THE CHURCH. In the NT Christ is described as "the head of the church" (Eph. 1:22; 5:23), and "head of the body, the church" (Col. 1:18; cf. Eph. 4:15). This figure speaks of the pre-eminence of Christ, His authority, and the complete dependence of the church upon Christ. It must not be pressed to mean that Christ is the intellectual center of His people, through whom the members are passively governed, for to the Jewish mind, the heart, not the head, was the seat of the intellect. In Colossians 1:18 the headship of Christ over the body denotes His priority of rank.

HEART (Heb. *lēv, lēvāv,* Gr. *kardía*). Although the word occurs more than 900 times in Scripture, it is almost never used in a literal sense, the principal exception being in Exodus 28:29,30, which speaks of the breastplate of judgment upon the heart of Aaron. Commonly the "heart" is regarded as being the seat of the intellect, the feelings and the will; e.g., "every imagination of the thoughts of his heart" (Gen. 6:5) would imply intellect; "comfort ye your hearts" (Gen. 18:5; or "strengthen your heart" as in ASV) would imply feeling; while "that seeking him with the whole heart" (Ps. 119:2) means the will. It is often used to signify the innermost being, i.e., "It grieved him at his heart" (Gen. 6:6). In modern usage, "heart" is used to imply affection, as "I have you in my heart," as found in Psalm 62:10, "If riches increase, set not your heart upon them" and in scores of other passages.

Both in ancient times and today, different parts of the body are used figuratively as the seat of different functions of the soul; and the ancient usage often differs from the modern. In expressing sympathy, we might say "This touches my heart," where the ancient might say "my bowels were moved for him" (S. of Sol. 5:4). Psalm 7:9 in KJV has "the righteous God trieth the hearts and reins," whereas ASV has "the minds and hearts." Here ancient "hearts" is equated with modern "minds" and ancient "reins," i.e., "kidneys" with modern "hearts." This is not a question of truth and error as between ancient and modern psychology, but reflects a difference in common figurative usage. The NT was written mostly by Jews and so is colored by Hebrew thinking and usage; e.g. "They do always err in their heart" means "They are wrong in their thinking" though probably the affections are included as well. Often the word "heart" implies the whole moral nature of fallen man, e.g. "The heart is deceitful above all things, and desperately wicked" (Jer. 17:9) whereas the next verse in KJV has "search the heart, try the reins" but in ASV "search the mind, try the heart." A.B.F.

HEARTH. In ancient times homes were heated very differently from today. In the poorer houses the hearth consisted of a depression in the floor of a room in which a fire was kindled for cooking or for warmth. Chimneys were unknown: smoke escaped from the house as it could, or through a latticed opening for the purpose. The better class of houses were heated by means of a brazier of burning coals. This was a wide, shallow pan which could also be used for cooking. (See Gen. 18:6; Ps. 102:3; Isa. 30:14; Hosea 13:3; Jer. 36:22,23; Zech. 12:6.)

HEATH, a shrub with very small, narrow, rigid leaves. The species *Erica verticillata* grows on the W slopes of Lebanon. (See Jer. 17:6; 48:6).

HEATHEN (hēē'th'n, Heb. *gôy,* pl. *gôyim,* Gr. *éthnos, people, nation*). [Anglo-Saxon, *dweller on the heath.*] In the OT *gôy* is rendered "Gentiles," "heathen," and "nation," but it is usually used for

a non-Israelitish people, and thus has the meaning of "Gentiles." Sometimes, however, it refers to the Israelites, as in Genesis 12:2; Deuteronomy 32:28, but the word ordinarily used for the people of God is *'ām.* In the NT *Éthnos* is the equivalent of *gôy* in the OT, while *laós* corresponds to *'ām.* Sometimes in the KJV the Gr. *Héllenes* renders "Gentiles" (John 7:35; Rom. 2:9,10).

The differentiation between Israelites and Gentiles was more sharply accentuated in NT times than in OT times, the reason for this being chiefly that the Jews had suffered so much from Gentile hands. Gentiles were looked upon with aversion and hatred. This is evident in the NT (John 18:28; Acts 10:28; 11:3).

God's interest in and concern for the heathen is seen in the OT, especially in the Book of Jonah. In the NT Jesus commanded the apostles to preach the Gospel to all the world; and we find them proclaiming it to Gentile nations throughout the Mediterranean world.   S.B.

HEAVEN (Heb. *shāmayim,* Gr. *ouranós*). 1. Cosmologically, one of the two great divisions of the universe, the earth and the heavens (Gen. 1:1; 14:19; etc.); or one of the three — heaven, earth, and the waters under the earth (Exod. 20:4). In the visible heavens are the stars and planets (Gen. 1:14-17; Ezek. 32:7,8). Later Jews divided the heavens into seven strata, but there is no evidence for this in the Bible, although Paul spoke of being caught up into the third heaven (II Cor. 12:2). The term, "heaven of heavens" (Deut. 10:14; I Kings 8:27; Ps. 148:4) probably means the "height of heaven."

2. The abode of God (Gen. 28:17; Ps. 80:14; Isa. 66:1; Matt. 5:12) and of the good angels (Matt. 24:36); where the redeemed shall some day be (Matt. 5:12; 6:20; Eph. 3:15); where the Redeemer has gone and intercedes for the saints, and from which He will some day come for His own (I Thess. 4:16).

3. The inhabitants of heaven (Luke 15:18; Rev. 18:20).   S.B.

HEAVE OFFERING (See Offerings)

HEAVING AND WAVING (See Offerings)

HEBER (hē'bēr, *associate*). 1. A great-grandson of Jacob through Asher and Beriah (Gen. 46:17).

2. The Kenite whose wife Jael killed Sisera (Judg. 4:11-21). He had been friendly with the Canaanites who had been oppressing Israel.

3. A son of Ezrah (KJV "Ezra") of the tribe of Judah and probably of the family of Caleb, the good spy (I Chron. 4:18).

4. A man of the tribe of Benjamin, and son of Elpaal (I Chron. 8:17). In KJV the name of these other men, whose name should be Eber as in ASV.

5. The head of a family in the tribe of Gad (I Chron. 5:13).

6. A Benjamite, son of Shashak, mentioned only in I Chronicles 8:22.

7. One mentioned in Christ's genealogy (Luke 3:35 KJV), father of Peleg and Joktan. He is properly called "Eber" elsewhere (e.g. Gen. 10:24, 25; Gen. 11:12-16). See EBER, HEBREWS.

HEBREW OF THE HEBREWS. When Paul in Philippians 3:4-6 so described himself, he meant that he was a pure-blooded Hebrew who had retained the language and customs of his fathers, in contrast to other Jews who had adopted Greek language and customs.

HEBREWS, EPISTLE TO THE. Authorship. The writer of Hebrews does not attach his name to his letter. I John is the only other epistle in the NT to which a name is not attached. Because of this fact, there has been much discussion since the first century as to who wrote Hebrews.

Early Christians held various opinions. Those on the eastern shore of the Mediterranean and around Alexandria associated the book with Paul. Origen (185-254 A.D.) held that the thoughts of the book were Paul's, but the language and composition were someone else's. In North Africa, Tertullian (155-225 A.D.) thought that Barnabas wrote Hebrews. Although the epistle was first known in Rome and the W (I Clement, dated around 95 A.D. cites Hebrews frequently), for 200 years Christians in Rome and the W were unanimous in their opinion that Paul did not write Hebrews. Who did write Hebrews these early Christians did not say.

Present day Christians should hardly be dogmatic about an issue which from the very beginning of the church was surrounded with uncertainty. A careful study of the epistle in the Greek text discloses some important things about the author: 1. The letter has a polished Greek style, like that of a master rhetorician. The continuous use of this style is unlike Paul who frequently picks up a new stream of thought before he finishes the one he is treating. 2. The vocabulary, figures of speech, and manner of argument show an Alexandrian and Philonic influence (Philo, 20 B.C. to 50 or 60 A.D.). Paul, having come from Tarsus and having been educated in Jerusalem, did not have such a background. 3. Both Paul and the writer of Hebrews quote the Old Testament frequently. But the way they introduce their quotations is quite different. Paul's formulas — "just as it has been written" (19 times), "it has been written" (10 times), "the Scripture says" (6 times), "the Scripture proclaims good tidings beforehand" (1 time) — never occur in Hebrews. Paul's manner of introducing quotations puts the reader's attention on the content quoted. The writer of Hebrews, as an orator, puts the stress on the one who speaks. For him God, Christ, or the Holy Spirit is speaking.

Along with many present day scholars, this author favors Apollos as the possible writer of Hebrews. He was a Jew, born in Alexandria (Acts 18:24), a learned and cultured man. He was well-versed in the Scriptures (Acts 18:24). Being orally taught the way of the Lord, Apollos was teaching about Jesus even when he knew only John's baptism (Acts 18:25). He was a man of enthusiasm. Priscilla and Aquila, Paul's friends, led Apollos to a full knowledge of Christ (Acts 18:26). After he received this fuller knowledge, he was a man of courage. He left Ephesus for Achaia to help the believers there (Acts 18:27). He consistently used the Scriptures in his public preaching (Acts 18:25). Paul testifies to Apollos' capability in I Corinthians chapters 1-4. His polished rhetorical style may have been a contributing cause to the Apollos party which was found in Corinth (I Cor. 3:4,5,6). Apollos' modesty and desire to avoid friction are seen in I Corinthians 16:12. He was still an active co-worker of Paul late in Paul's ministry (see Titus 3:13). In Apollos one can explain all of Hebrews' similarities with Paul as well as the distinct differences from Paul.

Assuming Apollos to be the author, one can best date the letter between 68-70 A.D.

Original Readers. The letter was first known in Rome and the West. Its first readers were Jewish Christians who spoke and wrote Greek. The brief statement: "They from Italy salute you" (Heb. 13:24) certainly favors the readers' being located in Italy. If the writer had been in Italy, he would have named the precise place. A letter from any city in the United States would not say: "Those from the United States send greetings." But if the letter came from an interior city of India or Brazil, such a greeting would be appropriate. Hence, it appears there were Italian Christians with the writer somewhere outside of Italy as he penned this letter. The writer knows the readers well. He refers to their spiritual dullness (5:11-14), their faithful ministering to the saints (6:9-10), their experiences after their conversion (10:32-36). The term used for their spiritual leaders or rulers is *hoi hēgoumenoi* (13:7,17,24), a technical term found nowhere else in the New Testament, but other writings coming from Rome and the West have this same term (cf. I Clement 1:3; 21:6; Shepherd of Hermas II, 2:6, 9:7 [*proegoumenoi*]). Their first leaders seem to have died (13:7), while their present leaders are continually engaged in the task of watching over the flock (13:17). To these the writer sends greetings (13:24).

Although absolute certainty cannot be reached, it seems best to regard the original readers as being located somewhere in Italy. Many roads led to Rome. These believers may have been in one of the cities nearer or farther from the capital. Paul himself spent seven days with the brothers in Puteoli (Acts 28:13-14). They could have been in Rome or its suburbs. As the writer pens this letter, Timothy has departed [from him] and is absent (perfect tense) — very likely on some tour of churches. As soon as he appears (or if he comes soon), the writer and Timothy together will visit the readers (Heb. 13:23).

Outline and Summary of Content — An outline shows the centrality of Jesus Christ in the book of Hebrews.

PROLOGUE: COURSE AND CLIMAX OF DIVINE REVELATION (1:1-3)

I. PRE-EMINENCE OF CHRIST HIMSELF (1:4-4:13)
   A. Superiority of Christ to Angels (1:4-14)
   B. Warning: Peril of Indifference to These Truths (2:1-14)
   C. Reason Christ Became Human (2:5-18)
   D. Christ's Position is Greater than That of Moses (3:1-6)
   E. Warning: Unbelief Brings Temporal and Eternal Effects (3:7-4:13)

II. PRIESTHOOD OF JESUS CHRIST (4:14-10:18)
   A. Importance of His Priesthood for a Believer's Conduct (4:14-16)
   B. Qualifications of a High Priest (5:1-10)
   C. Warning: Immaturity and Apostasy are Conquered Only by Faith, Longsuffering, and Hope (5:11-6:20a)
   D. Melchizedek's Eternal Successor (6:20b-7:28)
   E. Heavenly Sanctuary and New Covenant (8:1-13)
   F. Priestly Service under the Old Covenant and the New (9:1-28)
   G. Inadequacy of the Sacrifices under the Law contrasted with the Efficacy and Finality of Christ's Sacrifice (10:1-18)

III. Perseverance of Christians (10:19-12:29)
A. Attitudes to be Sought and Attitudes to be Shunned (10:19-38)
B. Faith in Action—Illustrious Examples from the Past (11:1-40)
C. Incentives for Action in the Present Scene and in the Future Goal (12:1-29)

Postscript: Exhortations, Personal Concerns, Benediction (13:1-25)

Although God spoke to the fathers by the prophets, He has now spoken by His Son. In the prologue we see the distinctiveness of the Son. He is before history, in history, above history, the goal of history, and the agent who brings about a cleansing of men from sins committed in history. He shares the essence of Deity and radiates the glory of Deity. He is the supreme revelation of God (1:1-3).

The writer's first main task is to make clear the pre-eminence of Christ (1:4-4:13). He is superior to angels. They assist those who will be heirs of salvation. Christ, by virtue of who He is, of God's appointment, and of what He has done, stands exalted far above them. It would be tragic to be careless of the great salvation which He proclaimed. He will achieve for man the promise that all things will be in harmonious subjection to man. He can do this because He is fully man and has provided the expiation for sins. He is superior to Moses, for Moses was a servant among the people of God, while Christ is a son over the people of God. It would be tragic to cease trusting Him. Unbelief kept one entire generation of Israelites from Canaan. Christians are warned of such unbelief. Faith is emphasized as well as zeal to enter into the eternal rest of God. Both the Gospel of God and God Himself scrutinize men.

The second major emphasis in the letter falls upon the priesthood of Christ (4:14-10:18). Qualifications, conditions, and experiences of the Aaronic priesthood are listed in comparison to Christ as a priest. Before further developing this theme, the writer warns his readers of their unpreparedness for advanced teaching. Only earnest diligence in things of God will bring them out of immaturity. Christ as a priest, like Melchizedek, is superior to the Levitical priesthood because His life is indestructible. He was both priest and sacrifice. His priesthood is eternal. His sanctuary is in heaven and His blood establishes the validity of the New Covenant which is also an eternal covenant. His one offering on behalf of sins is final; i.e., it is for all time. Likewise He has made perfect for all time those who are in the process of being sanctified.

The last main section of Hebrews deals with the response of Christians. Perseverance on the part of Christians springs out of fellowship with God, activity for God, faith in God, and a consciousness of what lies ahead (10:19-12:29).

In concluding the letter the writer puts stress on the cross as the Christian altar and the resurrection of the Shepherd of the sheep as the basis for God's action. Such redemptive-historical events move the believer to action (13:1-25).

Teaching. Although more space is devoted to Christ, the letter has a fully developed set of teachings about God the Father.

Much is said about Christ. He is fully God and fully man. He is active in creation. The atonement of Christ, as both priest and sacrificial victim, is developed in detail. In the role of a priest, He is a leader and guide. He also is the revealer of God. Great depth is achieved in all of these teachings about Christ's person and work.

Very little is said about the Holy Spirit in Hebrews. The Spirit is mentioned only seven times: three times in reference to the inspiration of the OT, once in regard to the work of Christ, once in regard to the apostate's rejection of Christianity, and twice in regard to the believer.

The Old and New Covenants are compared and reasons for the superiority of the New or Eternal Covenant are given.

The doctrine of sin in Hebrews focuses attention on unbelief and the failure to go on with God to the eternal city.

Shadow and reality are carefully contrasted. Heaven is the scene of reality. Earth is concerned both with shadow and reality. Christ is the bridge between the temporary and the eternal.

The people of God are looked upon as migrating from a transitory setting to an abiding city. This migration involves God's Word, the matter of testing, discipline or punishment, faithfulness, and God's activity in sanctifying or making holy. The Christian life is developed in the framework of this heavenly pilgrimage.

Eschatology or last things involves the obtaining of eternal rest, a final shaking of heaven and earth, the personal return of Christ, and glory belonging to God for ever and ever.   A.B.M.

HEBREW, HEBREWS, traditionally considered designations for Abraham and his descendants, especially through Jacob, the equivalent of Israelite(s). I Samuel 14:21 may suggest that the terms are to be equated. Jews quite uniformly have used "Israel" and "the children of Israel" (later "Jews") in referring to themselves, finding in such terminology treasured religious and national associations. Foreigners thought of them as "Hebrews" (Exod. 1:16; 2:6), and they so identified themselves in speaking to non-Jews (Gen. 40:15; Exod. 10:3; Jonah 1:9). Also, in contexts involving contrasts between Israelites and those of other nations, the same phenomenon appears (Gen. 43:32; Exod. 1:15; 2:11; I Sam. 13:3; 14:21).

One must reckon, however, with the possibility that in OT times the names "Hebrews," "Habiru," "Khapiru," "'Apiru," and 'pr were forms of the same word, (equivalent to the Akkadian SA.GAZ), a designation without national significance. Rather, they indicated wandering peoples greatly restricted as regards financial means and without citizenship and social status. Ancient records show "Habiru" to be scattered over western Asia for centuries until about 1100 B.C. Nomadic peoples, mostly Semitic — sometimes raiders, sometimes skilled artisans — they frequently offered themselves as mercenaries and slaves, with individuals occasionally rising to prominence. In Egypt, the Israelites were reduced to a lowly position and later moved about in the wilderness. Conceivably they could, therefore, have been known as "Hebrews." Interestingly enough, in taking oaths the Habiru swore by "the gods of the Habiru," whereas identical phraseology, "The God of the Hebrews," is found in Exodus 3:18; 5:3; 7:16. "Hebrews" and "Habiru" were terms employed prior to the name "Israel," and both were discontinued generally about the time of the Judges.

NT "Hebrew" references contrast people (Acts 6:1) and language (John 5:2; 19:13,17,20; 20:16)

TRANSLATION.

1st line. "*(Behold) the excavation !   Now this had been the history of the excavation.   While the workmen were still lifting up*
2nd „   "*the axe, each towards his neighbour, and while three cubits still remained to (cut through), (each heard) the voice of the other who called*
3rd „   "*to his neighbour since there was an excess in the rock on the right hand and on (the left).   And on the day of the*
4th „   "*excavation the workmen struck, each to meet his neighbour, axe against axe, and there flowed*
5th „   "*the waters from the spring to the pool for a thousand two hundred cubits ; and . . . . .*
6th „   "*of a cubit was the height of the rock over the heads of the workmen.*"   [2 Kings xx., 20.   2 Chron. xxxii., 30].

THE SILOAM INSCRIPTION, with translation. It was found carved in the walls of Hezekiah's Tunnel, built in the 8th century B.C. The tunnel was constructed when the Jerusalem water supply was threatened by the approach of the Assyrian Army. The inscription records the tunnel's construction.

to differentiate between the Greeks and Hellenistic culture on the one hand and Jews and their traditional life and speech on the other. What is called "Hebrew language" may in John's Gospel refer to Aramaic, but in the Apocalypse to Hebrew proper (Rev. 9:11; 16:16).

Etymologically, it has been debated whether "Hebrew" is to be traced to Eber, the father of Peleg and Joktan (Gen. 10:24,25; 11:12-16) or is derived from the Hebrew root "to pass over." and has reference to "a land on the other side," as the dweller E of the Euphrates might think of Canaan. However, the possible equating of the Hebrews and the Habiru might suggest that the Hebrews were "those who crossed over" in the sense of trespassing, i.e. "trespassers."   B.L.G.

HEBREW LANGUAGE. With the exception of Aramaic in Ezra 4:8-6:18; 7:12-26; Daniel 2:4-7; 28 and Jeremiah 10:11, Hebrew is the language of the OT. The term "Hebrew" was first used as a designation for individuals or a people and only later denoted a language. The OT refers to the language not as "Hebrew" but as "the language of Canaan" (Isa. 19:18) or "the Jews' language" (II Kings 18:26,28 and parallel passages; also Neh. 13:24). Josephus, Ecclesiasticus and the NT (Rev. 9:11; 16:16), however, speak of it as "Hebrew." With close affinity to Ugaritic, Phoenician, Moabitic and the Canaanite dialects, Hebrew represents the northwest branch of the Semitic language family. Its sister languages include Arabic, Akkadian and Aramaic. With few exceptions, extant texts of Ancient Hebrew are those of the OT and certain of the apocryphal and pseudepigraphic works. Inscriptions employing the language include the Siloam Inscription from the eighth century B.C. and the Gezer Calendar from the tenth century B.C.

In large measure, the OT Hebrew must be self explanatory. However, the Ugaritic Ras Shamra tablets shed much light upon the meaning of the Hebrew Bible, and since the structure and vocabulary were so very similar in the various Semitic tongues, much cognate language help is available for the understanding of the language of the Israelites. The Greek translation of the OT, the LXX, is also of much value in interpretative study of Biblical Hebrew.

As the language encountered Aramaizing and Hellenizing influences in the half dozen centuries preceding the advent of Christ, its use as a spoken language became less and less. Some of the Dead Sea Scrolls were written in Hebrew, and Hebrew was the vehicle for the writing of such Jewish religious literature as the Mishnah and the Midrashim in the early part of the Christian era and in medieval times for Biblical commentaries and philosophical and literary works. In modern Israel, Hebrew has again become a living tongue.

The historical origins of the language are somewhat obscure but go back beyond 2000 B.C. The OT literature, written over a period of more than a thousand years, reveals a minimum of stylistic changes, although loan words and new ways of expression became more or less noticeable with the passing of years, especially after the Exile. It is also true that at a given time dialectical differences existed, a fact attested by the narrative in Judges 12, in which Ephraimites were unable to pronounce the "sh" of their neighbors to the south.

With its short sentences and simple coordinating conjunctions, ancient Hebrew lent itself well to the vivid expression of events. These features, together with parallelism and rhythm and special meanings and constructions made Hebrew poetry, as found in the Psalms and to a large extent in the Prophets, most expressive and strikingly effective.

Basic tools for the understanding of the language include the latest revisions of Gesenius' grammar and lexicon, and the lexicons of Koehler & Baumgartner and Davies-Mitchell, and the concordances of Mandelkern and Lisowsky.   B.L.G.

Ancient Semitic Alphabets

(With modern Hebrew, in column at right, for comparison)

Inscr. of Dibon. 9th. cent. B.C. Gram. §2,2. §5,1.	Phoenician Coins and Inscript.	New-Punic.	Old. Hebr. Coins and Gems.	Samaritan.	Aram.-Egyptian. 5th.—1st. cent. B.C.	Palmyra Inscript. 1st cent. B.C.—4th. cent. A.C.	Heb. Inscr. Christ's Time.	Square Char.	Raschi.	Modern Hebrew	
										א	'
										ב	b, bh
										ג	g, gh
										ד	d, dh
										ה	h
										ו	w
										ז	z
										ח	ch
										ט	ṭ
										י	y
										כ ך	k, kh
										ל	l
										מ ם	m
										נ ן	n
										ס	s
										ע	ʽ
										פ ף	p, ph
										צ ץ	ṣ
										ק	q
										ר	r
										שׁ	sh
										ת	t

GENERAL VIEW OF HEBRON. The mosque in the center is built over the Cave of Machpelah, traditional burial site of Abraham, Sarah, Isaac, Rebekah, Jacob, and Leah.

HEBRON (hē'brŏn, Heb. *hevrôn, league, confederacy*). 1. One of the oldest cities of the world, and one which has had several names at different times. It is located 19 miles SW of Jerusalem on the main road to Beer-sheba, and has one of the longest records for continuous occupation. Though lying in a shallow valley, it is about 3,000 feet above sea-level and 4,300 feet above the Dead Sea which lies a few miles E of Hebron. The hills about the city still bear choice grapes, and the Jewish people there make a fine wine. The brook of Eshcol from which the spies brought an immense cluster of grapes (Num. 13:22-24) ran quite near Hebron. Hebron's original name was Kiriatharba, i.e. "fourfold city" (Josh. 14:15; 15:13).

Hebron is replete with historical interest. It was early a camping place for Abram, to which he removed his tent, and dwelt by the oaks of Mamre (Gen. 13:18 mistranslated in KJV "the plain of Mamre"). This was close to Hebron, and here Abram built an altar unto the Lord. The only land that Abram owned, though God had promised him Canaan (Gen. 15:18-21), was the field of Machpelah, which he purchased from the Hittites as a burial place for Sarah (Heb. 11:8-10; Gen. 23:17-20). In this cave Sarah and Abraham, later Isaac and Rebekah, then Jacob and Leah were buried. At the partition of Canaan after the partial conquest, Hebron and its environs were given to Caleb to conquer (Josh. 14:6-15), which he did (15:14-19); but later the city itself was given to the Kohathite Levites (I Chron. 6:55,56), though Caleb's descendants kept the suburban fields and villages. When David was king over Judah, but not yet over all Israel, his capital city was Hebron for seven and a half years, and there the elders of Israel anointed him king over all Israel. He removed the capital to Jerusalem, but when Absalom rebelled against his father, he made Hebron his headquarters and there prepared his coup-d'état (II Sam. 15:7-12).

2. Third son of Kohath, and so an uncle of Moses, Aaron and Miriam (Exod. 6:18). His descendants, 1,700 men of valor in the days of David, had the responsibility for the Lord's business and for the service of the king west of Jordan (I Chron. 26:30).

3. A town in Asher (Josh. 19:28 KJV). ASV has "Ebron," but "Abdon" (Josh. 21:30, copied in I Chron. 6:74) is almost certainly the correct reading.

4. A descendant of Caleb, son of Hezron, son of Perez, son of Judah (I Chron. 2:42,43), not to be confused with Caleb the good spy, who was a distant cousin.

HEDGE, loose stone walls without mortar, or cut thorn branches or thorny bushes, common as "hedges" and "fences" in Palestine. The word can be rendered, *fence, wall* or *hedge.* The use of a hedge about a vine or tree was mainly for protection (Ps. 80:12). Figuratively, prophets should make up a hedge for the people's protection (Ezek. 13:5), and God is pictured as so doing (Mark 12:1) for His people. The very poor live in highways and hedges (Luke 14:23).

HEGAI or **HEGE** (hĕg'ā-ī, hē'gē), the eunuch employed by Xerxes the Great ("Ahasuerus") as keeper of the women in the king's harem (Esth. 2:3,8,15). Some think that "Hegai" 'is not a proper name but means "eunuch."

HEIFER, a young cow (Gen. 15:9; Deut. 21:3; I Sam. 16:2). Heifers were used in religious rites only in the ceremony of Deuteronomy 21:1-9.

HEIFER, RED (See Animals)

HEIR (See Inheritance)

HELAH (hē'là), one of the two wives of Ashur (ASV Ashhur), posthumous son of Hezron (I Chron. 4:5,7).

HELAM (hē'lăm, Heb. *hēlām*), a place in the Syrian desert E of the Jordan where David defeated the forces of Hadarezer, king of Aram-zobah (II Sam. 10:16,17). The exact location is unknown.

HELBAH (hĕl'bà, *a fertile region*), a town in the tribe of Asher from which the men of Israel failed to expel the Canaanites. Near the River Leontes in Lebanon (Judg. 1:31).

HELBON (hĕl'bŏn, *fertile*), a city of northern Syria, celebrated in ancient times for its wine (Ezek. 27:18). Some think that a village in the Anti-Lebanon about 13 miles NW of Damascus is intended.

HELDAI (hĕl'dā-ī). 1. The captain over 24,000 men whose duties were in the 12th month under David (I Chron. 27:15). Probably the same as Heled in I Chronicles 11:30 and as Heleb in II Samuel 23:29.

2. One of three noble Jews who brought gold and silver from Babylon, and who were to surrender the metal to Zechariah (Zech. 6:9-15) that he might make crowns for Joshua the high-priest. (The name is spelled "Helem" in 6:14).

HELEB (hē'lĕb), one of David's valiant men of war (II Sam. 23:29). See HELED and HELDAI.

HELED (hē'lĕd), a mighty man of David's army (I Chron. 11:30). See HELEB and HELDAI.

HELEK (hē'lĕk), the second son of Gilead of the tribe of Manasseh and head of a family (Num. 26:30; Josh. 17:2).

HELEM (hē'lĕm, *health*). 1. A man of the tribe of Asher (I Chron. 7:35), called Hotham in verse 32. 2. An ambassador, mentioned only in Zechariah 6:14; but also certainly the same person as Heldai (Zech. 6:10).

HELEPH (hē'lĕf, *change*), an ancient village on the border of Naphtali (Josh. 19:33). Perhaps on the site now called Beitlif in Galilee.

HELEZ (hē'lĕz). 1. A man of Judah, of the family of Hezron, but also of Egyptian descent (I Chron. 2:39). 2. One of David's mighty leaders, called a "Paltite" in II Samuel 23:26, but "Pelonite" in I Chronicles 11:27; an Ephraimite (I Chron. 27:10).

HELI (hē'lī, Heb. *'ēlî*), the father of Joseph, the husband of Mary, in the genealogy of Jesus in Luke 3:23. According to another view, he is the father of Mary, the mother of Jesus, a view that is reached by punctuating the Gr. differently. See GENEALOGY OF JESUS CHRIST.

HELIOPOLIS (hē-lĭ-ŏp'ō-lĭs, Heb. *'ôn*, Gr. *Heliopolis, city of the sun*), a city near the S end of the Delta of the Nile, the site of a temple to the sun built by Amenophis I. It was a very old and holy city, with a learned school of priests. Joseph's father-in-law belonged to the priests of the Sun Temple (Gen. 41:45; 46:20). In the intertestamental period Onias built a Jewish Temple there. The modern site is the village El-Matariye.

HELKAI (hĕl'kā-ī, perhaps an abbr. of *Helkiah*), a priest of the Jews in the days of Joiakim (Neh. 12:15).

HELKATH (hĕl'kăth, Heb. *helqath, a field*), a town on the southern border of the tribe of Asher (Josh. 19:25) given to the Gershonite Levites (Josh. 21:31). Later called Hukok (I Chron. 6:75). Site uncertain .

HELKATH HAZZURIM (hĕl'kăth hăz'ū-rĭm, *the field of the sharp knives*), a piece of ground near the pool of Gibeon where the men of Joab fought with an equal number of the men of Abner, and all 24 fell down slain (II Sam. 2:12-16).

HELL. The real existence of hell is irrefutably taught in Scripture as both a *place* of the wicked dead and a *condition* of retribution for unredeemed man.

No formal statement of immortality occurs in the Old Testament, yet it constantly alludes to the "cutting off" of the wicked from God. While the word, *Sheol*, does not pointedly refer to a definitive doctrine of endless retribution, but rather to a shadowy existence beyond the grave, it nevertheless reflects the belief in a future and continued existence. Translated by KJV and ERV as "hell," the word carries the connotation of doom, hopelessness and futility. "The wicked in a moment go down into Sheol" (Job. 21:13). "The wicked shall be turned into Sheol, and all the nations that forget God" (Ps. 9:17). "If I ascend up into heaven, thou art there; if I make my bed in Sheol, behold thou art there" (Ps. 139:8). "The way of life is above the wise, that he may depart from Sheol beneath" (Prov. 15:24). The etymology of the word is uncertain. It may be translated merely as "grave" or "abode of the dead," or it may be given the stronger connotation of "hell." However it may be translated, its meaning is clear — it represents the place of future retribution (Job 26:6), the abode of the wicked (Prov. 23:4, Job 21:30), a place of punishment (Prov. 15:11). It is insep-

arably associated with spiritual death (Ps. 89:48), and is contrasted with the destiny of the righteous (Ps. 17:15).

In the Inter-Testamental period, both apocryphal literature and Rabbinical teaching continued the development of the association of immortality and retribution until, during the New Testament times, two words were used: Hades (Gr. *hádes*) and Gehenna (Gr. *geénna*). Gehenna, used 13 times in the New Testament, and with but one exception (James 3:6) always by Christ, indisputably refers to the place of retributive suffering. The word derives its meaning from the Hebrew, *ge-hinnom* (*the valley of Hinnom*) which was a pit into which refuse was dumped. A site which had long been contemptuously regarded in the Hebrew mind, as when Josiah dumped the filth of Jerusalem (II Kings 23:10) to be burned, and in which the bodies of executed criminals were tossed, it had become a technical term for unending torment, and is so used in Matthew 10:28 and Mark 9:43. *Hades,* used by the Septuagint translators for *Sheol*, and thus somewhat undefined in early usage, undeniably assumed definiteness of meaning by Christ's use of it in Matthew 11:23 (Luke 10:15), where it represents destruction, in Matthew 16:18, where it is synonymous with the kingdom of evil, and in Revelation 1:18, where it represents confinement in prison and is identified with death. In each of these cases, the reality of hell is established through Christ's reference to it.

The *nature* of hell is indicated by the repeated reference to everlasting punishment (Matt. 25:46); everlasting fire (Matt. 18:8); everlasting chains (II Thess. 1:8); the eternal fire (Jude 7); the pit of the abyss (Rev. 9:2,11); outer darkness (Matt. 8:12); the wrath of God (Rom. 2:5); second death (Rev. 21:8); eternal destruction from the face of God (II Thess. 1:9); and eternal sin (Mark 3:29). While many of these terms are symbolic and descriptive, they connote real entities, about which existence there can be no doubt.

The *duration* of hell is explicitly indicated in the NT. The word "everlasting" (*aionios*) is derived from the verb *aion,* signifying an "age" or "duration." Scripture speaks of two *aions,* or ages: the present age and the age to come (Matt. 12:32; Mark 10:30; Luke 18:30; Eph. 1:21). The present age — this world — is always contrasted with the age to come as temporal, while the future age is to be endless. As the everlasting life of the believer is to be endless, just so the retributive aspect of hell refers to the future infinite age. In every reference in which *aiōnios* applies to the future punishment of the wicked, it indisputably denotes endless duration (Matt. 18:8; 25:41,46; Mark 3:29; I Thess. 1:9; Heb. 6:2; Jude 6).

Hell is, therefore, both a *condition* of retribution, and a *place* in which the retribution occurs. In both these aspects, the three basic ideas associated with the concept of hell are reflected: (1) absence of righteousness, (2) separation from God, and (3) judgment.

The absence of personal righteousness, with its correlative of the presence of personal unrighteousness, renders the individual unable to enter felicity with the holy God (Mark 3:29). The eternal state of the wicked, therefore, will involve a separation from the presence of God (John 3:36). The concept of judgment is heightened by the note of finality in the warnings against sin (Matt. 8:12). It is a judgment, however, against man's sinful nature — still unredeemed though Christ died — (Matt. 25:31-46) and is decisive and irreversible.

When all else has been said about hell, however, there is still the inescapable fact of Scripture — it will be a retributive judgment upon the *spirit* of man — the inner essence of his being. The severity of the judgment will be upon the fixed character of his essential nature — his soul, which will involve the eternal loss of exclusion from Christ's kingdom and fellowship with God.   C.B.B.

HELLENISTS (hĕl'ĕn-ĭsts), non-Greeks who spoke Greek, a term used specially of Jews who made Greek their tongue, and with it often adopted Greek ideas and practices (Acts 6:1; 9:29). The KJV has Grecians, RSV Hellenists.

HELMET (See Arms, Armor)

HELON (hē'lôn, *valorous*), father of Eliab, a leading man of Zebulun at the first census (Num. 1:9).

HELPMEET, now often used as one word, meaning a helper, generally a wife; but in Genesis 2:18 it is two words. "I will make him a help, meet for him," i.e., suitable for or answering to him. It is often changed to "helpmate," which means the same.

HELPS. In the NT there are four lists of "gifts" which God has given to His Church (Rom. 12:6-8, I Cor. 12:7-11, 28-31, and Eph. 4:11,12) and these are not to be confused with the officers who are listed elsewhere. "Helps" are mentioned only in I Corinthians 12:28, and the Greek word occurs only here. It means *protector* or *assistant*, and probably refers to the ability to perform helpful works in a gracious manner .

HEMAM (hē'măm), a grandson of Seir the Horite (Gen. 36:22). "Homam" in I Chronicles 1:39.

HEMAN (hē'măn, Heb. *hêmân, faithful*). 1. A grandson of Judah through Zerah (I Chron. 2:6). He is listed as one of the most notable wise men, though Solomon was wiser.

2. The first of the three Levites whom David appointed to lead in the musical services (I Chron. 6:33). He was "the king's seer in the words of God to lift up the horn" (I Chron. 25:5) and had 14 sons and three daughters.

3. Psalm 88 is attributed to Heman the Ezrahite, and if "Ezrahite" means "Zerahite," as many think, he may be the same as 1. above.

HEMATH (hē'măth). In Amos 6:14 "Hemath" should be "Hamath" as in ASV. In I Chronicles 2:55 "Hemath" should be Hammath as in ASV. He was the father of Rechabites (Jer. 35:2-18). See HAMATH.

HEMDAN (hĕm'dăn, Heb. *hemdān, pleasant*), an early Horite in the land of Seir, who discovered hot springs in the wilderness (Gen. 36:26). In I Chronicles 1:41 the Heb. text and RV have "Hamran, but KJV has "Amram." Hemdan is probably the original form.

HEMLOCK (See Plants)

HEM OF A GARMENT, the fringes or tassels on the borders of the Jewish outer garment (Num. 15:38,39) containing a thread of blue. The word "hem" (Exod. 28:33,34, 39:24-26) should be "skirt." Cf. ASV *in loco*. To "touch the hem (ASV "border") of his garment" (Matt. 9:20,21, 14:36) denoted a reverent approach, not daring to lay hold of Him, but having faith in the efficacy of His miraculous power.

HEN (Heb. *hēn, favor*), a son of Zephaniah (Zech. 6:14), but RV margin has "for the kindness of the son of Zephaniah," in which case the son's name disappears.

HEN (Gr. *órnis*), a general term for "bird," "fowl," etc. (Matt. 23:37; Luke 13:34).

HENA (hēn'à, Heb. *hēna'*), a city on the south bank of the Euphrates, about 180 miles NW of ancient Babylon. It was mentioned by Rabshakeh, along with four other cities whose gods could not save them from destruction by Sennacherib, as a proof that Jehovah could not save Jerusalem (II Kings 18:34, 19:13, Isa. 37:13).

HENADAD (hĕn'à-dăd, *favor of Hadad*), head of a family of Levites who helped Zerubbabel (Ezra 3:9), and who in the next century helped Nehemiah in building (Neh. 3:18,24).

HEPHER (hē'fēr, *pit, well*). 1. Head of the family of the Hepherites (Num. 26:32). His son Zelophehad had five daughters who were commanded to marry within their tribe so as not to alienate any of the tribal property of Manasseh to another tribe (Num. 27:1-8, 36:1-9).

2. A son of Ashhur (KJV Ashur), the founder of Tekoa (I Chron. 4:5,6).

3. One of David's mighty men (I Chron. 11:36) from Macherah, a place otherwise unmentioned and unknown.

4. A royal city in Canaan listed among the 31 which Joshua conquered (Josh. 12:17). The land of Hepher (I Kings 4:10) was SW of Jerusalem.

HEPHZIBAH (hĕf'zĭ-bà, Heb. *hephtsî-vâh, my delight is in hĕr*). 1. Wife of King Hezekiah (II Kings 21:1) and mother of Manasseh.

HERD. Israel, before Joshua's time, like the Bedouin of today, was a nomadic people, and after the conquest of Canaan continued to be a pastoral people for the most part. For the property of such a people see Job 1:3 or 42:12. The herds consisted of the larger animals, as contrasted with the flocks of sheep, goats, etc. The cattle were used in plowing and threshing, and for sacrifice, but were not commonly fattened for food, though in contrast, see Ezekiel 39:18.

HERDMAN. Hebrew has three words rendered herdman in the Bible: *bôqēr, a cowherd* (Amos 7:14); *rō'eh*, a general term for any kind of herdman (Gen. 13:7,8; 26:20); *nôqēdh, one who spots or marks the sheep*, hence *a herdman* (Amos 1:1). Herdmen generally did not own the sheep; they were hirelings.

HERES (he'rez, *sun*). 1. A district around Aijalon from which the Amorites were not expelled (Judg. 1:35). The meaning is uncertain.

2. A place E of the Jordan from which Gideon returned after his defeat of Zebah and Zalmunna (Judg. 8:13).

3. An Egyptian city (Isa. 19:18). Undoubtedly Heliopolis.

HERESH (hē'resh, *dumb, silent*), a Levite who early returned from captivity (I Chron. 9:15).

HERESY (hâr'ĕ-sē, Gr. *haíresis*, from vb. *hairéo, to choose*). 1. A sect or faction, not necessarily representing a departure from orthodox doctrine, as "sect of Sadducees" (Acts 5:17), "sect of Nazarenes" (Acts 24:5). The Pharisees are called "the straitest sect" (Acts 26:5). Christianity is called a heresy in Acts 24:14; 28:22.

2. A doctrine or sect representing a departure from sound doctrine (II Pet. 2:1).